On the Other Hand
New Perspectives
on American Sign Language

LANGUAGE, THOUGHT, AND CULTURE: *Advances in the*
Study of Cognition

Under the Editorship of: E. A. HAMMEL
DEPARTMENT OF ANTHROPOLOGY
UNIVERSITY OF CALIFORNIA
BERKELEY

On the Other Hand

New Perspectives on American Sign Language

EDITED BY

LYNN A. FRIEDMAN

Department of Linguistics
University of California
Berkeley, California

ACADEMIC PRESS, INC.   New York   San Francisco   London   1977
A Subsidiary of Harcourt Brace Jovanovich, Publishers

Academic Press Rapid Manuscript Reproduction

HV
2474
. 05

ACADEMIC PRESS, INC.
111 Fifth Avenue, New York, New York 10003

United Kingdom Edition published by
ACADEMIC PRESS, INC. (LONDON) LTD.
24/28 Oval Road, London NW1

Library of Congress Cataloging in Publication Data

Main entry under title:

On the other hand.

    (Language, thought, and culture series)
    "An outgrowth of a course on the structure of the
American Sign Language (ASL) given at U. C. Berkeley
during the winter and spring quarters, 1975."
    Includes bibliographical references and index.
    1.   Sign language.   2.   Deaf—Means of communication.
I.   Friedman, Lynn A.
HV2474.05   419   77-5342
ISBN 0–12–267850–8

CONTENTS

FOREWORD

Since newcomers to linguistics sometimes find it hard to give up the assumption that a language exists basically in the medium of writing, it is traditional in textbooks and in introductory linguistics courses to give very early the argument that a language is first and foremost a system of speech, only derivatively representable in a visual medium, and that the organization and functioning of a language are in many ways dependent on the mechanisms of speaking and hearing. The lesson containing this argument is typically illustrated with a stylized diagram that shows the path taken by a message, presented as a train of sound waves, as it travels from a speaker's mouth to a hearer's ears.

This lesson is an important one if linguistics students are to appreciate that there are many impressive regularities in language that are not reflected in the writing system, and that there are rich resources for linguistic study in speech samples that have not appeared in written form. In emphasizing these points, however, linguists have frequently gone so far as to build the notion of the vocal/auditory channel into the very definition of language. That commitment, we find, has unhappily left linguistics with no easy way to cope with the realities of the sign languages of the deaf, such as the American Sign Language (ASL) treated in this book.

The layman's view that language is basically writing and the linguist's view that language is basically speech both independently support doubts that ASL and its counterparts could be "real languages." The question of whether ASL is a "language" is one that has two aspects: first, it can be taken as a purely academic question of whether the official doctrines on the domain of linguistics should be broadened so as to include sign language (i.e., should "language" be redefined?); second, it can be seen as an extremely consequential real-world question, concerning which makers of educational policy in this country need to be informed, of whether the people who use ASL as their main or as their only means of communication are for that reason cognitively or culturally deprived.

If as linguists we are inclined to bring sign language into our domain, we will have many excitements in store for us. These are excitements that I know, unfortunately, only at second hand—by observing the intense involvement in the study of sign on the part of the students in Lynn Friedman's class, by listening to papers on sign at linguistics conferences, by observing ongoing analyses of videotaped discourses in sign, and by reading the papers in this book. I find that learning about language in a gestural/visual modality can give us new ways of thinking about language in the oral/auditory modality. Matters of speech timing, the unidimensionality of the speech chain, certain kinds of limits on sentence complexity, and many other aspects of language structure and function, can now be thought of partly in terms of constraints imposed and opportunities offered by the modality itself. We can separate, in other words, aspects of language that appear to be modality-determined from those that we can attribute to the human capacity for language. And we are now free to ask what that language capacity can accomplish, and how it is constrained, within a different modality, one which allows the use of three-dimensional space, which encourages visual-iconic representations and allows easy transitions between "talk" and demonstrations or pantomime, which tolerates simultaneity of signals from the two hands, the face, and the body, and which requires constant visual monitoring.

Once the possibilities have been grasped, we find that there is no end to the research questions that come to mind on the differences between sign languages and oral languages. How, for example, does a language get along without such grammatical trappings as complementizers, case endings, agreement affixes and function words? And what functions do those trappings really perform in oral languages? How is visual imagery exploited in sign? How does the coherence and continuity of an image aid in the reception and comprehension of a signed discourse? And how, by comparison, is imagery aroused, sustained and manipulated in oral language? How does the speaker's location within the visible signing space figure in the presentation of a narrative "point of view"? How, indeed, is it possible in sign language to **avoid** assuming a point of view in a narrative? And how, in detail, does oral language differ from sign language in this respect? Is there anything in ASL corresponding to the syntactic roles of Subject and Object (distinct, that is, from rhetorical roles like Definite, Topic, Given, etc., and from semantic roles like Agent, Patient, Experiencer)? If not, what exactly is the function of these roles in oral language? How do sign languages change in time? How are new elements introduced? Is the importation of name signs and technical terms from written English evidence of an inherent deficiency in ASL, or is it completely analogous to the use of Latin and Greek elements in the construction of technical terms in English? How does the possibility of using points in space for anaphoric reference bear on the general question of cross-reference in grammar? Are, for example, the relative-clause constructions found in so many (all?) oral languages merely nonspatial devices for maintaining coreference? Is the apparent absence of such constructions in ASL merely a consequence of the possibility of exploiting space in this modality?

Methodological issues also contribute to the sense of excitement in this new field. Means of acquiring reliable data must be found, notations and terms for recording and comparing observations must be constructed, refinements or replacements of standard explanatory paradigms must be devised. Much of the ground work has been done of course, but there is obviously much more to do. As this work goes on, the relevance to oral language research of achievements in sign language research will doubtless frequently become apparent. It has been demonstrated with special clarity that for sign languages it is necessary to devise elicitation methods which yield discourse samples in natural conversational contexts; translation-based techniques, we learn, give uniformly misleading results. The possible lesson for the oral language field worker is obvious.

There will doubtless be readers who look to this book for an answer to the question of whether ASL "is a language". Such readers will quickly lose interest in the purely academic aspect of this question, seeing it as no more important than the problem of deciding whether Australia is the largest island or the smallest continent. Clearly, either the scope of linguistics must reach beyond "language" strictly defined, or the concept of language must be extended to include the rich and powerful symbolic systems of the kind we see described here. The readers of this book will also, I believe, come to see the second and more consequential version of the question as settled once and for all. It is simply very difficult to believe that children could be cognitively limited by being encouraged to learn and master ASL, or that the deaf community in this country could be hampered in any way by enriching, propagating, standardizing, and artistically exploiting their language.

Charles J. Fillmore

PREFACE

This volume is an outgrowth of a course on the structure of the American Sign Language (ASL) given at U.C. Berkeley during the winter and spring quarters, 1975. The papers presented here are the work of students in the class and the instructor, myself. The class was a close-knit, congenial, and conscientious working group, concentrating on field work in unexplored areas of the structure of ASL. Although the papers represent the original research of each author, no one paper can be said to have been written in isolation. All of the works presented here are interrelated, and as such, must be viewed as comprising a whole. In the course of our investigation and in the writing of the papers, the research and thoughts of each member of the group influenced those of every other member; each member sought to incorporate the views of his colleagues into his presentation. Our primary concern is to take a fresh look at manual/visual language without being bound by theories and models based on oral language. In doing so, we reconsider the role of iconicity in the formational properties of the signal ("phonology"), and the grammatical and semantic structure of ASL, with a critical attitude about what has gone before (including the work of the instructor). We come to the conclusion that iconicity—of sublexical units, lexical items, morphology, syntax, and semantics—is a fundamental component of ASL and of manual/visual language in general.

To summarize the contents briefly: Friedman presents a description and phonemic analysis of the four articulatory parameters, and a discussion of the importance of iconicity in ASL's phonological structure; Mandel describes and analyzes iconic devices—in lexical signs, nonlexicalized gesture and in grammatical constructions—and demonstrates the importance of iconicity to the formational structure of the language; DeMatteo presents formal arguments for a linguistically significant level of visual imagery in the grammar of ASL; Edge and Herrmann discuss the grammatical and semantic devices by which signer and addressee identify the relation of arguments to the verb; Thompson presents data and arguments in support of his claim that ASL lacks grammatical subordination; Cogen analyzes several troublesome notions of time expression, in particular the PAST CONTINUOUS marker and the manifestation of the concept 'until'; Baker presents a discussion of eye contact and eye movement as turn-taking regulators in discourse.

What follows here then is a multifaceted but in many ways integrated look at ASL. It attempts to delve into some old questions with new answers, and devises new questions (and some interesting, novel solutions) for further investigation into —not only ASL—but also the nature of the manual/visual modality of language. We hope such research may lend perspective to our understanding of the nature of language, as we allow ourselves to take our investigation of language to language in another modality. We may gain new insight into the difference between the effect on and constraints imposed by the channel of communication and that which belongs to language itself as distinct from the modality in which it is manifested.

On behalf of the authors, I wish to express our gratitude to our principal informant, Tommie L. Radford. It is in large part due to his tireless effort, intelligence, and unfailing enthusiasm that this volume has been written. We are grateful to Helmut Schmitt for the illustrations in Chapter Two and to the Educational Television Office of U.C. Berkeley for the use of videotape equipment and for the time and energy spent by its talented staff in our behalf.

I would especially like to thank Charles J. Fillmore and John H. Crothers for their comments, advice, support, and encouragement during the course and in the writing of the final manuscript, and Eileen Odegaard for her invaluable assistance during the course.

Lynn A. Friedman

INTRODUCTION

Lynn A. Friedman

American Sign Language (ASL) is a manual/visual language used by over half a million deaf (and countless hearing) people in the United States today. It is one of many sign languages; there is no one universal Sign Language. Various visual languages such as ASL, Israeli Sign Language, Chinese Sign, and Iranian Sign Languages are totally unrelated historically. Although others are related—such as American and French Sign Languages—their historical relationship does not in any way correspond to that of the oral languages spoken in the same areas.

ASL (like other sign languages) is not derivative of any oral language. Its "phonological," syntactic, and semantic structure is unique. It is not an alphabetic code for English, although the one-handed manual alphabet is used in limited ways in ASL, for instance to borrow technical terms or names from English. These languages are not comparable to those visual **codes** which have been called sign languages, such as American Indian Sign Language, or Neapolitan Sign Language, which are derivative at least in part from the oral language(s) of the community. Use of the "sign language" of the Plains Indians

> was confined to situations of fairly limited and predictable contexts. Its users always had their native languages in which to express things not covered by the sign lexicon and grammar, so that matter of moment could be referred to an interpreter or translation. [Stokoe, 1972, p. 82]

ASL, however, is capable of all the range and diversity of expression possible in any language, although the means of expression is quite different from that of oral language. The study of ASL is not merely an investigation of another language, but a study of the ways in which the channel of communication—the mode of the signal —can affect language. The study of ASL and other sign languages will hopefully give us a new perspective on our understanding of the nature of language.

American Sign Language is historically related to French Sign Language (FSL). It was introduced to the United States in 1816 by Thomas Gallaudet, founder of the American Asylum in Hartford, Connecticut. There had already existed in the U.S. various local sign languages, and it was these local "languages" in combination with the language brought from France that resulted in ASL. ASL and FSL are still to some extent mutually intelligible today. The most noticeable difference is seen in linguistic borrowing from the local oral languages, English and French.

The earliest documentation of FSL comes from the records of the Abbé de l'Epée, a teacher of the deaf whose career began in 1752. (Publication of his teaching theories dates from 1776.) Epée discovered that his students, although they knew no French, could communicate with each other by means of what he called "la langue des signes naturels." Since his goal was to teach them French, he devised a system of "signes méthodiques" to augment the "language of natural signs" (or the "natural sign language"), adding signs corresponding to grammatical elements in French that did not occur in the natural sign language. For instance, he invented signs for some French prepositions and for plural and other inflectional affixes. He invented signs for *le* and *la* so that his pupils would be able to make necessary gender distinctions in French; although their hand shapes differ, the present-day ASL and FSL signs BOY and GIRL are derived from those signs, an extended index finger (representing the number one) at the forehead for *le* and a finger at the cheek for *la*. Epée incorporated elements of the natural sign language when devising new forms; for examples, he modified the simple past index (flat open palm (*B*) or extended index finger (*G* facing or pointing over shoulder to space behind body to indicate past time), having one "coup de la main" indicate past, two indicate present perfect, and three pluperfect. Today, ASL retains only the simple past index. (A reduplicated index to the space representing past time indicates 'very distant past' in present-day ASL.)

It was the combination of "la langue des signes naturels" and Epée's "signes méthodiques" that became the French Sign Language that was brought to the U.S. in 1816. Over time, FSL and ASL have come to lose many of Epée's "systematic" signs and to incorporate others into the "natural" language.[1]

Educators carried FSL through Europe and the United States. Stokoe (1972) presents the following diagram indicating its dispersal (following Stokoe, 1972, figure 8, p. 93):

FIGURE A

**Sign Languages Acquired
As Natural Languages**

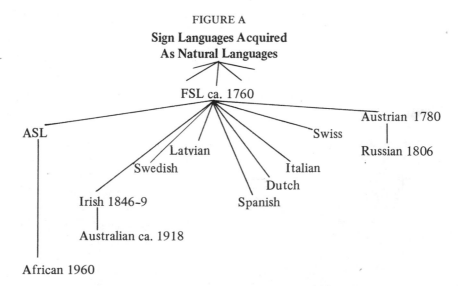

Interestingly, the sign language or languages used in Britain developed independently and are not intelligible to signers of ASL.

> The language situation involves the language of a sub-culture, whose members must also know the language of the larger community. The situation differs from the typical one in that here the sub-culture language is articulated and perceived in the manual/visual modality, but is not written; thus the community is one in which there is literacy only in a second language. [Friedman, 1975b, p. 940]

A fact which complicates the investigation of ASL is that in addition to ASL, there is another variety of Sign Language—Signed English—which is a pidgin of ASL and English. It is composed of signs from ASL, words from English (articulated by means of the manual alphabet), and has primarily English syntax. There are also several manual/visual codes for English, used mainly for pedagogical purposes; these codes constitute a morpheme-to-morpheme representation of English.

> The literate signer, therefore, controls several visual languages, ranging from ASL to any one of a variety of visual codes for English . . . It is also apparent that there is no definite line of demarcation between varieties. Thus we may say that there is a continuum of visual language, and the point on the continuum chosen by a signer is determined by the sociological and sociolinguistic circumstances of the discourse. [Friedman, 1975b, p. 941]

This Sign Language Continuum presents obvious problems to the investigator of only one extreme of the continuum—ASL. Educated signers can easily "talk" at all points along the continuum and can switch from one point to another with facility. Most linguists working on ASL are nonfluent signers, who tend to evoke Signed English; it is a lot easier for English speaking linguists to understand Signed English than to understand ASL, and signers know this. Therefore, the linguist has to be extremely careful (lucky?) to elicit ASL, rather than Signed English.

> In analyzing various video-taped portions of text (discourse) and series of isolated sentences translated from English cue sentences, I have found a striking difference between the two types of elicitation, in regard to grammar. These findings are not surprising when viewed in terms of the Sign Language Continuum . . . .
>
> In the light of the continuum, it is easy to see why signers, when asked to translate written English sentences, might tend to produce signed strings which look remarkably like English (even with repeated instructions to the informant not to do this). In the data I have examined, elicitation of isolated sentences show a marked resemblance to English. Textual data, however, bears no resemblance to English. [Friedman, 1976a, p. 127–128]

Whenever possible, throughout our investigations, we attempted to overcome this difficulty by using textual data. Further discussion of this problem will be found in the papers by Edge and Herrmann, Thompson, and Cogen.

Articulatory Parameters of ASL

There appear to be four major articulatory parameters in ASL—and in all other manual/visual languages: (1) hand configuration—the shape of the articulator(s); (2) movement—the movement of the hands in the formation of the sign; (3) place of articulation—that area on the body, or in the articulation space defined by the body, at which or near which the sign is articulated; and (4) orientation—the orientation of the hands in relation to the body.

We can demonstrate the existence not only of these four sublexical parameters in ASL, but also of finite sets of distinctive features within the parameters. However, the component structure of ASL (or of any given sign language) is not entirely analogous to that of oral language structures.

The most striking difference in the manifestation of ASL (in fact of all sign languages) is that the structure of the language—on all levels—maximizes the use of visual imagery and the use of space. Essentially, all the differences between oral and visual language structure discussed here derive from the fact that the language completely exploits the modality in which it is manifested—it makes complete use of all the iconic cues available in the manual/visual mode.

Oral language segments are necessarily produced in a strictly linear sequence. It is impossible to articulate either two phones or two lexical items simultaneously using the oral/auditory signal. The situation with regard to linearity is quite different in language using a manual/visual signal. Sublexical components in sign language—units of each of the four parameters—must be articulated simultaneously within a given (simple) sign. An individual component (of a parameter) in ASL **cannot** be articulated separately—that is, cannot be articulated (or perceived, for that matter) when not in combination with components of the other parameters. For example, a distinctive unit of the movement parameter cannot be articulated without a component of the hand configuration and the place of articulation parameter. Clearly, this is not the case in oral language where any segment may be articulated separately. (Of course, we must bear in mind that in the actual production of oral language, segments are not entirely discrete. For example, we perceive the characteristics of a stop, which after all entails silence, by the formant structure of the transitions from the preceding and to the following vowel. The stop can be articulated but may not be perceived if articulated alone.

There are a number of monomorphemic signs that have two different places of articulation or two hand configurations (i.e., the hand shape changes during the production of the sign). In those signs, of course, there has to be a linear sequence of components. (That is, for example, one hand shape must precede another.) However, for these signs as well as for simple signs, each place or each hand shape can be articulated only in combination with components from the other parameters. (Also, we find [See Friedman for discussion] that the two parts [syllables?] of signs like HEAD [fingertips of *B*-hand touch first the upper cheek and then the temple] and LIKE [5-hand, facing signer at chest, closes to 8—tip of middle finger and thumb make contact] function as a unified whole [see Figure 1, Friedman, for handshape drawings]. For instance, in the manifestation of emphatic stress, it is the movement between the two places of articulation that changes. In signs in which the hand shape changes, the characteristic movement of those signs is the opening or closing of the hands [or bending of the joints] and the beginning or ending shapes are predictable [from the end or beginning shapes, respectively].)

It is also possible to articulate two lexical items simultaneously in ASL. For instance, the sentence 'Has he eaten?' may be rendered

$$\left[\begin{array}{l} \text{--------------------?-----------------} \\ \text{R \quad EAT \qquad\qquad FINISH} \\ \text{L \quad HE (index) --------------------} \end{array}\right.$$

in which the dominant hand signs EAT, the nondominant hand signs the indexical proform (an extended index finger pointing to a previously established location for the 3rd person referent), while the face carries the question intonation (in this case raising the eyebrows and furrowing the forehead).[2]

Furthermore, I think it can be argued that word order—that is, the linear sequence of/lexical items—plays an insignificant role in ASL's grammar. Edge and Herrmann come to this conclusion in their discussion of the determination of the relation of arguments to the verb in ASL.[3] They conclude

> ... that the use of space to indicate grammatical mechanisms is the basis of the grammatical structure of ASL ...
>
> A description of the grammatical structure of ASL which stops at the level of word order fails to describe many of the basic mechanisms employed in ASL—mechanisms which optimally exploit the manual/visual modality through the use of space to indicate grammatical relationships and create visual representations of those relationships. [p. 176]

The grammar of ASL need not depend on fixed word order or case markings (it has none) to indicate the relation of argument to verb. The signer is able, for example, to move action verbs around in space from the direction of source to the location of goal of the action. Person, location, and temporal proforms are established in space (in conventional locations); first and second person (the interlocutors) are always present. Nonaction verbs, e.g., "psych" verbs, may not be moved from source to goal, as they are necessarily made at or near the body (that is, their place of articulation is always some location on the body, not in neutral space). To indicate grammatical subject (agent or experiencer) and object (patient/beneficiary) of these verbs, the signer either orients his hands away from agent and toward patient (multiorientation verbs) or actually moves his body (or merely his head) into the previously established location for the 3rd person referents (primarily bodily anchored verbs). Edge and Herrmann present a detailed discussion of these and other grammatical mechanisms that are only possible with a manual/visual signal (and which exploit the use of that signal).

Hockett (1966) discusses a number of features he claims are found in all human languages but not all of which are found in nonhuman communication systems. I suggest that at least three of these proposed design features are not necessary properties of human language but only of language in the oral/auditory modality.

> Arbitrariness. The relation between a meaningful element in language and its deno-
> tation is independent of any physical or geometrical resemblance between the two . . .
>
> Discreteness. The possible messages in any language constitute a discrete repertory
> rather than a continuous one. [p. 10]

DeMatteo briefly discusses these features in the light of facts concerning the continuous (as opposed to discrete) nature of ASL's coding system. DeMatteo's primary concern is to argue that a notion of visual imagery is crucial to an accurate grammatical representation of ASL. He proposes that much of ASL's grammar can be viewed as analogic representations of real-world continuous phenomena. Oral language, constrained to the use of discrete (and arbitrary) elements, must codify real-world continuous phenomena like movement, size, and intensity in discrete terms: there must be distinct lexical items (which rarely, if ever, resemble each other phonologically) for each variant or nuance the language chooses to distinguish. Manual/visual language is not constrained to discrete or arbitrary elements; many constructions in ASL may be viewed as a mapping of continuous code elements onto continuous real-world phenomena. DeMatteo offers as an example of analogic representation, variations of the sign glossed in English as MEET. If the signer wishes to convey for instance the sentence 'The boy and the girl met', he will normally (if this is the beginning of a discourse mentioning this particular boy and girl) articulate the sign BOY and then immediately establish a proform representing the preceding nominal—a marker for BOY.[4] A marker for a person is most commonly a *G*-hand, index finger pointing upward. Then the sign GIRL is made and a marker established with the nondominant hand. To convey the reciprocal meaning of the verb (i.e., 'they met'), the two markers are brought in contact with one another in the center of the signing space (about mid-chest). (Past tense may be indicated in a variety of ways, most commonly by an indexical gesture toward the space behind the signer's body, representing past time. Noncalendric temporal reference is usually made, when necessary, only at the beginning of the discourse.) However, if the signer wishes to convey 'The girl met the boy', only the marker representing GIRL moves until it "meets" the BOY marker; in 'The boy met the girl', the BOY marker moves to come in conatct with the GIRL marker.

DeMatteo states that this type of phenomena could easily be handled (as Friedman [1975b] suggests) by referring to the location of the source and goal of the action, if it were not for the fact that there are other related expressions that do not lend themselves so easily to this analysis. Once the person markers have been established, quite a number of "sentences" may be conveyed, distinguished by the movements of the hands. For example, the hands may move past each other without making contact, meaning something like 'they passed each other by'; the hands may approach each other and then turn away; they may make contact and then move outward while touching and then one may abruptly veer rightward ('they met and walked away; then the boy left her'). Either we claim that each of these movements (and the variations are seemingly endless) represent distinct signs, in which case

> we give up all hope of placing finite bounds on the number of lexical items, and all hope of accounting for the productivity of the process. [DeMatteo, p. 114].

or we view these variations as conventional representations of continuous real-world phenomena.

An examination of the formational properties of the signal (phonology) of ASL provides further evidence that language can sustain elements that are neither discrete nor arbitrary. Analogic phonological alternation is a widespread phenomenon in ASL. As Friedman points out later, no accurate description of ASL phonological structure can fail to take into account the pervasive use of nondiscrete and iconic (nonarbitrary) elements. The fact is that many lexical items and sublexical components are iconic in some form and that in large part, (synchronic) phonological alternation depends on a direct and nonarbitrary relation between *signifiant* and *signifié*. This is not to say that all elements of ASL are iconic or nondiscrete. The system sustains arbitrary and discrete elements as well as iconic and scalar components. The claim also does not maintain that iconic signs or elements entirely depict the referent or perform the referent action since

> such an action would be pantomime and such depiction would be drawing. I doubt that a language could sustain such a large amount of unconventional elements. The fact is that **the iconicity and iconic phonological and grammatical mechanisms in ASL and in other sign languages are highly conventionalized. Iconicity, at least in sign language, does not in any way indicate lack of conventionality**. [Friedman, p. 52, emphasis added]

Among types of nonarbitrary and nondiscrete elements of ASL discussed by Friedman are variations in signs like TABLE and WALK. TABLE can be altered to indicate the size of the table—a small table is simply smaller than a big table. The movement of verb signs like WALK can be altered to show manner, e.g., 'walk slowly', 'trudge', 'march', 'walk like Charlie Chaplin', etc. Whole subsystems in ASL such as (noncalendric) temporal reference rely on nonarbitrary and nondiscrete components. In addition, Friedman argues that we would be unable to account felicitously for the formation of and relations among certain sets of signs, such as signs for times of the day, **without** reference to nonarbitrary and nondiscrete components.

It should be pointed out that the kinds of iconic devices available in ASL are numerous and their interrelationship complex. Mandel's article is devoted to analyzing the complexity and presenting as complete a picture as possible of the types of devices available. As he points out, iconicity and conventionality are two separate parameters. However, the relation of the two continua is implicational at least in part, in that the less conventional a sign or a construction is, the more iconic it must be, and the less iconic it is the more conventional it must be, but not the inverse. That is, although a sign may be 100% iconic and 100% conventional (in Mandel's terms), no sign may be wholly noniconic and wholly nonconventional. Mandel divides all iconic signs and constructions into two major categories: (1) **presentation**, in which either the referent action is performed (**mime**), or a token of the referent is presented or indexed (**presentation**), and (2) **depiction**, in which a "picture" of the sign is made, either by pretending to "draw" the picture with all or part of the articulator (**virtual depiction**) or by having the articulator actually become the picture or stand in for parts of the picture (**substitutive depiction**). There is a factor cross-cutting all of these major categories: whether the presentation or the depiction in the sign or construction represents the entire referent or only a part of the referent or something commonly associated with the referent (that is, whether the surface manifestation is metonymic or nonmetonymic of the *signifié*).

Edge and Herrmann's description and discussion of the manifestation of grammatical relations relies almost entirely on recognizing the nonarbitrary nature of ASL's structure. Cogen comes to the conclusion that all (noncalendric) expression of time depends on the visual icon that has been called the **time line**—even those aspectual markers like the PAST-CONTINUOUS that were not recognized before as relating to the icon. In essence, as I stated in the preface to this volume, the primary conclusion to our study to date is that iconicity and continuity of expression (i.e., nondiscreteness) are fundamental components of ASL's structure on all levels. Given these principles, and if we are in agreement that ASL and other sign languages are, in fact, languages (a conclusion that is, I believe, inescapable), then we have to conclude that total arbitrariness and discreteness are not necessary conditions for language.

I began this discussion of Hockett's design features by suggesting that three of the features are not necessary properties of languages, but I have only discussed two features—arbitrariness and discreteness. The third property that is not a necessary feature of language, and about which I hope I need not argue here is that "the channel for all linguistic communication is vocal/auditory" (Hockett, p. 8). As every study of ASL has shown, language in the manual/visual channel is not only viable, but is a highly complex and, if I may add, a most aesthetically pleasing linguistic system.

There is one other design feature that must be mentioned to complete this discussion of Hockett's proposed universals—duality of patterning. Hockett states that

every language has both a cenematic subsystem and a plerematic subsystem . . .

By virtue of duality of patterning, an enormous number of minimum semantically functional elements (pleremes, morphemes) can be and are mapped into arrangements of a conveniently small number of minimum meaningless but message-differentiating elements (cenemes, phonological components). [p. 12]

It is evident that ASL has duality of patterning in that it has both a cenematic and a plerematic subsystem. Stokoe (1972), in speaking about this point, states that

ASL grammar has the same general form as other grammars. There is in this language
a small closed set of distinctive features, meaningless in themselves which nevertheless
combine in ways peculiar to this language to form morphemes, i.e., signs which
denote meaning as do the morphemes of other languages. [p. 94]

There is ample evidence for a sublexical level in ASL. However, I suggest that the
degree to which ASL has duality of patterning is somewhat less than that of oral
languages. I mentioned briefly earlier (and I will discuss it in more detail later) the
fact that some sublexical units are iconic and thus have meaning. Frishberg and
Gough (1973) discuss a large number of sets of signs which have a formational
similarity and a consistent corresponding semantic similarity; that is, some hand
shapes, movements, orientations, and locations have a consistent corresponding
meaning. What this amounts to is that some phonemes are also morphemes, which
of course entails a (partial) lack of duality. For the most part, one hand shape, for
instance, corresponds to two or three meanings, rather than only and always having
one meaning if it carries semantic import at all. For example, the *V*-hand shape can
have one of two meanings (although it does appear in signs in which it functions as
an arbitrary element): the two extended fingers can iconically represent the eyes,
in, for example SEE, LOOK-AT, and BLIND, or the fingers can represent legs, as in
SIT, STAND, JUMP and TOSS-AND-TURN ('fidget'). It is significant that when new
signs are formed, or ad hoc variations produced (in conventional phonological or
grammatical ways), these semantic constants are maintained and are productively
used. I do not mean to imply that all sublexical components of ASL have meaning;
the majority do not—but are arbitrary elements. However, there are too many
meaningful sublexical elements to dismiss the class as analogous to those troublesome
sound symbolic sublexical elements in oral language, like *sn-* in *sneeze*, *sniff*,
snicker, etc. It seems clear that although languages in the manual/visual mode have
duality of patterning, its nature is somewhat different than that in oral/auditory
language.

NOTES

1. For further discussion of FSL and historical change see Stokoe, 1972; Frishberg, 1975a, 1975b; Fischer, 1973b, 1975.
2. Friedman (1975b) presents a fuller discussion of this kind of simultaneous articulation. See also Friedman, 1976b, for physical correlates of question intonation.
3. Friedman, 1976a comes to the same conclusion.
4. See Mandel and Edge and Herrmann for discussion of markers in ASL.

HOW TO READ (AND UNDERSTAND)
ASL TRANSCRIPTS IN THIS VOLUME

Transcripts in this volume, whenever possible, entail standard (and nonstandard where necessary) English glosses for signs. As it would be extremely difficult for the reader entering for the first time into this unfamiliar territory to assimilate a "phonetic" or "phonemic" notational system for ASL, we present all ASL material in terms of sign glosses and interpretive directions.

The following information is necessary for the interpretation of transcripts.

1. All sign glosses appear in upper case: SIGN.
2. Fingerspelled English words appear in lower case, hyphens separating letters of the manual alphabet: f-i-n-g-e-r-s-p-e-l-l.
3. There are often times when the right and left hands are simultaneously articulating two forms. Transcripts indicate this simultaneous articulation by two coordinated lines of glosses—the top line for the dominant hand (right hand in right-handed signers), the lower line for the nondominant (left) hand.

> R BOY MARKER---------------------------------- MEET
> · L   GIRL MARKER ------- MEET
> *The boy and the girl met.*

A marker (usually a *G*-hand pointing upward for a person) is a kind of proform. (See Mandel for discussion.)

4. When it is necessary to indicate the position of the signer's body or the direction of movement of a sign (verbs and indices), these positions and directions appear in lower case print **above** the dominant hand gloss line (and **below** the nondominant hand gloss line where necessary). (See, for example, Edge and Herrmann.)
5. Glosses for nonlexicalized gestures are indicated in lower case print on the (appropriate) gloss line.

upward (toward previously
established 'mother' position)

CHILD jump-up / LOOK-AT
'The child jumped up and looked up at her mother.'

11

6. For ease of interpretation, **all** transcripts throughout the volume are simplified to indicate only information relevant to the particular discussion in each paper.
7. A plus (+) following a sign indicates that the sign is repeated.
8. A virgule (– / –) indicates a substantial pause.
9. A question mark (– ? –) indicates question intonation on sign directly preceding it. Question intonation entails holding (or slightly raising) the questioned sign for an extra "beat", raising the eyebrows and furrowing the brow.
10. A broken line (--------) following a sign indicates that the (handshape of the) sign is maintained while the other hand articulates other forms. (See 3.)

FORMATIONAL PROPERTIES OF AMERICAN SIGN LANGUAGE

Lynn A. Friedman

0. Introduction

0.1 This paper presents a discussion of the basic formational properties of American Sign Language (ASL). Most languages have a physical signal in the oral/auditory channel; ASL and other sign languages, however, are articulated and perceived in the manual/visual modality. The term 'phonology' is used throughout this paper to refer to the description and analysis of the formational properties and organization of any language, whether it has a manual/visual signal or an oral/auditory one.

0.2 This presentation is a departure from earlier analyses of ASL parameters in that it represents on the phonetic level, discrete units of the language. In part, my presentation is derived from Stokoe's (1960, 1965) description of the parameters. Stokoe's description and 'phonemicization'[1]—the first of its kind in ASL and a momentous effort does not, in my opinion, quite capture the system. I will present alternative phonetic and phonemic analyses for three parameters—hand configuration, place of articulation and orientation—and a phonetic and feature analysis of the movement parameter. The analysis of the phonological system of ASL presents a variety of problems (many of which are discussed later). In a departure from my own previous work and that of others,[2] I intend to demonstrate that no phonological description of ASL, depending entirely or even in large part on the notion of discreteness on the phonetic level can account for the formational structure of the language.

0.3 There appear to be four basic articulatory parameters in Sign Language: hand configuration, place of articulation, movement, and orientation (of the hands in relation to the body). A simple sign involves one hand configuration, made with both hands or with the dominant hand, combined with one place of articulation (which can be the nondominant hand), and specifications of orientation and movement features.

0.4 There are two types of signs which involve both hands: (1) those in which both hands move, or in other words in which both act as articulators, and (2) those in

13

which the dominant hand (the right in right-handed signers) acts as the articulator and the nondominant hand (left) as the place of articulation. In signs of the second type, only the dominant hand moves. In signs in which both hands have a movement component, both hands must maintain the same configuration **and** the same movement throughout the sign (although the movement may be an alternating one, e.g., the hands alternately move up and down). There is one exception that I know of—the sign for the technical term TOTAL COMMUNICATION—in which the hand shapes differ (one has T, and other C), although the movement of the two hands is the same. However, this sign has been recently coined, and is a borrowing from English. We shall see later that loan signs tend to behave oddly, at least at the time of their entry into the language, especially in regard to hand configuration (see section 1.3). Examples of double articulator signs are: TALK—two 4's, facing each other alternate toward and away from the body at the mouth (see Figure 1 for drawings of hand configurations), and BUT—two G's, pointing upward, sometimes crossed, in neutral space, diverge.

In those signs in which one hand acts as the articulator and the other as the place of articulation, there are two possibilities in regard to hand shape: either (1) both hands have the same configuration, i.e., the signs are symmetrical regarding hand shape, or (2) the nondominant or place-of-articulation hand assumes one of six neutral hand shapes: $A, B, 5, G, C,$ or O. Examples of the first type are SCHOOL —B-hand taps B-hand twice, NAME—H-hand (facing leftward) twice contacts H-hand (facing rightward). Signs of the second type are HELP—B-hand moves up under and makes contact with A-hand, thumb up, and PRACTICE—A-hand, fingers downward moves back and forth across the extended index finger of G pointing rightward.[3]

0.5 Signs may also have two places of articulation. Of these, we can distinguish polymorphemic (compounds) and monomorphemic signs. Compounds such as BELIEVE and SISTER, which derive from two distinct signs—e.g., BELIEVE < THINK + JOIN, SISTER < FEMALE + SAME—are subject to regular phonological processes by which distinct hand configurations and movements of the two signs assimilate.[4]

0.6 The articulation space available to the signer is functionally limited to that area at or near his body which his addressee can see. This space is limited to the area of an approximate rectangle, the limits of which are a line approximately six inches above the head, a line at the waist, the width being the extent of the arms bent at the elbows connecting the upper and lower limits. This seemingly trivial limitation imposes constraints on the phonological structure of the language in that no sign may be made outside of this area, although it is quite possible to do so (e.g., behind one's back). [5]

1. Hand Configuration

1.1 Figure 1 gives the discrete hand shapes of ASL. It is clear that not all physically possible configurations occur. For example, there are sixteen possible combinations of fingers extended from the fist (excluding thumb extension as a variable). That is, all fingers can be extended, or none; each of the four may be extended separately; six combinations of two extended fingers and four combinations of three are possible. Of these 16, ten possible variations occur in ASL represented by: *A, B, G, I, H, Y , W, F, 8, 7.* By this example I wish to point out that there are physically possible hand shapes (and movements, places of articulation, as well) that happen **not** to occur in ASL—as there are sounds which do not occur in any given oral language. For example, the extended ring finger as a hand shape does not occur in ASL but does in Chinese Sign Language.

1.2 It would be possible to analyze the hand shape parameter in terms of features. We could, for example, describe hand shapes as having spread or unspread fingers; there could be an *n*-ary feature which describes thumb position—e.g., drawn inward, at the side of the hand, extended forward, extended sideward. Various feature descriptions have been (informally) suggested for the analysis of the hand shape parameter.[6] However, while the use of the diacritics ° and ¨ (bent fingers) amounts to a partial feature analysis, there would appear to be little or no motivation for taking on the trappings of a **full** feature analysis. Except for a few cases (involving the spread thumb and finger bending, for example), there would seem to be only arbitrary reasons for making specific choices of features. Until it can be demonstrated that generalizations about variations in hand shapes, either historical or synchronic, can best be formulated in terms of recurring features—thereby giving the feature analysis explanatory value—I do not believe we need such an analysis. It is possible to explain occurring synchronic variation in hand configuration in terms of a phonemic analysis.

1.3 The analysis presented here is not a classic phonemicization. Given sign language and its unique typology, such an analysis is impossible. The first departure is necessitated by the fact that there is something odd about the configurations *T, M, N, D, bD, E, G_2, K, I, W,* and *R,* shapes forming a fairly large class of extrasystematic elements. These configurations are only marginally available in that they only appear in loans from English. ASL, a nontechnical language, borrows items from the oral language surrounding it by relatively straightforward means, using the existing one-handed manual alphabet that has hand-shapes for each letter of the Roman alphabet (and one for ampersand). (The reader will note that whenever possible the name given for the hand shapes in Figure 1 corresponds to the appropriate letter of the manual alphabet.) The initial letter of the English word, rendered in the manual alphabet, becomes the hand shape of the loan. This hand configuration is then usually combined with the same movement, place, and orientation of an existing, semantically related sign. For example, the signs **MATH, ALGEBRA, CALCULUS,** and **GEOMETRY** are all formed using the initial letters *M, A, C,* and *G* respectively with the same movement, place, and orientation of the original sign **FIGURE-OUT.** Name signs (signs for individual people) are usually invented (for

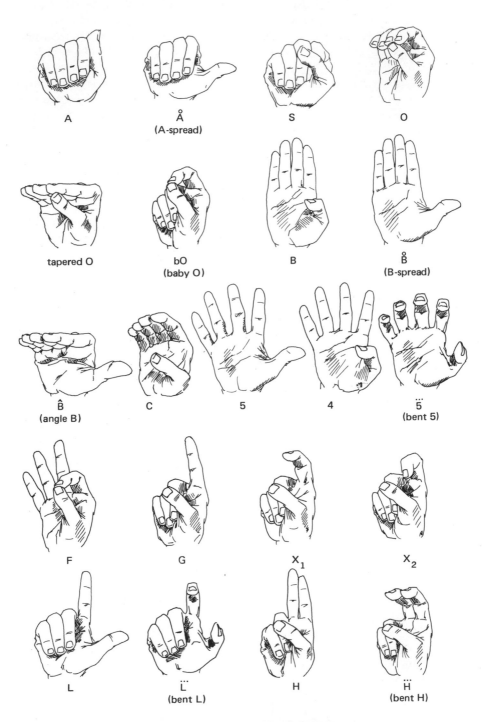

FIGURE 1   HAND CONFIGURATION

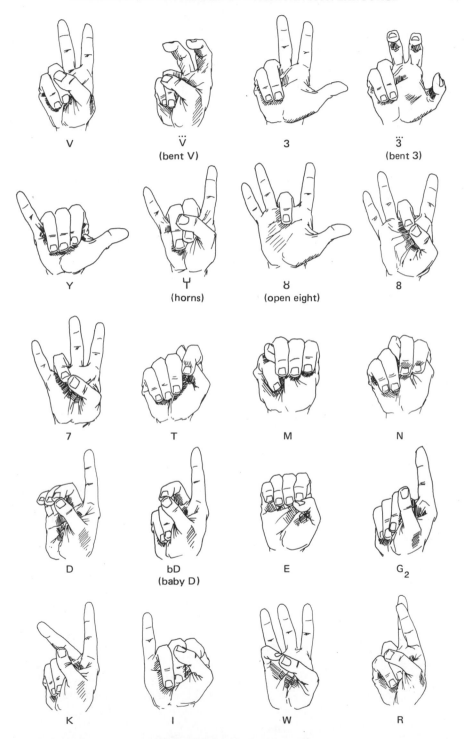

FIGURE 1   HAND CONFIGURATION

each person) based on some personal characteristic of the individual using the initial letter of the person's English name. For example, a recently invented name sign for Nixon uses an N, moved leftward under the mouth, based on the sign LIE (prevaricate), which has the same movement and place, but with the G-shape. As the configurations T, M, N, D, bD, E, G_2, K, I, W, and R only appear in loan words, we might say that they have not been fully incorporated into the phonological system of the language. This is not to say that they should not be considered in our analysis, but only that they must be considered marginal. It is interesting to note that if we did wish to analyze hand shape in terms of features, these shapes do not conform to regular patterns apparent among the other frequently occurring configurations. With the exception of I and W, each of the "marginal" shapes have "features" that belong to no other hand shape in the language. (T, M, and N share the same "odd" feature.) For example, R entails the crossing of the middle finger over the index finger—no other hand shape has any finger crossing over any other; K is characterized by the thumb tip making contact with the middle finger—not at the tip which is common among regular shapes, e.g., O, bO, F, 8—but at the middle or third joint. Whether or not we ultimately opt for a feature description of this parameter, given the distribution in the language of this class of "loanshapes" ("loanphones"?), it would appear that they will have to be considered odd or marked.

1.31   There are six hand configurations which may be said to be **neutral** or **unmarked**[7]: A (and its variant S), B, 5, G, C, and O. These hand shapes can be classed as neutral because of various observations regarding their appearance and acquisition. These six shapes appear the most frequently of all possible shapes in the language (with A, B, and G being most prominent). They occur in all known sign languages. Presumably they are the least complex shapes the hand can assume (in terms of muscular arrangement). As further evidence, it is just these hand configurations that are the first acquired by the child learning Sign. When the child overgeneralizes in regard to hand shape, she tends to choose these. (She initially has only A, B, and G.) One significant aspect of the "unmarkedness" of these configurations was mentioned earlier in regard to the formation of two-handed signs: in a sign which entails the use of both hands, if both do not have the same shape, one must assume one of these six neutral shapes. Also, when there is a hand shape change in the articulation of a single monomorphemic sign, the sign must either begin or end in a neutral shape, as for example in the sign CATCH (a rapid closing of 5 to S, representing grabbing) or CHOOSE (a closing of 5 to F). Given this constraint, I would prefer to analyze signs of this type as having a single hand shape and an opening or closing action. Stokoe (1960, 1965) has the elements opening and closing action in the movement parameter, with the final hand shape given for individual items. I concur with his analysis except that it would not appear to be necessary to stipulate the final (or initial for "closing action" signs) configuration in that they are either predictable or variable (and as such of no importance to the phonemic make-up of the sign). Such insignificant variability is the case when a sign closes to a fist—it is irrelevant whether the final shape is A or S. (S is a variant of A—see below for phonemic inventory.)

1.32   Another significant departure from classical phonemic analysis is that in the analysis of ASL we need to take into account the visual picture that the sign makes—its iconicity. The iconic value of a sign appears to have a considerable impact on its phonological structure. As I have stated earlier, and as I will elaborate (section 5), I believe that an accurate phonological description of ASL will have to include principles of iconicity as well as a description of arbitrary elements, even among such discrete elements as individual hand shapes.

1.4   Phonemic Inventory

We can now proceed with a phonemic inventory of the hand configuration parameter, including the environments in which the variants of each set occur. Please refer to Figure 1 to interpret symbols. (See Table 1 for summary of phoneme sets.)

1.41   /A/. The most frequent allophone is $\overset{\circ}{A}$ (A with thumb extended), occurring when contact is made with the thumb tip, in, for example, YESTERDAY and GIRL, **or** in signs in which the thumb extension is necessary for iconic purposes, e.g., SCIENCE, with two $\overset{\circ}{A}$-hands, representing pouring something into a beaker or test tube.

Another allophone of /A/ is S, which occurs when contact of the two hands is made on the side (where the thumbs would be if the shape were A), as in SHOE(S). Clearly it is easier to make this kind of side contact if the thumbs are not in the way. However, A occurs in signs where one hand makes contact on the thumb side, as in PATIENT (A-hand, thumb-side in contact with mouth, moves downward). S also occurs in a few loan words such as STRIVE. As stated in section 1.31, S also occurs as a neutral final shape in signs with changing hand shape, as in CATCH.

1.42   /O/. *Tapered-O (flat-O)* and O occur in free variation in all signs having /O/, e.g., EAT, NUMBER, FLOWER.

One variant of /O/ is bO (which may also be a variant of F—see 1.48), given signs like '20' which entail a closure of the L shape to bO. Given the morpheme structure condition (cited above) that signs with two different hand shapes must begin with or end in a neutral hand shape, it is reasonable to analyze some bOs as variants of /O/.

1.43   /B/. B and $\overset{\circ}{B}$ (B with extended thumb) occur in free variation in signs such as THING, CHILD, TROUBLE, the possessive index, and the future modal WILL. In fact $\overset{\circ}{B}$ seems to appear more frequently than B, so we might as easily call this phoneme /$\overset{\circ}{B}$/. A convenient reason for calling it /B/ is that the hand shape B corresponds to the manual alphabet B.

The only condition on the occurrence of the variants of /B/ is that in signs with thumb tip contact,[8] e.g., STUBBORN (two $\overset{\circ}{B}$-hands thumb at sides of forehead, bend to $\hat{B}$); only the $\hat{B}$ variant, for obvious reasons, may occur.

$\hat{B}$ *(angle-B)* may be considered an allophone of /B/, occurring when the movement designation is *BEND-FROM-KNUCKLES*. The reduced form of the sign BOX has this shape. $\hat{B}$ also occurs in highly iconic, often nonlexicalized gestures[9] such as one indicating the surface and sides of a table.

1.44   I want to digress for a moment to return to the discussion about motivation for a feature analysis. In both the phoneme sets /A/ and /B/ we have seen the extension of the thumb (in $\mathring{A}$ and $\hat{B}$) as a conditioned variable—$\mathring{A}$ and $\hat{B}$ both occur in signs entailing thumb tip contact. Here we have an allophonic variation based on a possible feature distinction, say ±thumb extension, or as I mentioned earlier, an *n*-ary feature including all four possible thumb positions. Other evidence in support of the thumb-position feature may be found in an ongoing phonological change—the extension of the thumb on hand configurations that previously did not entail the extension. Not all signs with appropriate hand shapes have undergone the change nor do all signers extend the thumb. Signs in which the thumb is now found in its extended position are those that previously had the hand shapes *G, H, V, V̂, Ϥ, X, R*, and *I*, as in the signs RED, NAME, VOICE, BLIND, KIDS, FRIEND, RESTAURANT, and INSTITUTION. This ongoing change results in a "neutralization in progress" in that distinct hand shapes merge; for example, *G* adds the thumb extension and consequently has the same shape as *L*, and *V* with thumb extension merges with *3*.[10] Although there would seem to be motivation for a distinctive thumb position feature, we still do not have motivation for any other features (and one ingredient will not make the cake).

1.45   /C/. /C/ has no variants. Signs with the shape *C* include DRINK (*C* curves toward signer at mouth) and BASKETBALL (two *C*-hands facing away from signer twist upward, as if tossing a basketball into a basket).

1.46   /5/. The hand shape *4* may be considered a variant of /5/. *4*, a relatively infrequent shape, occurs for example in the signs TALK, LECH (a metaphorical variant of DROOL, which is made with *G*), a form of MEET or MEETING, and in the plural pronominal index. It does not contrast with *5* and basically can be analyzed as the non-thumb-extended variant of /5/. There is always an element of plurality (or quantity) involved in signs having the *4*-shape: the form of TALK with two *4*-hands is used only when referring to conversation among several people (TALK, when referring to two people, is made with two *G*-hands); MEET(ING) with two *4*s is the "plural" form of MEET made with two *G*s.[11] Therefore, if we view the *4*-hand as having a correlating semantic constant, we might say that *4* is the "plural" variant of /5/. Since in some signs which (in citation form) have *4*, the thumb may now be extended (in free variation with its nonextension)—as it may be with other hand shapes already discussed—it is possible that the phonetic distinction between *4* and *5* may eventually be lost—or that *4* and *5* would appear in free variation.

1.47   /5̈/. /5̈/ (also called 'claw' for obvious reasons) has no variants. *5* and *5̈* can be shown to be distinct given the close to minimal pair CONFUSED and

COLLEGE. CONFUSED has two $\ddot{5}$-hands facing each other in neutral space making two circular motions; in COLLEGE with two 5-hands facing each other, the dominant hand starts in contact with the nondominant hand and moves upward in a circular motion, palm downward throughout.

However, a case could be made for $\ddot{5}$ being a variant of /5/, given signs like BUG (INSECT), in which the fingers of the 5-hand (thumb tip in contact with the nose) bend during the articulation of the sign, i.e., 5 becomes $\ddot{5}$. If we include BEND or BEND-FINGERS as an element of the movement parameter (c.f., $\hat{B}$ above), then we would have to say the $\ddot{5}$ is the bent variant of /5/. We would not say that the $\ddot{5}$ in CONFUSED is the bent variant of /5/ because the movement element 'bend' does not occur in the sign (i.e., the fingers are bent throughout).

One possible solution is to posit $\ddot{5}$ as a variant of /5/ and to say that the $\ddot{5}$ in CONFUSED is a result of some kind of metaphoric iconicity of the sign in that the muscular tension entailed in the formation of $\ddot{5}$ may represent emotional tension (or something like that) in a way that 5 could not. In support of this kind of solution, I would add that $\ddot{5}$ appears very infrequently, except in those signs where 5 becomes $\ddot{5}$.

For the moment, however, it seems best to say that the $\ddot{5}$ appearing in signs like BUG is the bent variant of /5/ while the $\ddot{5}$ in CONFUSED is a distinct phoneme.

1.48   /F/. bO is an infrequent reduced variant of /F/ in, for example, JOIN. The term reduced refers to those hand shapes (movements and places) and hand shape (movement and place) changes occurring in colloquial and/or rapid signing (analogous to rapid speech), or when the signer is tired.[12] One aspect of rapid signing or "tired signing" is that possible nondistinctive elements of hand shape are altered. (Another prominent aspect is that neutralization of clearly distinctive elements of all parameters occurs.) The use of bO in signs that in citation form have F may be an example of such an alternation. (Note that bO is actually F without the extended fingers.) Reduction as a variant is discussed again in the phoneme set /Y/.

One variant of bO (not shown in Figure 1) places the thumb over the index finger—in a sense gripping it—rather than having the fleshy parts of the fingers touching. This variant occurs when the sign's movement is a flicking, opening motion as in SURPRISE—two bOs flick open at the midface area, accompanied by a rapid (closing and) opening of the eyes. (c.f., 8 in /8/, which has a similar variant.)

1.49   /G/. /G/ has no variants. G is one of the three most frequently occurring hand shapes, occurring in signs such as THINK (G contacts forehead) and BORING (G in twisting motion in contact with side of nose). Interestingly, G is not the shape of the letter G in the manual alphabet—G_2 is.

1.50   /X/. X_1 and X_2 are allophones of the phoneme /X/. X_2 (the "squished" variant) occurs when the sign entails contact on the body with the (extended) knuckle of the middle joint, as in ONION, APPLE, and KEY. X_1 occurs elsewhere, in signs such as FRIEND, TEASE, and MUST.

1.51   /L/. $\ddot{L}$ may be considered an allophone of /L/ for two reasons. One is that it appears in apparent free variation with L in signs such as BIG—two Ls separated sharply in neutral space. ($\ddot{L}$ appears especially in the stressed form of BIG.)[13] The second reason for the inclusion of $\ddot{L}$ in /L/ is similar to the one cited earlier for the inclusion of $\hat{B}$ in /B/: we may analyze signs such as RUN—two Ls, the index finger of one hooked to the thumb of the other, moving forward with the "free" thumb and index finger bending and straightening repeatedly—as having a movement component 'bend at the fingers' (*BEND-FINGERS*). Thus $\ddot{L}$ occurs in signs having an /L/ shape and such a movement component.

The only other signs—mostly nonlexicalized gestures—in which $\ddot{L}$ occurs are highly iconic: for example, a *bent-L* moved horizontally across the area in which TABLE had just been signed to indicate the amount of dirt on the tabletop. As has been pointed out above, iconicity plays an important role in the phonological structure of the language. The degree of iconicity[14] a sign shows may determine the degree to which the formational properties of the sign will vary from the "conventional" phonological structure.

A variant of $\ddot{L}$ (not shown in Figure 1) has the thumb bent while the index finger remains straight. This configuration appears in two types of signs. In one, the index finger is "anchored" to a place or articulation on the body, e.g., COKE, an iconic representation of shooting a hypodermic needle into the upper arm. (The sign COKE, meaning the soft drink, thus borrows the English metaphor for the same referent.) Clearly, if the index finger must maintain contact during the sign, it would not bend as well. The second type of sign (and COKE really fits into this class as well) is one that iconically represents the referent, as in GUN, where the index finger forms the barrel, and the bending thumb represents the cocking of the trigger. Again, this variant need not be a problem in the phonemic analysis, if we allow for principles of iconicity to operate. (See section 5 for discussion of iconicity.)

1.52   /H/. *Bent-H* ($\ddot{H}$), an infrequently occurring shape, is an allophone of /H/, occurring in signs that entail contact with the palm-side of the fingers, as in SIT (CHAIR) in which the *bent-H* of the dominant hand makes palm-side contact with the H (palm toward signer) of the nondominant hand. Given the morpheme structure condition that in two-handed signs where the nondominant hand is place of articulation, either both hands must have the same shape, or one must assume a neutral shape, it would appear that *bent-H* is a member of the phoneme set /H/. Since H is **not** a neutral hand shape, both hand shapes must be the same—at least phonemically.

1.53   /V/, /$\ddot{V}$/. The analysis of /$\ddot{V}$/ presents another potential problem in that it appears to be both an allophone of /V/ and a distinct phoneme. $\ddot{V}$ and V contrast in some environments, for example, in two-handed signs in neutral space, and in the signs PROBLEM ($\ddot{V}$-hand makes contact with sharp movement on $\ddot{V}$-hand) and WORSE (two Vs cross sharply—usually at the wrist—in neutral space). Another environment in which V and $\ddot{V}$ contrast is at the eyes, for example in the near minimal pair SEE (V moves outward from the eye area) and BLIND ($\ddot{V}$ moves inward sharply to eyes). However, for this particular pair, it may be that $\ddot{V}$ may be considered a variant of /V/. It has been pointed out (cf., Frishberg and Gough, 1973) that the use of the hand shape $\ddot{V}$ often correlates with the semantic notion *DIFFICULTY*. We could analyze BLIND as having the /V/ phoneme if we say that BLIND is SEE + *DIFFICULTY* and that *DIFFICULTY* entails the use of the bent variant of /V/.

In signs having $\ddot{V}$ such as TRAVEL, WALK, SIT-IN-A-CIRCLE, ROLL-IN-THE-AISLES-WITH-LAUGHTER, and JUMP, $\ddot{V}$ may also be analyzed as a variant of V, in that in many signs both V and $\ddot{V}$ iconically represent legs. Signs of this type having V include STAND, LIE (DOWN), and TOSS-AND-TURN (in bed). The choice of V or $\ddot{V}$ is determined by the shape of the legs in the referent; the bending of the fingers represents the bending of the knees.[15] For example, when standing the legs are typically straight—thus the V-shape is used: when jumping or walking the legs are typically bent or bending—JUMP has the $\ddot{V}$-shape and WALK has $\ddot{V}$ with fingers wiggling. TRAVEL ($\ddot{V}$, palm downward, in a circular motion in neutral space) and SIT-AROUND-IN-A-CIRCLE ($\ddot{V}$ "placed" several times with downward movement in circle in neutral space) are phonologically derived from SIT (*bent-H* makes palm-side contact with H toward signer). When two-handed signs become one-handed (in for example "encumbered" signing) the dominant hand is always used. In signs in which the nondominant hand is the place of articulation, this "abbreviation" results in the loss or substitution of the place of articulation.[16] TRAVEL and SIT-AROUND-IN-A-CIRLCE entail this kind of reduction. Given the V-legs "morpheme," we might say that $\ddot{H}$ is a variant of /V/ as well, when it appears in signs such as SIT.

Other evidence in support of $\ddot{V}$ as a variant of /V/ comes from an examination of signs such as DOUBT and FROG in which V becomes $\ddot{V}$ in the course of the sign. As with $\hat{B}$ and $\ddot{L}$, we could analyze the $\ddot{V}$-shape in these signs as resulting from /V/ with a *BEND-FINGERS* movement.

It seems clear that $\ddot{V}$ occurs sometimes as a variant of and sometimes in contrast with /V/. Signs such as STUCK and VAMPIRE (where V makes contact with center and side of neck respectively) in which either V or $\ddot{V}$ occur in free variation, make it clear that the contrast between /V/ and /$\ddot{V}$/ is neutralized in certain environments and under certain iconic conditions.

1.54   /3/. 3 and $\ddot{3}$ may be analyzed in much the same way as V and $\ddot{V}$. $\ddot{3}$ appears to be an allophone of /3/ when it occurs as a result of the movement *BEND-FINGERS* in signs like BUG (a variant of the one given in 1.47 with /5/)—3 with thumb tip contact at the nose sharply bends to $\ddot{3}$. However, 3 and $\ddot{3}$ are in contrast in other environments; for example, in neutral space, in AWKWARD (two $\ddot{3}$s move back and forth in neutral space) and in CAR (3, palm sideward, moves forward and usually abruptly stops in neutral space). Thus we would want to say that $\ddot{3}$ is both an allophone of /3/ and a distinctive phoneme /$\ddot{3}$/.

1.55   /Y/.   The phoneme /Y/ and two of its variants, $\overset{\circ}{\mathsf{T}}$ and $\mathsf{8}$, are interesting in that they demonstrate the kind of departure from the 'core' phonological structure that occurs in ASL in the presence of iconicity or reduction. The shape ȣ (*open-eight*) occurs as a reduced form (as in colloquial or "tired" signing) of /Y/, e.g., in the reduced form of WHY. Y reduces to its ȣ variant **only** in those signs in which the hand closes to Y during the sign's articulation. In citation form, WHY entails the closing of the hand (palm toward signer) to Y while it moves outward from the forehead; when reduced, the hand (usually unmoving, located somewhat below the forehead) has the ȣ-shape with the lowered middle finger wiggling. Although it is clear that ȣ is a reduced variant of /Y/ in this environment, in all other circumstances ȣ contrasts with /Y/. (See section 1.57 for discussion.) Thus we find another case of neutralization of distinction, this time due to phonological reduction.

The shape ᶙ can easily be shown to be an allophone of both /Y/ and /ᴴ/ (see also section 1.56–/ᴴ/). That ᶙ is a variant of /Y/ can be demonstrated with the sign CALIFORNIA, a ᶙ-shape beginning at the ear and moving downward with a twisting motion; as the hand moves downward the extended index finger gradually lowers. The appearance of ᶙ in the sign and the phenomenon of the index finger of the ᶙ-shape lowering, which appears only in this sign (as far as I know), can be explained as a result of an unusual assimilation of two hand shapes. CALIFORNIA was originally an unassimilated compound composed of EARRING (thumb and index finger grasp earlobe) and GOLD (or YELLOW) (Y-hand twisting in neutral space). (Signers are aware of this original compound.) The twisting motion accompanying the downward movement in the current sign is a result of an anticipation of the movement of the second part of the unassimilated compound. The beginning hand shape—ᶙ—can be analyzed as a Y-shape (in anticipation of the Y in GOLD) with the superimposition of the extended index finger remaining from the original first element of the compound. The prominent aspect of the hand shape in EAR-RING is the extension and closing (grasping) of the thumb and index finger. It would seem that the prominence of the index extension is great enough (possibly iconically) to allow it to remain an element of the assimilated form in this unusual type of phonological assimilation.[17] Most likely, the ᶙ-shape in CALIFORNIA will eventually be seen as distinct from /Y/, as signers forget the unassimilated form. Clearly, there is a potential in the language for splits as well as mergers.

The ᶙ-shape also occurs in the sign AIRPLANE (hand moves across upper neutral space, palm downward). I would say that the occurrence of ᶙ in this sign is due to iconicity, since the shape can easily be construed as visually representing the basic elements of an airplane: i.e., the wings and fuselage by the extension of the three digits. As already mentioned, the presence of iconicity or iconic elements in the structure of the sign seems to allow for relaxation of phonological restrictions. Again, it would appear that iconicity plays an important role in the phonological structure of ASL.

All other occurrences of ᶙ may be explained as allophonic variants of /ᴴ/.

The Y variant occurs most frequently of the allophones of /Y/ in signs such as STAY, WADDLE (an iconic variant of WALK with V-legs), PLAY, MISTAKE, and TELEPHONE.

1.56   /Ч/. That Ч contrasts with Y can be seen in, for example, the following two minimal environments: the nondominant hand as place of articulation, as in the signs THAT (Y contacts nondominant palm) and CIGARETTE (Ч contacts extended index finger (G) of nondominant hand); the lower face, for example, SILLY (Y nods at wrist in front of nose—midface area—and KID (slang for 'child') (Ч, palm downward, twists under nose—representing wiping a runny nose).

As I mentioned earlier, there is an ongoing change in some hand shapes, entailing the addition of the extended thumb to shapes that previously had the thumb "tucked in". Ч is one shape that sometimes adds the thumb extension, forming Ч̊. Signs with /Ч/ that sometimes appear with Ч̊ include CIGARETTE, WHISKEY, and BIG-WORD (a variant of WORD, made with *bent-L*). It would appear that the Ч̊ variant, occurring in free variation (so far) with Ч in these signs, is an allophone of /Ч/. I would predict an eventual across-the-board merger, with the potential loss of Ч as an element of the language.

1.57   /8/. 8 is a frequently occurring shape, appearing most prominently in verbs of feeling, both physical and emotional, e.g., TOUCH, SICK, HATE, PITY, TASTE (DELICIOUS) and DEPRESSED.

It is clear that 8 and Y contrast, despite the fact that 8 is a variant of /Y/ under the conditions described in 1.55 (see /Y/). as can be seen in the near minimal pair PITY (8-hand makes small circles in neutral space—orientation depends on location of agent and patient) and STAY—which also has the meaning 'uh-huh' or 'oh yeah, I got it', (Y-hand, palm away from the signer, moves back and forth in small motion in neutral space).

The shape *8* is an allophone of /8/, occurring in signs with the movement element *CLOSE* or *OPEN*. That is, *8* only appears in signs which open to 8 from *8* or close to *8* from 8. For example, HATE entails a flicking motion of the *8*-hand— middle finger flicks out from the thumb (orientation determined by location of patient); LIKE is formed by closing 8 to *8* at the chest. It should be noted that the *8*-shape in signs like HATE has the thumb over the middle finger (gripping it), rather than having the fleshy parts touching—presumably because of the flicking motion. (The same phonetic distinction under the same conditions appears with the shape bO—see /F/ in section 1.48.)

1.58   /7/. 7, a very infrequently occurring shape, has one variant. It appears (as far as I know) in only two signs: the number '7' and a sign meaning 'obedient' or 'good boy' (usually used to describe a child or dog), which has 7 with the fingers unspread, in a slightly circular or back-and-forth motion in neutral space. (7 contrasts with 8 in the minimal pair PITY and GOOD BOY.)

1.6   Loan Phones

Loan phones are those hand shapes which only occur in loan words from English —using the hand shape corresponding to the first letter of the English word.

/T/.   *T* occurs, for instance in the sign TRY (two *T*-hands—in neutral space—move down and outward), derived from an original sign TRY made with *A*. (Now, in some circles, mostly schools, there are TRY, STRIVE, and ATTEMPT. These signs differ only in hand shape. The invention of these new signs reflects an attempt to augment the teaching of English.)

/M/ and /N/.   *M* and *N* can be made with the fingers folded down, almost making a fist (as shown in Figure 1), or with the fingers extended outward, like *B̂*. Both variants of each are seen as the same element by the signer, in fingerspelling, for instance. The folded variants appear in MONDAY (*M* makes a circular motion in neutral space) and NATURE (or NATURAL) (*N* makes a circular motion ending in contact with back of nondominant hand). Signs having the extended variants include DOCTOR (*M*, for French *médecin*, contacts pulse-side of wrist) and NURSE (*N* contacts wrist).

/D/.   An example of a sign with *D* is DENTIST (*D* contacts mouth or sometimes teeth). *bD* is a variant of /D/ which appears in free variation with *D*.

/E/.   *E* occurs in EAST (*E* moves rightward in neutral space). There is one sign (that I know of) which has *E* but is not an initial letter borrowing, that of the California "dialect" sign CUTE (*E*-hand, palm toward signer, brushes downward twice on or slightly above the chin).

/G_2/. G_2 appears in, for instance, GROUP (two G_2s circle forward and make contact on pinky side of hand in neutral space) and GREEN (G_2 twists in neutral space). G_2 is also used in loans in which the English word begins with *Q*, like QUEEN (G_2 contacts contralateral shoulder and ipsilateral side of waist), because *G* and *Q* have the same shape in the manual alphabet, differing only in orientation.

/K/.   *K* appears in loans beginning with the letter *K* like KING (where *K* contacts the contralateral shoulder and ipsilateral side of the waist), and also in those English words beginning with *P* like PURPLE (*K* twists in neutral space), because *K* and *P* (like *G* and *Q*) have the same shape in the manual alphabet, differing only in orientation.

/I/.   *I* occurs in loan words whose initial letter in English is *I*, e.g., INSTITUTION (based on SCHOOL), and IDEA (based on THINK), or *J*, e.g. JAPANESE. Actually, *I* may be considered a "full-fledged" phoneme at present, since it also occurs in a few nonloans, e.g., SPAGHETTI. In the manual alphabet, *J* is formed with the *I*-shape, moving downward in a curved line, as if drawing the letter *J*.

/W/.   *W* is basically a loan shape, appearing in loans in which the initial letter of the English word is *W*, e.g., WORLD, WEIRD, and in one nonloan, the number '6'.

/R/.   *R* occurs in such signs as RESTAURANT, REASON, and RESTROOM. *R* is the only hand shape in which one finger crosses over another.

2. Movement

2.0   Stokoe (1960, 1965) describes the movement parameter in terms of the following distinctive elements: upward movement, downward movement, up and down movement, rightward movement, leftward movement, side to side movement, movement toward signer, movement away from signer, to and fro movement, supinating rotation (palm up), pronating rotation (palm down), twisting movement, nodding or bending action, opening action, closing action, wiggling action of fingers, circular action, convergent action (approach), contactual action (touch), linking action (grasp), crossing action, entering action, divergent action (separate), and interchanging action.

In this section, I will present a reanalysis of the movement parameter in terms of features.[18] Here I am concerned with the kinds of motion the hands and arms are capable of doing, the movements that specifically occur in ASL, and the interrelation of those movements within the structure of the language. We can analyze the movement parameter in terms of four fundamental aspects of movement: (1) whether one or both hands move and if both hands are articulators, whether they have the same movement or interact with each other; (2) whether or not the articulator makes contact with the body; (3) the direction of movement; and (4) the manner of movement.

2.1   To begin with (and as mentioned in section 0.3), in the citation form of a given sign, either one hand (the dominant) is the articulator—in which case the nondominant hand either acts as the place of articulation or does nothing[19]—or both hands act as articulators.[20] In encumbered signing only the dominant hand moves; often, for signs in which the nondominant hand is the place of articulation in citation form, the "lost" location is replaced by a convenient surface such as the hip, a tabletop and so on. For those signs in which both hands move, either their movements are the same or the hands interact in a relatively simple movement, e.g., alternating up and down or approaching each other. No sign requires the hands to perform different actions (like patting the head and rubbing the stomach at the same time). There are five mutually exclusive types of movement in which the hands are required to interact, all of which only occur in signs made in neutral space and thereby entail no contact with the body.

2.11   The most frequently occurring interacting movement entails an alternating or interchanging movement of the hands (*ALTERNATE*)—side to side, toward and away from the signer, or up and down, as in AWKWARD (two $\ddot{3}$s, palm downward, alternately move toward and away from signer), IF (two *F*s, palms facing each other alternately move up and down). Alternating movements always entail straight movement on any of the three axes (two horizontal, one vertical—see section 2.3)

2.12   The approaching of the hands (*APPROACH*) and their separation (*SEPARATE*) are interacting movements that occur only in the horizontal (side-to-side) axis.

TABLE 1. SUMMARY: PHONEMIC INVENTORY

Phoneme	Variant	Environment
/A/	A	
	$\mathring{A}$	contact with thumb tip
		iconic signs
	S	side contact
		loans
		neutral end or initial shape
/O/	O	
	tapered-O	free variation
	bO	end shape (in double-shape signs with closure of L)
/B/	B	free variation
	$\mathring{B}$	free variation
		required in signs with thumb tip contact
	$\hat{B}$	end shape in double-shape signs with *BEND KNUCKLES* movement
/C/	C	
/5/	5	
	4	plurality
	$\ddot{5}$	end shape in signs with *BEND FINGERS* movement
/$\ddot{5}$/	$\ddot{5}$	
/F/	F	
	bO	reduction
/G/	G	
/X/	X_1	
	X_2	contact with middle joint
/L/	L	
	$\ddot{L}$	end shape in signs with *BEND FINGERS* movement
	L w/bent thumb	iconic signs
		anchored index finger
/H/	H	
	$\ddot{H}$	palm-side contact
/V/	V	
	$\ddot{V}$	end shape with *BEND FINGERS* movement
		iconic signs
/$\ddot{V}$/	$\ddot{V}$	
/3/	3	
	$\ddot{3}$	end shape in signs with *BEND FINGERS* movement

Phoneme	Variant	Environment
/3̈/	3̈	
/Y/	Y	
	𐊪	reduction
	𐊲	assimilation
		iconic signs
/Ⴕ/	Ⴕ	
	𐊲	free variation
/ծ/	ծ	
	8	*CLOSE* or *OPEN* movement
/7/	7	
	unspread-7	
/T/	T	
/M/	M	
/N/	N	
/D/	D	
	bD	free variation
/E/	E	
/G$_2$/	G$_2$	
/K/	K	
/I/	I	
/W/	W	
/R/	R	

Approaching and separating motion differ from alternating action in that they can co-occur with movement other than straight-line action (see below), i.e., circular, open, close, and wiggling (of the fingers). Examples of signs with approaching and separating motions are MEETING (two 5-hands close to Os while approaching each other) and BUT (two G-hands separate). I do not mean to designate those signs in which **one** hand moves toward or away from the other stationary hand (acting as place of articulation) as having approaching or separating movements, like NEAR (B-hand approaches B-hand) or BASIC (FUNDAMENTAL) (B-hand, palm downward moves downward in a circular motion under B-hand, palm downward). The movements in these signs do not require **interaction** of the two hands (as only one moves); their movements can be described by stating the manner and direction of the movement of the single articulator.[21]

2.13   The only other interacting movements are the crossing of the hands (*CROSS*), e.g., MATH (two M-hands, facing downward, cross, making light contact several times), and the linking or grasping of the fingers or hand (*LINK*), as in JOIN (two F-hands link) and MARRY (two C-hands grasp each other).

2.14   In my 1974a and b discussions of the movement parameter, I attempted to handle the movement of the hands separately in double articulator signs. I described alternating action as, for example, the upward and subsequent downward movement of the right hand while the left hand simultaneously moves downward and then upward; *APPROACH* and *SEPARATE* were described as: [right hand moves left, left hand moves right] and [right hand moves right, left hand moves left], respectively. (This description of *APPROACH* and *SEPARATE* does not work in any case; the right hand can move left and the left hand move right and never **approach** each other.) However, the fact that the language is constrained in such a way that the hands **must** have the same movement if they are both articulators—whether or not that movement entails interaction of the hands—leads me to the inescapable conclusion that the movements of the two hands ought to be treated as a single entity, be that movement interacting or noninteracting. I suggest that we analyze this aspect of movement as a single feature *INTERACT* with six values: *ALTERNATE, APPROACH, SEPARATE, CROSS, LINK,* and *NONINTERACTING*. Signs with *NONINTERACTING* movement include those in which both hands move but do not interact, as in ROAD (two Bs, facing each other, move outward away from signer), and those in which only one hand moves, whether or not the nondominant hand is the place of articulation.

2.2   The second fundamental aspect of movement is whether or not the hand makes contact with the body during the production of the sign. During my investigation into the physical aspects of emphatic stress, it became apparent "that the particular manifestation of stress on a given sign chosen by the signer is dependent on the nature of the movement in its citation form" (Friedman, 1974a, p.2).[22] One significant aspect of the particular manifestation of stress is whether or not contact is made. The general tendency in the manifestation of stress is for *CONTACT* signs to become *NONCONTACT* and for *NONCONTACT* signs to entail *CONTACT* (specifically *END CONTACT*).[23] It would appear that the feature *CONTACT* has six values: (1) the first of these is *CONTINUOUS CONTACT*,[24] in which contact with the body is made and maintained throughout the sign while the articulator moves from the point-of-origin-place-of-articulation. For example, GIRL is made with the *Å*-hand, making contact first at the upper cheek, and drawn down the side of the face toward the mouth, while continuously maintaining contact. (2) The second value is *HOLDING CONTACT*, in which one part of the articulator, usually an extended digit, starts with and maintains contact with the body throughout the sign, but in which the articulator does not move from the point-of-origin–place-of-articulation. For example, the sign LATER entails a *BEND-WRIST* movement with the *L*-hand, the extended thumb maintaining contact in the same position at the palm of the nondominant hand. (3) The third value is *END CONTACT*, in which the articulator makes contact with the body at the end of the sign, whereas the sign begins without contact. Examples of signs with end contact are ME—ending with index finger of *G* making contact with the chest, and DUMB ('stupid')—whose movement entails the palm-side contact of *A*, making contact with the forehead. (4) The fourth value is *BEGINNING CONTACT*, in which the sign begins with the articulator in contact with the body. An example is NOT, in which the *Å*-hand begins with the thumb in contact with the underside of the chin; the hand then moves outward into neutral space. (5) The fifth value of the feature *CONTACT* is *DOUBLE CONTACT*, in which the articulator makes separate contact at two different places of articulation in a monomorphemic sign. Two signs which have double contact are HEAD, in which contact is made at the temple and at the upper cheek (with the fingertips of *B*), and KING, in which the *K*-hand contacts the body at the contralateral (to the dominant hand) shoulder and then at the ipsilateral side of the waist. (6) The sixth value is *NONCONTACT*, in which the hand does not touch the body. All of the signs entailing interacting movement are noncontact signs.

2.3   The third aspect of movement is the direction in which the hands move. We can view the possible directions of movement in terms of three spatial axes: vertical, horizontal-width (describing sideward movement), and horizontal-depth (indicating movement direction toward and away from the front of the body). Within each axis there are three possible movements.

2.31   The vertical axis. Possible movements on the vertical axis are: *UPWARD*, e.g., FEEL (⅄, middle finger in continuous contact with chest, moves upward), *DOWNWARD*, e.g., HUNGRY (*C*-hand, fingertips in continuous contact with chest, moves downward), or *UP-AND-DOWN*, e.g., HURRY (*H*-hand moves up and down in neutral space). *UP-AND-DOWN* movements may also combine with *ALTERNATING* action, e.g., IF (*F*s, facing each other, alternately move up and down). There is a general tendency is ASL for signs' movements to be repeated once or twice; whether or not a movement is repeated apparently depends on the type of movement (see section 2.6). Because of this tendency, it is sometimes difficult to determine whether the movement of a particular sign is, for instance, *UP-AND-DOWN* or simply *DOWN*—repeated several times. (After all, the hand has to go up before it can go down.) However, in quite a number of signs, the type of movement may be determined by the visual image the sign makes—its iconicity. For example, the sign RAIN is made with two 5-hands moving up and down; since we know that rain always moves downward, I think we can safely say the the movement in RAIN is a repeated downward one.

2.32   The horizontal–depth axis. Movements along this axis are: movement *TOWARD* the signer's body, as in ME (*G*-hand, pointed toward signer, moves toward and makes contact with the chest), movement *AWAY* from the signer's body, as in *DELICIOUS* (୪, beginning with middle finger in contact with mouth, moves outward with a twisting motion), and *TO-AND-FRO*, either with alternating action, e.g., TALK (*4*s, facing each other, alternately move back and forth at mouth area), or noninteracting, e.g., 1st person plural inclusive—'we: you and I' (*V*-hand, palm upward, moves back and forth in the direction of addressee).

2.33   The horizontal–width axis. Movements along this axis are: *RIGHTWARD*, e.g., BLACK (*G* in continuous contact with forehead moves rightward), *LEFT-WARD*, e.g., LIE ('prevaricate') (*G* brushes leftward under mouth), and *SIDE-TO-SIDE*, either interacting, as in SHOES (*S*s approach (and contact) and separate sideward in neutral space), or noninteracting, as in SONG (*B* moves from side to side (wrist bends), pointing toward *B*-hand palm up). (Designations for right and left are reversed for the left-handed signer.)

2.34   There is a (potential) problem with these values, in that assigning values of *RIGHT* and *LEFT* to a sign's movement does not always accurately describe the direction of the horizontal movement. Consider, for example, the sign WEEK—*G*-hand (pointed upward palm away from signer) moves rightward in continuous contact with *B*-hand, palm toward signer. It is entirely possible if, for example, the signer is facing leftward while signing (which he could be doing for a variety of rhetorical purposes), that the *G*-hand would move **outward** across the nondominant palm to form WEEK, rather than rightward. Given that the values *RIGHT* and *LEFT* do not always reflect a surface movement rightward or leftward, it would be better to **define** the values *RIGHT* and *LEFT* as movement in the direction of the dominant side (side of the dominant hand) (and away from the nondominant side) and in the direction of the nondominant side (and away from the dominant side), respectively.

Given that these directions of movement are mutually exclusive, and that they co-occur with values of the three other features proposed here,[25] I suggest a feature *DIRECTION* with ten values: *UP, DOWN, UP-AND-DOWN, TOWARD, AWAY, TO-AND-FRO, RIGHT, LEFT, SIDE-TO-SIDE*, and *NONDIRECTIONAL*, in which there is no gross movement in space (e.g., BORING—*G* in contact with side of nose, twists several times).

2.4   The fourth aspect of movement is what I will refer to as the manner in which the hands move. There would appear to be two (nonsignificant) subparameters of manner of movement: one in which the joints of the hand (and wrist) move (micromovement), and one in which the entire arm is required to move (macro)—but not in a particular direction.

2.41   We can isolate six types of micromovement which occur in ASL.
(1)–(3)   The bending of the hand at the finger joints, at the knuckles, and at the wrist (*BEND-FINGERS, -KNUCKLES, -WRIST*). *BEND-WRIST* corresponds to Stokoe's element *NOD* (or *BEND*), occurring for instance in YES (*A* bends at wrist several times in neutral space). The values *BEND-FINGERS* and *BEND-KNUCKLES* arc needed to explain the changes in hand configuration in signs like FROG (*V*, palm down under chin sharply bends to become *V̂*) and STUBBORN (two *B̊*-hands, thumb tip contact at sides of forehead, bend at the knuckles to become *B̂*s). (See discussion in section 1.)
(4)   The wiggling of the fingers (*WIGGLE*), as in FINGERSPELL (*5*-hand, with wiggling fingers, moves rightward in neutral space).
(5)–(6)   The opening and closing action of the hands (*OPEN, CLOSE*), as in the signs BOY (*C* closes to *O* while moving outward from forehead) and HATE (*8* opens to *5* in flicking motion while palm faces direction of patient). Opening and closing movements could be handled with changes in hand configuration. However, as mentioned earlier (section 1.31), signs in which hand shape changes occur always begin or end in a neutral and predictable shape. If we analyze opening and closing action as hand shape changes, we would be forced to add redundancy by marking predictable elements in the description. Also, the movement in signs with opening and closing action (i.e., the "change in hand shape") is relatively rapid and would seem to contrast with changes from one shape to another in, for example, a nonassimilated compound.

2.42   There are three types of nondirectional macromovements.
(1)   *STRAIGHT* action, in which the hand traces a straight line from one point to another, whether those points are located on or near the body or in neutral space (i.e., the shortest distance between two points). All alternating movements discussed above have *STRAIGHT* movements.
(2)   The twisting of the wrists (*TWIST*), as in BORING (*G* twists repeatedly while in contact at the side of the nose).
(3)   *CIRCULAR* motion of the hand and arm, as in CONFUSED (two *5̈*-hands facing each other make alternating circular motions).
        I propose a feature *MANNER* with nine values: *STRAIGHT, CIRCULAR, TWIST, BEND-FINGERS, BEND-KNUCKLES, BEND-WRIST, WIGGLE, OPEN, CLOSE*.

2.5   A case could be made for handling some of the other movements described here in other ways. For example, the motion described by *TWIST* could be thought of as entailing a change in orientation, for example, from palm down to palm leftward. If one's interest lies in reducing the number of features (or phonemes, for that matter) to the fewest possible, then this analysis would be appealing. However, it seems to lose something of the essential nature of the movement. In signs with a clear-cut change of orientation as in COOK (*B*-hand palm down taps *B*-hand palm up; then dominant *B*-hand turns to palm up and taps the nondominant palm again), the movements and changes of orientation can be described as discrete elements in the sense that each has its own definite beginning and end. In a sign such as FRENCH (*F*-hand twists upward in neutral space), the movement is continuous and the twist relatively rapid. Change in orientation resulting from the twist cannot be viewed as composed of discrete elements. Also, the twisting motion in many signs, e.g., ONION (X_2 twists at upper cheek) is repeated several times. This fact would seem to constitute evidence for the value *TWIST* as a unified whole which can easily be repeated several times.

   BEND-WRIST could be reformulated as something like *UP-AND-DOWN, WRIST*. This formulation seems to lose something of the gestalt of "bending at the wrist," especially since in most signs with bend-wrist movement, the nodding or bending is repeated several times (e.g., YES—*A*-hand nods several times in neutral space). Since the same formulation could not be applicable to bend-fingers and bend-knuckles, because they do not go up and down, we would lose the correlation of the three bending movements (i.e., that hands can bend in these three places), if we opted for this alternative formulation.

2.6   As I have already mentioned briefly, there seems to be a general tendency for some signs' movements to be repeated once or twice during normal production.[26] Whether or not a sign's movement is repeated would appear to depend on the type of movement occurring in that sign. In general, movements tend not to be repeated when the signs are (emphatically) stressed,[27] maybe because they also tend to become larger and more rapid (and entail tense musculature) when stressed. All of the interacting movements tend to be repeated in nonstressed production. The bending of the fingers is usually repeated, as are twisting and circular motions; opening and closing of the hand are usually not repeated. Movements involving *END CONTACT* and *HOLDING CONTACT* are generally repeated (although the contact is not reestablished in *HOLDING CONTACT* signs); there is generally no repetition of movement in signs with *CONTINUOUS, BEGINNING,* or *DOUBLE CONTACT*. Further investigation may lead us to an explanation of this phenomenon.

3. Place of Articulation

3.0   In some ways, the place of articulation parameter is the most difficult to analyze in discrete terms. The basic constraints on place of articulation are not language specific, but rather articulatory and perceptual. As I stated earlier (section

TABLE 2.   MOVEMENT FEATURES

INTERACT

ALTERNATE
APPROACH
SEPARATE
CROSS
LINK
NONINTERACTING

CONTACT

CONTINUOUS ⎫
HOLDING   ⎪
END   ⎬ CONTACT
BEGINNING   ⎪
DOUBLE   ⎭

NONCONTACT

DIRECTION

UPWARD   ⎫
DOWNWARD   ⎬ VERTICAL
UP-AND-DOWN ⎭

RIGHT   ⎫
LEFT   ⎬ HORIZONTAL-WIDTH
SIDE-TO-SIDE ⎭

TOWARD   ⎫
AWAY   ⎬ HORIZONTAL-DEPTH
TO-AND-FRO ⎭

NONDIRECTIONAL

MANNER

STRAIGHT ⎫
TWIST   ⎬ MACRO
CIRCULAR ⎭

BEND-FINGERS   ⎫
BEND-KNUCKLES ⎪
BEND-WRIST   ⎪
OPEN   ⎬ MICRO
CLOSE   ⎪
WIGGLE   ⎭

0.6), the articulation space available to the signer is limited to that area at or near his body which his addressee can see. This space is limited to the area of an approximate rectangle surrounding the head and chest area. There are (rather limited) occasions when a gesture is made out of the signing space, for example, in a variation of the sign BIG in which the signer conveys the meaning 'gigantic' (the arms may be extended fully to the sides), but these need not be of concern here. There is one lexicalized sign (that I know of) that is articulated out of the signing space—the sign DOG, in which the *B*-hand pats the thigh twice.

In addition to the area of *NEUTRAL SPACE*—that area off the body (limited by the extent of the arms forward, bent at the elbows) in the center of the signing space, i.e., on the horizontal plane of the upper chest, neck, lower face region—signs may be articulated practically anywhere on the body area limited by the signing space (i.e., head, neck, trunk, nondominant arm). *NEUTRAL SPACE* is that area in which the greatest number of signs are articulated—including all action verbs such as GO, WALK, WORK.

We can distinguish one area from another, but it is clear that there are very few clear-cut lines of demarcation. Also, we will see that iconicity plays an important role in the place of articulation parameter.

3.1   One aspect of the sublexical components in ASL (and in Sign Language in general) is their lack of discreteness in comparison to phonetic segments in oral language. We think of phonetic segments in oral languages as discrete signals. Of course, we could not claim that segments are completely discrete units of sound. We know that speakers with different larynx sizes and sizes and shapes of oral and nasal cavities produce different formant structures for the same vowel even if they speak the same phonological dialect of the same language and do not perceive these differences as distinct. The same is true of different speakers' production of tone in tone languages. However, despite this seeming lack of discreteness in sound production, speakers are able to articulate and perceive fine distinctions within a very small and discrete range of acoustic signals. This situation is quite different in visual language. In sign language, possibly due to the size of the articulators and of the articulation space, and due to the nature of visual perception, sublexical units are not required to be discrete. There is certainly no need to maximize the use of the articulation space, as it is so large (as compared with the articulation space in oral language production). (In fact, the very lack of discreteness allows for advantages in phonological alternation for the purpose of semantic variation that the phonological structure of oral languages cannot allow. See section 5 for a more detailed discussion.)

3.2   With this in mind, we can now proceed to discuss the place of articulation parameter. There appear to be four major areas of the body in regard to place of articulation: the head (including the neck), the trunk, the arm, and the hand. The salience of these major areas can be seen in morpheme structure conditions entailed in signs whose articulation involves contacting the body twice (double contact signs).

Battison (in Friedman and Battison, 1973) points out that for double contact signs "the observed tendency is to make both contacts within the same major areas" (p.8). There are signs in which contact points cross these boundaries, but not all possible sequences of contact that cross boundaries occur in ASL. (Battison finds that only 56% of all possible sequence types are utilized.) The only occurring sequences are those in which contact is first made at the head area and then on the trunk (e.g., GENTLEMAN), first head then arm (e.g., DAUGHTER), first the head then hand (e.g., SISTER), first hand then head (e.g., LEARN), but **disallowed** are first trunk then head, arm, or hand; first arm then head, trunk, or hand; and first hand, then trunk or arm. Thus we find that only when the first contact is made at the head area can the second contact be made at any other major area.[28]

Within each major area, we can further delimit distinctive places of articulation, as follows. (Before continuing, I should add that signs need not actually touch the body to be considered made at any given place of articulation. When describing a sign's place of articulation, we are describing that area of the body at which or **near** which [i.e., next to which] the sign is made. For instance, there seems to be a taboo especially among middle-aged and older women, against touching the chest. But we would still want to say that for example the sign FEEL [୪-hand, palm toward chest, middle finger drawn upward in continuous contact with the chest] has *CHEST* as its place of articulation.)

3.3   Head

3.31   The *WHOLE FACE*, as opposed to any part of the face, is a distinctive place of articulation, occurring for example in the signs TROUBLE (two *B*-hands facing each other alternate in a downward movement across the face) and MIRROR (*B*-hand, palm toward signer, in a quick twisting motion). Rather than viewing *WHOLE FACE* as a distinctive component of the place parameter, it might be better to think of it as the neutral or unmarked 'head area' place, lacking any further distinction in that major area. (That is, not the nose, chin and so on specifically, but the whole front of the head—and basically the front is the only part of the head that **can** be a component of Sign.)

If we consider *WHOLE FACE* as the neutral or unmarked *HEAD* location, then we can say that the *TOP of the HEAD* is its variant. Signs made at the top of the head are iconic, having to do with the top of the head or the hair, e.g., HAIR (grasp hair), CUT-HAIR (*V* closes to *H* repeatedly while moving over head, representing scissors), and HAT (*B*-hand pats head).

3.32   The *UPPER FACE*, including the forehead and the eyes constitutes a distinctive place. Signs articulated at the *FOREHEAD* include THINK (index finger of *G* contacts forehead) and BLACK (*G* moves rightward in continuous contact with forehead).

Signs made at the *SIDES of the FOREHEAD* are all double articulator signs— i.e., signs in which both hands act as articulators, as in STUBBORN (two *B̂*s, thumb tip in contact with the sides of the forehead; *B̂*s bend to *B̂*s). In other words, the variant *SIDE-FOREHEAD* occurs in double articulator signs.

Signs made at or near the *EYES* are all iconic; they all have something to do with the eyes or with functions of the eyes (for example, seeing, crying). Signs made at the *EYES* include SEE (*V*-hand toward signer moves outward—in the direction of patient) and BLIND (*V*-hand bends sharply to $\ddot{V}$). Signs articulated at the *SIDE of the EYES* (sometimes at the cheekbone) all entail contact with the face; presumably these signs are made at the side of the eyes because no contact may be made **in** the eyes. *SIDE-EYES* signs include ONION (onions make the eyes tear) (X_2-hand—middle joint in contact at side of eyes or upper cheek—twists repeatedly), CRY (two *G*-hands move downward quickly as if tracing the path of the tears), and CHINESE (slanted eyes) (*G*-hand, contact with index finger, twists repeatedly).

In Stokoe's (1960, 1965) analysis, the *EYES* place is a variant of his *MIDFACE* (or *NOSE*) 'chereme'. However, *EYES* and *NOSE* contrast, as can be seen in the minimal pair CHINESE and BORING (*G*-hand twists at side of nose).

3.33   The *NOSE* place of articulation has three variants: *CENTER, SIDE(S)*, and *UNDER*. Signs made *UNDER the NOSE* are iconic, having to do with a runny nose, as in KIDS (slang; refers to kids wiping their noses with finger) (Ч -hand, index finger pointing rightward twists under nose) and COLD (the sickness) (*X* with thumb extended moves downward under nose and closes to *A*, imitating blowing nose).

Signs made at the *SIDE of the NOSE* are either double contact signs, e.g., FLOWER (*O*-hand contacts both sides of the nose) or have a twisting movement, e.g., BORING (*G*-hand twists repeatedly). and DON'T-CARE (*G*-hand moves outward with a twist).

All other signs with the *NOSE* place of articulation are made in contact with or near the center of the nose. *CENTER-NOSE* signs include BUG (insect) (*5*-hand, thumb touching tip of nose, bends to $\ddot{5}$), SMELL (*B*-hand, palm toward signer, moves upward twice at nose), and FUNNY (*H*-hand, palm downward, brushes past nose twice).

3.34   The *LOWER FACE* area includes the *MOUTH* and the *CHIN*. Signs made at the mouth all have referents having to do with the mouth or (real or metaphoric) functions of the mouth, e.g., eating, talking, smoking. Examples of signs made at the mouth include EAT (*O* contacts mouth), ICE CREAM (*S*-hand in circular motion), DELICIOUS, (୪ contacts mouth and twists outward) LIP-READ ($\ddot{V}$ in circular motion), SAY, (*G* pointing leftward at mouth makes circular motion) and DEAF (*G* contacts mouth and upper cheek near ear, representing the non-functional mouth and ear).

There is evidence supporting the claim that the *MOUTH* and the *CHIN* are variants of the same distinctive area in that signs requiring contact at the mouth are never made at that location by many women but rather lowered to the chin (presumably to avoid smudging their lipstick).

All other signs of the *LOWER FACE* are made at the *CHIN*, e.g., OLD (*C*, toward signer closes while moving downward), PATIENT (*A* with thumb-side contact at chin moves downward), MOTHER (5-hand, fingers wiggling, thumb contacts chin), COLOR (5, palm toward chin—fingers wiggle), TALK (4s facing each other at chin, alternately move to and fro), WRONG (Y-hand, palm toward signer, contacts chin).

3.35   A relatively small number of signs are made *UNDER the CHIN*, including NOT (Å-hand, contact with thumb, moves sharply outward), FROG (V, palm downward, under chin bends to V̇ twice, representing the frog's pulsating throat), and DIRTY (5-hand, palm down under chin, with wiggling fingers). *UNDER-CHIN* must be considered a distinctive place of articulation, since there are no conditions which would allow it to be considered a variant of *LOWER FACE*. (However, since there are so few signs made under the chin, there are no contrasting environments either. That is, there are no signs made on the lower face that have the same hand shape, orientation, and movement as signs made under the chin.)

3.36   The *CHEEK* is a distinctive place of articulation. Specific place of articulation within the cheek area depends on hand configuration and in some cases on the meaning of the referent. (That is, iconic signs resemble their referents, whether or not they violate phonological constraints.) In signs made with thumb tip contact at the *CHEEK*, the sign is made at the side of the cheek, near or at the jaw, e.g., GIRL (Å, thumb in continuous, contact, moves down the side of the cheek), and YESTERDAY (Å-hand contacts side cheek twice, moving backward along the time line).

Most *CHEEK* signs are made in the center of the cheek (the unmarked cheek location), including CANDY (G-hand, finger in contact, twists several times)—which contrasts with SOUR (same hand shape, movement, made at the chin)—and BLUSH (B-hand moves up cheek, back of hand in continuous contact). The contrast *CHEEK* and *EYE (UPPER FACE)* is seen in the minimal pair APPLE (X_2 twists in contact with cheek) and ONION (X_2 twists at side of eye). HEAD is a double contact sign—B-hand first touches the upper cheek and then the temple; the fact that the sign is made at the upper cheek may be due to anticipatory assimilation to the location of the second point of contact.

The *EAR* may be considered a variant of *CHEEK*. All signs made at the *EAR* are iconic and refer to the ear in some way, as in EAR, HEAR, EARRING, and an assimilated compound of EARRING and GOLD, meaning CALIFORNIA. Evidence for *EAR* as a variant of *CHEEK* may be found in the sign DEAF (G-hand contacts mouth and upper cheek). The sign originally entailed the contact of the G-hand at the mouth (as in the paralinguistic gesture for 'hush') and again at the ear (to indicate the "hushing" of the ear). In the assimilated form, the second contact is at the upper cheek, which would seem to indicate that the cheek and ear locations are not distinctive (except that signs having to do with 'ear' are made at the ear).

3.37   Relatively few signs are made at the distinctive location *NECK*. Most of those that are made at the neck have a meaning related to the neck or the throat, including NECK, VOICE (V-hand palm down, moves upward along neck), THIRSTY

(*C*-hand moves down neck), and REPRESS (one's feelings, i.e., keep them down) (*C*-hand closes while moving sharply downward). However, there are signs made at the neck which are not iconic (or at least not in any obvious way), for example CURIOUS (*Ľ*-hand grasps neck and moves up and down; this could represent the movement of the larynx while swallowing, but the relation of this to 'curious' eludes me) and STUCK (also slang for 'pregnant') (fingers of *V*-hand sharply contact center of neck).

There is one (clearly) iconic sign made at the side of the neck—VAMPIRE (fingers of *V*-hand sharply contact side of neck). Since VAMPIRE and STUCK have the same form except for their location, one might want to say that the center and side of the neck were distinctive locations. However, given the nature of iconicity and its effect on the phonological structure, and given the fact that VAMPIRE is the only sign made at the side of the neck, it seems more appropriate to ignore the contrast.

3.4   Trunk or Chest

3.40   There are far fewer distinctions in place of articulation made on the chest than on the face; only four **phonetic** distinctions may be made: the center of the chest (*CHEST*), the shoulder, the stomach, and the waist. The greater number of distinctive places of articulation on the face as opposed to the other major areas may be accounted for in the light of information regarding visual acuity. It is known that the addressee primarily focuses on the signer's face during the communicating period and derives linguistic information with a modicum of eye movement to other areas. Siple (1973) observes that visual acuity

> is best at the point of fixation and drops off rapidly as the distance from that point increases . . . If a person stands six feet from a signer and stares at his nose and eyes, that is the area of greatest acuity. (p. 1)

She goes on to offer this as an explanation for the relatively greater fineness of distinction in the area of the face than in any other area of the body.

In addition to Siple's explanation for the greater fineness of distinction regarding place of articulation in the facial area, I would point out that the physical properties of the body itself would tend to impose this difference in fineness or number of distinctions. Human beings are so constructed as to have many more obvious physical "landmarks" on the face than on the chest (or any other body part). That is, that on the face there are the forehead, eyes, mouth, nose, cheeks, etc., while on the chest, besides breasts on a female (and there is a definite taboo against touching them in signing), the only obvious landmarks are the chest itself and the shoulders. It seems clear that a language in the visual mode would tend to use those distinctions already present and perceptible to construct and constrain its phonology.

3.41   The greatest number of signs made on the trunk are made at what may be considered the neutral or unmarked trunk location, the center of the *CHEST*. Signs made at the chest include FEEL, LOVE, ME (1st person index), LIVE, SCARED, and WHITE.

There are a number of signs made at the lower chest—in the area of the *STOM-ACH*. However, the stomach area may be considered a nondistinctive variant of *CHEST*, in that all signs made there iconically represent something to do with that area, either the stomach or the womb. Examples of lower chest signs include PREGNANT, BORN, BABY, CRAMPS (menstrual), BELLY-LAUGH, and STOMACH-ACHE.

3.42   The *SHOULDER* or shoulder area is a distinctive place of articulation. Both shoulders are contacted in double articulator signs like VACATION—two *L*-hands make thumb tip contact with midshoulder area. Signs made at one shoulder include COP (*C*-hand contacts contralateral shoulder), LAZY (*L* contacts contralateral shoulder), PAST-CONTINUOUS aspectual marker (usually translates as 'have been' or 'up to now' in English) (two *G*-hands move outward from contact at dominant shoulder), and RECENTLY (*B*-hand contacts ipsilateral shoulder). It should be pointed out that the shoulder location is odd in that **all** signs made at the shoulder(s) show a high degree of iconicity. For example, RECENTLY and PAST-CONTINUOUS make use of the visual time line—an imaginary plane running along-side the body: the body (and the area immediately in front if it) represents present time, the space behind the body past, and the area in front of the body future time. RECENTLY indexes the near past by touching the past "border"—the shoulder; PAST-CONTINUOUS traces a line from the past to the present. VACATION represents pulling at suspenders (like the farmer with a piece of corn silk in his mouth). COP requires placing a *C*-hand at the place where the policeman's badge would be worn. KING—a *K*-hand touching first the contralateral shoulder and then the ipsilateral side of the waist—represents the image of a king's sash. Because no "arbitrary" (noniconic) signs are made at the shoulder, we might want to consider *SHOULDER* a somewhat marginal distinction.

3.43   The *WAIST* is an extremely infrequent place of articulation, also occurring only in iconic signs like KING, HIPS (outlining hips with $\overset{\circ}{B}$-hands), and RUSSIAN ($\overset{\circ}{B}$-hands contact waist twice, representing typical dancer's pose). Because of the iconicity of signs made there, it might be best to consider *WAIST* a nondistinctive variant of *CHEST*.

3.5   Arm

3.51   The *UPPER ARM* is a distinctive place of articulation, occurring in signs such as HOSPITAL (*H*-hand traces cross on upper arm), COKE (both cola and cocaine) (index finger of *L*-hand contacts upper arm, thumb bends repeatedly; represents insertion of hypodermic needle), and SCOTLAND (*4*-hand moves down and then rightward, tracing tartan). No distinction is made between what I will call the dorsal side (outside surface) and the ventral side (inside surface) of the upper arm—the choice of dorsal or ventral depends on either the picture the sign makes, or the physical constraints imposed by the hand shape and movement. For example, the red cross suggested by the sign HOSPITAL typically appears on the outside of the sleeve, hence it is made on the dorsal portion of the arm; it would be very difficult to make contact with the *L*-hand in COKE at any other location than the inside (ventral) part of the arm.

3.52   The ELBOW is also a distinctive location on the arm, occurring relatively infrequently. Signs having the elbow as place of articulation include POOR (hand surrounding elbow closes to *O* while moving downward) and PUNISH (*G*-hand brushes past elbow).

3.53   Unlike the upper arm, there are two distinctive locations on the *FOREARM* –*DORSAL* side and *VENTRAL* side. I should point out that the place of articulation may be dorsal forearm or ventral forearm regardless of the arm's orientation in space (e.g., ventral side up or down). Signs whose place of articulation is the dorsal side of the forearm include LONG (*G*-finger moves upward along arm) and IMPROVE (*B*-hand, toward signer, moves upward along arm). Ventral forearm signs include BRIDGE (*V*-hand makes fingertip contact in two places on ventral side, which is facing downward), and STEAL (*V* bends to $\ddot{V}$ while moving toward hand on ventral side of crooked arm).

3.54   Relatively few signs are made at either the ventral or dorsal side of the wrist. It seems that the dorsal side of the wrist is a distinctive place of articulation (distinct from the forearm), occurring in signs such as TIME (*G* taps wrist) and POTATO ($\ddot{V}$ taps wrist). The ventral side of the wrist must also be considered distinct, occurring in signs such as DOCTOR (*M* contacts ventral wrist, as if taking pulse) and LOCK (*A*-hand turns over and contacts ventral side of wrist, facing upward).

However, both *DORSAL* and *VENTRAL WRIST* ought to be considered only marginal locations, since most of the signs made at the wrist have referents having something to do with the wrist, e.g., TIME (points to imaginary wristwatch, or real one, if there is one), DOCTOR (takes pulse). LOCK and POTATO are notable exceptions in that they are not iconic signs; it is because of these signs that we have to consider the two sides of the wrist as two distinct locations.

3.6   Hand

Theoretically, the nondominant hand can assume any configuration that the dominant hand can. However, as mentioned earlier, there are several conditions restricting the shape of the nondominant hand.

In double articulator signs, in which both hands have a movement component, both hands must have the same configuration, as well as the same movement. Signs of this type include IF (two *F*-hands alternate in an up and down movement) and ROAD (two *B*-hands, facing each other, move forward).

In signs in which the nondominant hand acts as place of articulation there are two possibilities in regard to the shape that hand can assume. One possibility is that both the articulator and the hand acting as location have the same shape. Signs which are symmetrical in regard to hand shape include NAME (*H*-hand taps *H*-hand twice) and SCHOOL (palm of *B*-hand taps palm of *B* twice). The second possibility is one in which the nondominant place of articulation hand assumes one of six neutral hand shapes: *A, B, 5, G, C, O*. Examples of this type are HELP (*B*-hand palm upward moves upward to contact *A*), PRACTICE (*A* brushes back and forth across extended index finger of *G*) and TEA (*F*-hand, palm downward, in circular motion over *O*).

4. Orientation

4.0   The components of the orientation parameter describe the relation in space of the hand to the signer's body. With the *B*-hand, for example, the hand (palm) can be said to be oriented *TOWARD* the signer, *AWAY* from the signer, *UP*, *DOWN*, to the *LEFT*, or some combination of directions, such as to the *LEFT* and *UP*. Only the left hand can have its palm facing rightward. We know that the hands' orientation is an essential aspect of the sign's description, given pairs of signs whose only difference lies in their orientation. The sign DANGER (*A*-hand toward signer bends at wrist while in contact with the nondominant arm, palm downward) differs from BEAT (DEFEAT) (*A*-hand away from signer bends at wrist while in contact with arm, palm downward) only in the orientation of the articulating hand. SCHOOL has two *B*-hands tapping twice, nondominant palm up, dominant palm down; MONEY also has two *B*-hands tapping twice, with the dominant as well as the nondominant hand palm up.

4.1   Orientation has to be defined for each hand shape, so that we know which part of the hand is "facing" which direction in relation to the body. Many hand shapes can be marked for two orientations: one for the direction that the palm faces, and one for the direction toward which the extended fingers point. For example, the *G*-hands in the sign SOCKS can be said to be oriented downward and away from the signer—the palm-sides face downward and the extended fingers away from the signer. (SOCKS has two *G*-hands alternating to and fro in neutral space). Table 4 defines orientation in terms of each hand configuration. Orientation of the arm is defined as the direction that the ventral side of the arm faces.

4.2   It is clear that for many signs the designations *TOWARD, AWAY, UP, DOWN, RIGHT,* and *LEFT* (and combinations of the six) are not sufficient descriptions. I discussed earlier a similar problem regarding components of the movement parameter (section 2.34), citing the sign WEEK (*G*-hand facing *B* moves across nondominant palm toward fingers) as an example. A description of the movement in WEEK as rightward will not account for that movement if the hands are oriented slightly differently, say with the fingers of the *B*-hand pointing slightly away from the signer, in which case the *G*-hand would move outward and not to the right. I attempted to solve this problem by defining rightward and leftward movement as

TABLE 3.   PLACE OF ARTICULATION

Place	Conditions of Occurrence
NEUTRAL SPACE	
HEAD	
WHOLE FACE	
WHOLE FACE	
TOP OF HEAD	iconic signs
UPPER FACE	
FOREHEAD	
SIDE-FOREHEAD	double articulator signs
EYES	iconic signs
SIDE-EYES	contact
NOSE	
CENTER	
UNDER	iconic signs
SIDE	double contact; twist
LOWER FACE	
CHIN	
MOUTH	iconic signs
(UNDER-CHIN)	
CHEEK	
CENTER	
SIDE	thumb tip contact
EAR	iconic signs
NECK	
CENTER	
SIDE	iconic signs
TRUNK	
CHEST	
CENTER	
STOMACH	iconic signs
WAIST	iconic signs
SHOULDER	
ARM	
UPPER ARM	
ELBOW	
DORSAL FOREARM	
VENTRAL FOREARM	
DORSAL WRIST	
VENTRAL WRIST	
HAND	

TABLE 4.   ORIENTATION DEFINED

Hand Configuration	Orientation in the Direction of . . .
A	finger or palm-side
O	fingertips (palm)
B	palm and/or fingertips
$\hat{B}$	palm
C	palm
5	palm and/or fingertips
4	palm and/or fingertips
$\ddot{5}$	palm
F	palm and/or fingertips
G	palm and/or fingertips
X	palm
L	palm and/or fingertips
H	palm and/or fingertips
V	palm and/or fingertips
$\ddot{V}$	palm
3	palm and/or fingertips
$\ddot{3}$	palm
Y	palm
8	palm
8	palm
7	palm
M	finger or palm-side
D	fingertips (palm)
E	palm
G_2	palm and/or fingertips
K	palm and/or fingertips
I	palm and/or fingertips
W	palm and/or fingertips
R	palm and/or fingertips

movement toward the dominant and the nondominant side of the body respectively. Describing the hands' orientation in WEEK presents the same problem: the
designations *PALM TOWARD* for the nondominant $B_r$hand and *PALM AWAY* for
the dominant *G*-hand will not account for nondistinctive variations in orientation as
when the hands are held horizontally.

4.3   A related problem arises for the orientation specifications in signs with one
hand acting as place of articulation like NAME and LAW, or in signs made on the
face like GIRL and ONION. Discrete designations that accurately describe orientation cannot be given for these and many other signs. NAME is made with two *H*-
hands—dominant hand taps nondominant hand twice; an accurate description of
the hands' orientation would be something like the following: (palm of) right hand
faces half way between the directions *LEFT* and *TOWARD* signer, left hand faces
halfway between *RIGHT* and *TOWARD* signer. However, how then do we account
for a nondistinctive variation of NAME in which the right hand faces *TOWARD* the
signer while the left faces *RIGHTWARD*? LAW is formed by having the *L*-hand
(palm away, pointing upward) make contact sharply with the palm of the *B*-hand,
facing away from the signer. Given discrete orientation components, we would be
unable to indicate that variations in orientation in these instances are irrelevant and
are neither phonologically nor semantically distinctive. Discrete specifications for
orientations are even more difficult to give for signs like GIRL and ONION. GIRL
entails thumb tip contact of $\mathring{A}$ on the cheek, and a downward movement in continuous contact; ONION is formed with a twisting movement of X_2, the middle
joint in contact at the side of the eye. We could say that the orientation in GIRL is
AWAY (from the signer) and in ONION is *DOWN* and/or *AWAY*. However, these
descriptions are not only inaccurate but they do not seem to grasp the significant
aspects of the hands' relation to the body. I suggest that the essential feature of the
hands' relation to the signer's body in these signs is **not** the orientation of the hands
in space but rather those parts of the hand that make contact with the body. Therefore, I propose that we add the notion of what I will call *POINT of CONTACT* to
the orientation parameter, giving designations as to that part of the hand that makes
contact with the body.
    Some evidence in favor of point of contact specification comes from examining
the hand configuration parameter. For example, the condition for the occurrence
of $\mathring{A}$ and $\mathring{B}$ (in noniconic signs) is that signs with these shapes must entail contact
with the tip of the thumb.
    I propose that for signs in which the hands (or hand) make contact with the
body (contact signs), the orientation specification designate the point of contact—
that part of the hand that touches the body. For noncontact signs—those in which
the hands do not make contact anywhere on the body—there is, of course, no point
of contact; specifications for orientation have to be marked as above; i.e., palm
facing (or extended finger pointing) *RIGHT, LEFT, UP, DOWN, TOWARD, AWAY*.

4.4   We can now reconsider the signs mentioned above in terms of point of
contact. Instead of trying to account for all possible (nondistinctive) variations of

the hands' spatial orientaion, WEEK can be analyzed as having a *PALM-SIDE* contact point: the palm-side of the *G*-hand contacts the palm-side of the *B*-hand; *G* moves toward fingers in continuous contact with *B*. Variations in orientation in NAME can be accounted for with reference to the *H*-hands' point of contact—the *SIDE* of the fingers: the *SIDE* of the dominant *H*-hand makes contact with the *SIDE* of the nondominant *H*-hand. In LAW, the *DORSAL* (back) side of the *L*-hand sharply contacts the *PALM* of the nondominant *B*. GIRL has the thumb tip of the $\mathring{A}$-hand making continuous contact down along the cheek. ONION entails middle joint contact of X_2 with a twisting movement at the side of the eyes.

4.5   The following points of contact may be isolated as elements of contact signs:

4.51   *FINGERTIP(S)*. The signs HEAD (with *B*), EAT (with *O*), THINK (*G*), COKE (*L*), POTATO ($\ddot{V}$), and FEEL (8) all have the fingertip(s) as point of contact.

It is clear that fingertip as well as other points of contact have to be defined for each hand shape. For example, fingertip contact with the 8-hand involves the bent middle finger's touching the body. Since the 8-shape allows for no other point of contact, we are justified in defining fingertip contact as midfingertip contact. Not all hand shapes permit all points of contact. For instance, no fingertip contact may be made with the *A*-hand or any of its variants. Table 5 gives all possible points of contact and examples of each contact point for each distinctive hand shape.

One hand shape, X_2, always and only makes contact with the middle joint of the bent finger. This part of the hand is the point of contact with no other hand shape. Therefore, we can loosely define fingertip contact as contact with the **end** of the extended finger. Since the middle joint really is the end point of the extension of the bent index finger of X_2, we can characterize X_2's point of contact as a variant of fingertip contact.

4.52   *THUMB TIP*. That thumb tip and fingertip contact contrast can be seen in signs which have, for example, the *L*-shape. *L* allows for both finger and thumb tip contact, in for instance, COKE (index finger contacts upper arm) and LATER (thumb contacts palm of nondominant hand). Other signs with thumb tip as point of contact include GIRL (with $\mathring{A}$), STUBBORN ($\mathring{B}$), MOTHER (*5*), COW (*Y*), and BUG (*3*).

4.53   *PALM:* the palm or fleshy side of the hand. Examples of signs with palm-side contact are SCHOOL (with *B*), RED (*G*), TRAIN (*H*), TELEPHONE (*Y*), and WITH (A). Palm-side contact of *A* is defined as contact with the "finger-side" of the fist (as opposed to the back of the hand).

4.54   *SIDE*: the edge of the fingers or hand. Examples include HOT (*B*), BOY (*C* closes to *O*, COP (*C*), LECH (*4*) (in the manner of a "dirty old man"), KIDS ( ), and PATIENT (*A*).

TABLE 5. POINT OF CONTACT

	FINGERTIP	THUMB TIP	PALM	SIDE	DORSAL
A	–	GIRL	WITH	PATIENT	LOCK
O	EAT	–	–	BOY	BIRD (bO)
B	HEAD	STUBBORN	SCHOOL	HOT	BLUSH
C	x	DRINK	–	COP	x
5	x	MOTHER	COLOR	LECH (4)	DIRTY
5̈	COOKIE	x	–	x	DYING-INSECT
F	INDIAN	–	–	IMPORTANT	x
G	THINK	–	RED	LIE (prevaricate)	x
X₁	WRITE	–	FRIEND	HOT	x
X₂	ONION	–	–	–	–
L	COKE	LATER	LYNN (name sign)	–	LAW
H	x	–	TRAIN	NAME	x
V	VOICE	–	COPULATE	VICKI (name sign)	STUPID
V̈	POTATO	–	–	x	TOSS-AND-TURN
3	x	LOUSE	3-WEEKS	PARK-CAR	3-MONTHS AGO
3̈	x	DEVIL	–	x	x
Y	x	COW	MISTAKE	SHAVE	x
Ϥ	BIG-WORD	–	CIGARETTE	KIDS	x
8	FEEL	x	–	x	x
7	x	x	–	x	x
T	x	x	TEMPLE	x	x
M	x	–	DOCTOR	MATH	x
N	NATURE	–	NURSE	NIXON (name sign)	x
D	DENTIST	–	–	x	x
E	–	–	CUTE	x	x
K	x	–	KING	x	x
I	ITALIAN	–	x	x	x
W	x	–	x	WATER	x
R	REASON	–	x	RAT	x

Key: — = impossible, x = not occurring

4.55   *DORSAL*: the back of the hand. Signs in which the dorsal side of the hand makes contact with the body include BLUSH (*B*), LAW (*L*), and FROG (*V* → *V̈*).

4.6   As already stated above, contact points must be defined for each hand shape. In order to complete this discussion of point of contact, I will present here a brief description of contact points of hand shapes for which particular specifications for orientation given may not be obvious. (Refer to Figure 1 for hand configurations.)

1.   *PALM* of *A* = the finger-side of the closed fist. There can be no fingertip contact with *A* since there are no extended fingers.

2.   *SIDE* of *A* = thumb or pinky side of closed fist.

3.   *FINGERTIP* of *C* = tips of all fingers and thumb.

4.   *FINGERTIP* of *D* = tips of thumb and fingers in contact with thumb. The tip of the extended index finger never occurs as point of contact with *D*.

5.   *FINGERTIP* of *F* = tips of thumb and index finger (in contact with thumb). The tips of the extended fingers of *F* are never points of contact.

For hand shapes in which the thumb tip touches the fingertips(s) (cf., *O, bO, D, bD, F, W, 8, 7*), the tips of the remaining extended fingers (those not touching the thumb) are never points of contact.

6.   *FINGERTIP* of 8 = the tip of the bent middle finger.

7.   *FINGERTIP* of X_2 = the extended knuckle or joint of the bent index finger.

5. Iconic and Scalar Elements

5.0   In the preceding sections, I have demonstrated the existence not only of sublexical components in ASL (i.e., the four articulatory parameters) but also of finite sets of distinctive units within the parameters. However, it is evident that the component structure of ASL (or of any visual language) is not entirely analogous to that of oral language structures.

It is clear that although there are certainly finite sets of arbitrary elements in the language, a crucial element of ASL's formational structure lies in the nature of visual representation or suggestion of referents or parts of referents—in its iconicity. It is not within the scope of this paper to discuss the types of iconic devices available in ASL.[29] In this section, I will discuss the role of iconicity in the formational structure of the language and some principles of iconicity that must be included in an accurate phonological description. If we fail to consider the role of iconicity and insist on analyzing ASL with reference only to its arbitrary elements, we will fail to grasp the essential nature of its formational properties.

5.1   We have been concerned throughout this paper with not only the arbitrary but also the discrete elements of ASL's phonological structure. One significant aspect of ASL's structure is that nuance of meaning can be conveyed by means of systematic phonological alternation. Mandel discusses among iconic devices in ASL that which he calls **depiction**—basically making a picture of the referent, or part of it, or something associated with the referent. There are two types of depiction: one in which the signer "draws" the picture using his articulator (e.g., hand, finger, arm) as an implement (leaving an imaginary trace) as in HOSPITAL, in which the *H*-hand draws a cross on the arm, and TABLE, where *B*-hands move sideward and down, drawing the top and sides of the table; and one in which the signer uses his articulator as a substitute for the referent, as in WALK, in which the *B*-hands, representing the feet, move back and forth, and BIRD, in which the *L*-hand closes to *bO* at mouth, representing the bird's beak opening and closing. Signs that may be phonologically altered to convey nuance are nonmetonymic, depictive signs—that is, they depict the whole referent as opposed to some part of the referent. The signer may alter the shape of these signs by mapping "a continuous semantic feature continuously onto a continuous code feature" (Mandel, p. 65).[30] Such analogic (as opposed to digital) processes not only allow for lexical variation of the sort under consideration here, but also appear to be a major aspect of the grammar.[31] By such an analogic process, a sign like TABLE can be altered to indicate the size of the table; a big table is simply bigger than a small table. However, a metonymic sign like HOSPITAL cannot be altered to indicate for instance 'big hospital', even though the sign is depictive. The sign depicts a cross on the sleeve conveying by convention the meaning 'hospital'; if the signer were to make the sign HOSPITAL larger, he would merely convey something like 'big cross'. WALK may be phonologically altered to convey a variety of meanings including 'walk fast', 'walk slowly', 'trot', 'trudge', and 'march' because the referent action may be continuously mapped onto the action of the articulators, substituting for the referent feet. However, no such alternation is possible for BIRD because only the bird's beak is depicted in the sign.

To be sure, oral language has the ability to phonologically alter the shape of lexical items to convey degrees of meaning, but only in limited ways. In some languages, English, for example, one can intensify the degree of an item (usually a surface adjective or durative verb) by stressing it, as for example in the sentence *The fish was big*. In other languages, for example Hoysan, intensification or lessening of degree can be conveyed by various types of reduplication. In Hoysan [huŋ˩] 'red' when reduplicated with a rising tone followed by a low level tone [huŋ˦ huŋ˩] means 'very red'; when reduplicated and the tones are reversed, [huŋ˩ huŋ˦], the meaning is 'slightly red'. To some extent, onomatopoetic lexical items can be altered to represent real-world phenomena, for instance, by lengthening the vocalic portion of a word like *tweet* or by imitating long versus short or loud versus soft sounds in both onomatopoetic and nononomatopoetic items. However, phonological processes to show degree are quite limited in oral language.

However, in sign language, analogic phonological alternation is a widespread phenomenon. Visual language has the advantage of being able to use a much less discrete signal than can oral language. Any oral language is bound by its phonological structure: it must form its words from available, acceptable (language-specific) phones, in acceptable combinations. If a speaker wishes to convey various degrees of meaning (except in those cases cited above), he must carefully choose the lexical item which conveys that nuance, which rarely bears any resemblance to any other semantically related item.

5.2 Another striking example of the scalar (as opposed to segmental) properties of ASL's structure can be found in indexic locative and temporal expressions. Space, time, and person reference in ASL is achieved by the use of indexing, which entails the use of a neutral hand shape (usually *G, B,* or *A*) articulated in neutral space, pointed or oriented in given directions. The signer first establishes a frame of reference in the space in front of his body, and then establishes points of reference within that space identified with the objects, persons, and locations to which he intends to refer.[32]

> The relative distance of a locative referent from the signer in the real world is indicated by the relative angle of the extended finger in relation to the ground. The greater the angle of the hand in relation to the ground (up to but not including 90°) and the higher the arm is raised and the greater the length of the extension of the arm, the further the distance of the locative referent is from the signer. There are no definite lines of demarcation. In fact, a very distant location can be indexed by the superimposition of tense, sharp movement in which the arm is extended fully on the index (i.e. stress). [Friedman, 1975b, p. 949]

Relative distance from the signer from 'close to' to 'far from' the signer is indicated by a range of movements and orientations.

> It may be well to analyse the locative reference system as a continuum ranging from 'here' to 'very far from here' ... [ASL makes] use of all possible visual cues and spatial reality to form locative expressions. ASL appears to have less need for arbitrary combination of segments ... to indicate semantic components that can be (visually) iconically or metaphorically represented. [Friedman, 1975b, p. 949]

All temporal reference (excepting reference to calendric periods for which there are lexical items or time-adverbial phrases, e.g., YESTERDAY, LAST-WEEK) is made by indexic reference to points along an imaginary time line—a vertical plane running along the side of the body. The area of space coincident with and immediately in front of the signer's body represents present time; the area behind the body represents past time; the space in front of the body represents future time. By indexing various points along the time line, closer to and farther away from the body, the signer may indicate temporal reference relatively closer to and farther away from present time.

Given the type of analogic phonological alternation that is so prevalent in ASL, it seems clear that an analysis of ASL's phonology cannot depend solely on a description of discrete segments, the conditions of their occurrence, and their possible combination. I suggest that a phonological description of ASL has to include mapping or analogue rules of the sort mentioned here to account for the kind of variation found in the language. It is not sufficient to describe WALK, for example as two *B*-hands, palms downward or toward signer, with an alternating to and fro movement. Such a description fails to account for the depictive aspects of the sign, and more importantly, fails to relate the movement of the articulators—and the variations of that movement possible in the same sign—to the corresponding movement of the referent. My claim is **not** that the articulators actually perform the referent action or exactly depict the referent—such action would be pantomime, and such depiction would be drawing. I doubt that a language could sustain such a large amount of nonconventional elements. The fact is that the iconicity and iconic phonological and grammatical mechanisms in ASL and in other sign languages are highly conventionalized. Iconicity, at least in Sign Language, does not in any way indicate lack of conventionality.[33]

5.3   Given a description of the component parts of ASL and even given the notion of analogic representation, we would **still** not be able to account for the formation and relation of certain signs and sets of signs (paradigms?) without reference to further principles of iconicity.

5.31   Consider for instance the set of signs for times of the day. All signs for times of the day, and various signs like DAY and OVERSLEEP are based on an icon showing the typical position of the sun in relation to the horizon for any given time of the day. The position of the dominant hand indicates the sun's position in the sky; the horizontal nondominant forearm depicts the horizon. In NOON, the elbow of the dominant arm rests on the nondominant hand (orientation of the left hand is irrelevant); the dominant arm is perpendicular to the nondominant arm placing dominant hand in "high-noon" position, that is, directly above the nondominant arm. In MORNING the right (dominant) arm, facing the signer, makes contact with the left arm at about the middle of the right forearm; the sun, represented by the right hand, is in its typical morning position—about 45° from the horizon. EARLY-MORNING can be expressed by having the right arm's contact point be closer to the wrist—thus depicting the sun in a lower position in the sky. AFTERNOON reverses the orientation of the right arm—the sun is going down: contact with the nondominant "horizon" arm is made at the middle of the right forearm, which is facing away from the signer. Again the sun is in its typical afternoon position—at about 45° from the horizon on the other side of the sky. Clearly the sun's rising is depicted as coming toward the signer and its setting as moving away from the signer. NIGHT has the wrist of the right hand with the $\hat{B}$-shape (facing downward) making contact with the left wrist or hand; placing the right hand below the left arm depicts that the sun is below the horizon. ALL-NIGHT is formed by moving the *B*-hand around the underside left "horizon" arm—beginning with the position for NIGHT; the sun moves around the earth "under" the horizon during the night. ALL-AFTERNOON is made by moving the right arm from the NOON position to that of NIGHT—or almost to the NIGHT position. Similarly ALL-MORNING may be expressed by sliding the right forearm upward from the MORNING position until the left hand touches the crook of the right elbow.

In DAY, the right forearm, starting approximately perpendicular to the left arm, moves downward until it lies flat against the left arm. OVERSLEEP uses the *F*-hand shape which moves up from under the left arm until the right forearm contacts the left arm; the sign depicts the sun's movement as it reaches the midmorning position.

There are two reasons why I would like to treat this set of signs differently from signs discussed in sections 1–4. One possible insignificant reason is that the points of contact of the dominant arm in MORNING and AFTERNOON (and their variants) do not occur elsewhere; in no other signs is the forearm of the articulator the point of contact. It would be simple enough to add the forearm to the list of possible points of contact, but possibly a more elucidating solution would be to view the odd points of contact as incidental to the signs' depiction. I suggest that the depiction be described systematically and allow that description to account for the signs' formation rather than attempt to account for the formation in terms of discrete components of the four parameters.

Perhaps a more significant consideration regarding the times of day set is that if we describe these signs merely in terms of their component parts—that is their discrete 'phonetic' make-up—then we would fail to show the relation among the signs of the set—a relation based on the visual image the signs present. It seems counterproductive to describe all elements of a sign language—a language that makes full use of all possible visual cues, as well as of its lack of discreteness—solely in terms of arbitrary (and discrete) components. As an alternative, I suggest the following type of description.

Signs for times of the day are based on an iconic representation (depiction) of the position of the sun in relation to the horizon: the dominant hand—in the *B* shape—represents the sun; the nondominant arm in a horizontal position in neutral space represents the horizon. The rising sun (the sun's position in the Eastern sky) is depicted by having the hand (and forearm) face the signer and the setting sun (in the Western sky) by having the arm face away from the signer. Lexicalized distinctions: EARLY-MORNING, MORNING, ALL-MORNING, NOON, AFTERNOON, LATE-AFTERNOON, ALL-AFTERNOON, NIGHT, ALL-NIGHT. Variations: e.g., DAY—the dominant arm moves to the side and down rather than upward (for ALL-MORNING) or vertically downward (ALL-AFTERNOON).

5.32   Another example of a set of signs that may be described more felicitously in terms of the icon represented is the set including CHILD, TEENAGER, ADULT, and GROW-UP (people).[34] These signs are based on a depiction of people's typical

heights at certain ages. In CHILD, the dominant B-hand, palm downward, is placed
in neutral space at about waist level, indicating the typical height of a small child—
a short person. In ADULT, the B-hand is placed at head (eye) level or above, indicating the height of an adult. TEENAGER has the B-hand at about shoulder level,
somewhat nearer to adult than to child level. (It would appear that the sign TEEN-
AGER can only occur in conjunction with CHILD or ADULT or both and never in
an isolated construction.) Although varying heights of third person referents may
be indicated by various placements of the hand (i.e., 'Sarah was very tall, and her
friend Matilda was really short.'), the placement of the hand in CHILD, TEENAGER
and ADULT indicates nothing about the actual height of the referent individual.
That is, the sign ADULT means 'adult', regardless of height. In the verb sign GROW-
UP the B-hand moves approximately from the waist to the top of the head. It is
also possible to indicate 'grow to teenage-hood' and 'grow from adolescence to
adulthood' by moving the hand from waist to shoulder and from shoulder to head
respectively, but only in the context where both expressions are used.

Although we can easily describe this set solely in terms of arbitrary elements of
each parameter (e.g., CHILD = B-hand, palm down at waist), in doing so we would
fail to relate the signs to each other and to the visual icon they present. Instead, I
suggest that the phonological description of these and all depictive signs include a
systematic description of their iconicity.

5.4   Conclusion

5.40   I have attempted to present a comprehensive view of the component structure of ASL—a phonetic and phonemic description that takes into account the widespread iconicity of the language's formational properties. It seems clear that we cannot attempt to treat the phonology of a sign language exactly as we would treat
that of an oral language, in that language in the manual/visual modality avails itself
of every possible visual cue in its formation. It is clear that humans derive much of
their conceptual framework through visual stimulus and imagery. It is because of
this high sense of awareness of visual stimuli that language in the visual mode tends
to enhance its structure in ways that oral language cannot.

5.41   In de Saussure's definition of the nature of the linguistic sign, his first
principle is that the sign be arbitrary. He states that the "bond between the signifier
and the signified is arbitrary . . . the linguistic sign is arbitrary" (1959, p. 67). It
would appear that in many respects ASL does not follow this principle. Must we
then say that ASL is not a language comparable to languages in the oral/auditory
mode?

It is evident that de Saussure was not considering sign language (as a natural
language) in his description of the nature of the linguistic sign. It is true that in
oral language, the sign is arbitrary for the most part. He did not take into consideration (which is understandable in the light of claims made about sign languages at

the time of his writing) the possibility of a language in the visual mode, in which it is common and indeed **natural** to use all available visual cues to convey meaning. It is no longer necessary for us to prove that sign languages are viable and true languages. De Saussure's first principle applies only to those languages in which arbitrariness **is** an essential feature, namely oral language. It is important to remember in a discussion of the "phonology" of a sign language, that manual/visual language in many ways is **not** entirely comparable or analogous to oral/auditory language, with respect to both structural advantages and deficiencies.

The formational structure of ASL consists of conventional arbitrary and nonarbitrary elements, as well as discrete and nondiscrete components. The language makes full use of the possibilities of iconicity—available because of the visual modality—within the constraints of conventionality. It would be unnatural, given the nature of man—in terms of his reliance on visual imagery in thought—and the nature of language, if both iconicity and arbitrariness and both discreteness and nondiscreteness did not exist in any manual/visual language.

FOOTNOTES

1. Stokoe calls the units of ASL *chers* [kɛyɹz] and phonemes *cheremes* [kéyɹɪymz].
2. cf., Friedman, 1974a, b; Friedman and Battison, 1973; Stokoe, 1960, 1965.
3. For further discussion and explanation of these and other morpheme structure conditions, see Friedman, 1974b, 1976b.
4. See Frishberg 1975a, b; Friedman 1974b, 1975a, 1976b, for detailed discussion of phonological processes.
5. For further detail on this and other trivial and non-trivial constraints imposed by the modality of communication see Friedman 1974b, 1976b.
6. By Friedman, Battison.
7. Unmarked in relation to all other shapes; however, they are distinct from each other.
8. See section 4 for discussion of points of contact on the hand.
9. See Mandel for discussion of lexical versus nonlexical gesture.
10. The variation and its ongoing change are discussed in Battison et. al., 1974. Neutralization in ASL is discussed in Friedman 1975a, 1976b.
11. See Mandel, DeMatteo.
12. Phonological changes in rapid signing are discussed in Friedman 1975a, 1976b.
13. For details of stress manifestation see Friedman 1974a, b, 1976b.
14. See section 5 for more detailed discussion.
15. See Mandel for further discussion of *V*-legs.
16. For more detailed discussion see Friedman 1975a, 1976b.
17. See Friedman 1975a, 1976b, and Frishberg, 1975a, b, for discussion of phonological change in ASL.
18. The analysis presented here differs drastically from my analysis of the movement parameter derived from my preliminary study of the physical manifestation

of emphatic stress (Friedman and Battison, 1973, Friedman, 1974a, b). As I now believe that analysis to be incorrect, I will not burden the reader with any discussion of it. See Friedman, 1976b, for reanalysis of stress.

19. Unless of course two signs are simultaneously produced, as for example when the nondominant hand indexes a third person referent while the dominant hand identifies it or comments on it.

20. All signs may be "abbreviated" to become one-handed in rapid, or more commonly "encumbered" signing (when one hand is otherwise occupied).

21. Stokoe describes signs of this type as having approaching or separating action.

22. It is not within the scope of this paper to present a discussion of stress manifestation. See Friedman and Battison, 1973; Friedman 1974a, b, 1976b, for details.

23. This is a gross oversimplification. See Friedman, 1974a, b, 1976b, for details.

24. I called this value *CONTIGUOUS* in 1974.

25. There are, of course, constraints—perceptual, articulatory, and language-specific —for instance that *APPROACH* and *SEPARATE* only co-occur with movement in the width dimension.

26. There must be some perceptual reason for this phenomenon, but I do not know what it is.

27. See Friedman, 1976b, for further discussion.

28. See Friedman, 1976b, for further details.

29. For detailed discussion of iconic devices see Mandel.

30. This process is discussed in some detail in Mandel and DeMatteo.

31. See DeMatteo for discussion of analogic rules.

32. For discussion of space, time and person reference in ASL see Friedman, 1975b; indexing is discussed in regard to iconicity in Mandel.

33. Mandel presents a detailed discussion of iconicity and conventionality and their implicational interrelation in ASL.

34. GROW for plants is an entirely different sign.

ICONIC DEVICES IN AMERICAN SIGN LANGUAGE*

Mark Mandel

0. Introduction

0.0   What I Am Up To

An adequate account of American Sign Language must include the fact that the form various elements take in the language depends in part on the visual appearance of their referents.[1] Such an element is, to some degree, a picture. Its scope may be that of a whole paragraph of discourse, or it may be as small as a single component of a lexical item (forward motion in TOMORROW). Its visual similarity to its referent may depend on conventionalized (or not so conventionalized) actions comparable to acting (hefting the bat in BASEBALL), drawing (a rectangle for [monetary] CHECK), sculpting (the shape of a POT), puppetry (one hand following the other in FOLLOW), or simple pointing (to the signer's own nose for NOSE). Frequently in ASL *parole* the signer and audience seem unaware of the picture's underlying presence, and it does not interact syntactically with the rest of the discourse: although the sign GET-INTO-A-VEHICLE uses the *V*-legs morpheme in its formation, that may be irrelevant to the rest of a sentence like 'He drove up, I got in, and we left'. But often a picture proves necessary theoretically to account for the history of a sign, or its synchronic formational relationship to other signs, or its use in a particular discourse. For example, historically, the 'female'morpheme (chin or cheek as place of articulation) apparently derives from eighteenth century French women's sidecurls. To illustrate a synchronic paradigm, consider the numerous signs using the *V*-hand, referring to activities of the legs. An example of a particular use is changing the proportions of the sign HOUSE to approximate those of a particular, notably tall and narrow, house. (For the ASL history see Frishberg, 1975b; for data on synchronic paradigms see Frishberg & Gough, 1973, also Fant, 1972, *passim*; use in a particular discourse is discussed in this paper under **AD HOC** use.) Some of the pictures discussed in this paper are now dead, the signs containing them being no longer synchronically functional pictures—rather as, in English, no one any longer thinks of a cupboard as a board for cups (and the pronunciation confirms this). But the forgotten origin of lexical items is historically important. On the assumption (concerning which, see section 0.1.5) that signers see, may see, or once saw a picture in a gesture, my concern here is the relation between that picture and the formation ("phonological" form) of the gesture. The ways in which ASL forms a gesture to express a picture are the 'iconic devices' of my title.

The purpose of this paper, then, is to attempt to describe and classify the devices by which ASL has 'made pictures' and continues to make them. Taxonomy often seems to be considered a second-class kind of work, but a good classification has predictive value: it claims that its classes will prove to be natural ones (within the language) whose boundaries coincide with the limits of distributional patterns and constraints. This should also be true, **mutatis mutandis**, of a classification based on continua or fuzzy sets[2] rather than on well-defined sets (in the mathematical sense).

I have tried to order examples and analyses so that a reader who begins with no knowledge of ASL other than what is contained in the Introduction of this volume will neither be overwhelmed with data that he cannot comprehend, nor be faced with theoretical structures while lacking the material content to give them mental reality. This order of presentation has made it impossible to introduce every set of iconic devices systematically, since the presentation of any one of these systems presupposes knowledge of parts of others. So the introductory section of this paper offers a definition of iconicity, its place in ASL, and its often misunderstood relation to conventionality and arbitrariness. Section 1 is concerned with the devices with which ASL makes a simple picture (i.e., roughly, one that does not involve spatial relationships) and the principles governing these devices. Section 2 treats the more complex pictures ('constructs') that involve spatial relationships and are built up from simpler elements such as lexical signs, anaphoric devices, and movements. Section 3 is a brief return to the concerns of the introductory section, and a conclusion. The body of the paper is followed by an appendix of terms, most of which appear in **BOLDFACE CAPITALS** when introduced in the text; an appendix of tables summarizing the relationships between different concepts discussed in the paper and exemplifying their application; and the footnotes.

0.1   Iconicity, Arbitrariness, and Conventionality

0.1.1   ICONICITY

One of the defining characteristics of American Sign Language is that it is gestural-visual (though not simply manual-visual; see Baker, 1976a and in this volume) rather than oral-auditory. After that, perhaps the most salient feature to the casual observer is **ICONICITY**, its use of signs and other gestures perceived as bearing some visual relationship to their referents. (I will return to this in section 0.1.5.) Many signs of ASL can be analyzed as 'making a picture' in this sense. But some pictures are more pictorial than others. ASL uses a continuum of iconicity, from gestures with no apparent picture to ones that are, as closely as possible, reproductions of their referents. By **GESTURE** I mean any motion of the body, or of a part of the body, that is used meaningfully in ASL discourse. This is a broader class than that of **SIGNS**, which is limited to those gestures that are conventional in form and meaning and which generally obey certain formational rules (see Friedman, 1976b and Stokoe, Casterline, & Croneberg, 1965). I will usually distinguish these latter explicitly as 'lexical signs', but it is impossible, as well as undesirable, to make an absolute distinction between gestures that are sufficiently conventional and standard to be called 'lexical' and gestures that are not.

Remember that in speaking of the iconicity of lexical signs, I am not saying that an addressee has to see, e.g., the full citation form, formalized outline of a house ⌂ , or perceive the shape of the signer's gesture as that outline, in order to recognize the sign HOUSE. The iconic value of a lexical sign is irrelevant to its use much of the time. But lexical iconicity is important in diachronic studies and in the creation of new signs, in the underlying relationship between signs, and in the adaptation of a sign to a specific referent; and on a larger scale, propositional iconicity is a productive principle in ASL utterances.[3]

0.1.2   THE CONTINUUM OF ICONICITY

All noniconic gestures in ASL are lexical signs. One example is BLACK: draw the forefinger across the forehead.[4, 5] DARK seems a little more iconic: hold the palms facing back over the shoulders, on a plane in front of the face and about at eye level; then swing them down in the same plane to cross in front of the face and stop at about neck height. The effect is that of creating a barrier to the sight.

HOUSE sketches the conventionalized outline of a house ⌂ in the air in front of the signer with flat hands (B-hands; see Figure 1, Friedman, for hand configuration drawings): start with the hands together at the peak of the 'roof', then move them apart and down, turning them at the 'eaves' so they are always parallel to the surface they are describing. FOLLOW shows the very idea of following: using the fists, with the extended thumbs on top (double *thumbspread-A*), move one fist forward with the other in close pursuit. ON similarly shows a spatial relationship: flat hands, palm down, one lying on the other. In MIRROR the signer holds the cupped hand out and turns it slightly from side to side, as if holding a small mirror and looking at his face. BASEBALL represents a mime of hefting the bat at the shoulder (as far as the hands are concerned; stance and body posture do not normally enter into the sign). NOSE is signed by just pointing to the nose with the index finger. And the most literally iconic gestures I have seen are of the same sort as this example, which occurred in elicited narrative: 'I looked at my hand', signed[6] by the signer's simply looking at his own hand in the way he was telling about.

0.1.3   ICONICITY AND CONVENTIONALITY

For simplicity at this stage of the exposition, I have drawn only my last, most highly iconic example from nonlexical signing. The gesture 'I looked at my hand' was produced without reference to anything in the signer's previously existing repertoire of conventional gestures: it was totally **AD HOC**, referring only to the specific incident being described. The only conventional elements involved were, perhaps, rules of discourse governing the introduction of ad hoc mime. But degrees of "ad hocness"—or, to look at it from the other side, **CONVENTIONALITY**—are linked with iconicity in an implicational relationship that can best be represented by a two-dimensional continuum such as the following.

FIGURE 1

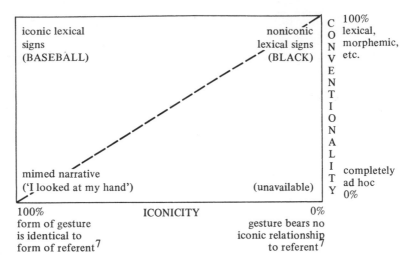

(I use the term 'conventionality' rather than 'lexicality' because some highly conventional elements of ASL, such as indexes [see section 2.1.1], are not clearly lexical.)

The diagonal dotted line, very roughly speaking, represents the lower boundary of the area used by ASL. Any meaning that is not borne by iconicity must be borne by conventionality, and vice versa. The southeast corner, zero-conventional and zero-iconic, is marked 'unavailable' because there can be no communication in that area. A gesture can communicate either by being or making a picture (in a broad sense) or by having a meaning agreed upon by convention, or by a combination of the two; there is no other possibility. (Most gestures of ASL are combinations.) A gesture with neither picture nor convention cannot communicate, and is therefore unavailable for use in a language. That is why all noniconic gestures must be lexical signs. (More generally and exactly, all noniconic elements are completely conventional.) The labels in the three 'available' corners describe the kinds of ASL element that occur there. All the ASL examples I have presented so far are on or near the '100%' edges of the graph, but there are other examples throughout the upper triangle.

0.1.4   ICONICITY AND CONVENTIONALITY IN ORAL LANGUAGE: ARBITRARINESS

This two-dimensional continuum of conventionality and iconicity—or, more generally, conventionality and **IMITATION**— can also be applied to oral languages. The best-known oral language instances of imitation are those of onomatopoeia, i.e., acoustic imitation, in which a lexical item referring to a sound sounds like its referent: 'buzz', 'hum', and 'hiss', (A case can also be made for direct quotation as a special case of onomatopoeia, especially when the original speaker's intonations and vocal mannerisms are mimicked in the quotation.) We also find chronological imitation, as in asymmetric **and**: 'Harry lit the joint and handed it to Clara' is not synonymous with 'Harry handed the joint to Clara and lit it'.

But most of oral language is nonimitative, and therefore, by the implicational relationship between imitation and conventionality, totally reliant on convention for its meaning. Since such conventions can vary almost without limit, those that a particular language uses are arbitrary.[8]

Concerning the oral language situation, then, most of a language's elements, including most of its lexical items, are arbitrary, and its imitative elements (notably onomatopoeia) stand out conspicuously as if a separate class. Since most linguists' familiarity with languages is limited to oral ones, the oral language situation has caused some confusion regarding the relationship between imitativeness and arbitrariness, even in ASL. Thus Frishberg(1975b) (in an argument incidental to the main point of the section) says:

> ASL uses the index finger in a vertical orientation as a sort of classifier for human beings. Lest the complaint be raised that this 'classifier' itself is iconic, we can show that this is **a language-specific symbol, and thus arbitrary** and subject to regular rule-governed change within the language. Chinese Sign Language uses the Y-hand [thumb and pinky extended, other fingers folded into the palm—MM] for a person classifier in a corresponding, although not identical, way. (p. 715) [emphasis added]

This form of argument, however, is invalid. An exact parallel of the argument would be to say that the English 'cock-a-doodle-doo', the French 'cocorico', and the Japanese 'kokekkoko', are not onomatopoetic because they are phonetically different forms: clearly an absurd conclusion. One the reasonable assumption that roosters sound the same the world over, it is evident that these languages have simply chosen different conventional forms with which to represent the sound. These forms must conform to the phonologies of the respective languages, and more or less to the cockcrow, but there is room for some arbitrary choice within these constraints; so there is no necessary reason in language or nature why the English representation of the cockcrow could not be 'keek-a-reeky', like the German 'kikeriki'. Similarly, the difference between the ASL and CSL person 'classifiers' is not evidence that either of them is noniconic: arbitrariness does not exclude iconicity. An element of language, whether signed or spoken, can be both conventional and imitative: that is, in oral language it can be both conventional and onomatopoetic; in sign language, both conventional and iconic.

0.1.5 THE EXISTENCE AND SIGNIFICANCE OF ICONICITY.
WHAT I AM NOT UP TO

There seem to be some linguists who do not consider iconicity a significant factor in ASL, at least at the lexical level. Presumably their arguments are motivated. at least in part, by de Saussure's declaration that the relation of the *signifiant* to the *signifie* is arbitrary, an assertion which until recently (see note 8) has not been seriously opposed with regard to oral languages. On the contrary, it is de Saussure's claim that requires support. Experience has supported it, by and large, in oral languages; but once we cross so important a line as the difference between the vocal-auditory and gestural-visual channels, we must be prepared to encounter facts and patterns at variance with our previous experience.

I have defined iconicity as the existence of a perceived visual relationship between the gesture and the referent. (The term would have to mean something similar in the context of ASL, in order to be etymologically relevant.) The word 'perceived' represents my best efforts to include all situations in which signers past, present, or future might conceivably see a picture in a gesture, because a picture that a signer thinks he sees may affect his use of the gesture, etymologically correct or not. Since I am trying to construct a framework in which to discuss the effects of pictures on gestures, I have to allow for as many possibilities as I can, but only within the range of what signers perceive. If the repeated contact-and-separation of the sign CITY reminds a nonsigning observer of a child clapping, that perceived picture is irrelevant to ASL.

This definition, by itself, is too general to use or test. But I can provide a description, in this taxonomy, (though probably not an exhaustive one) of the forms an iconic relationship between sign and referent can take. ASL, as well as other sign languages, can then be examined for uses of these forms of relationship—these **ICONIC DEVICES**—and for patterns in the language, such as domains of rule applicability, which can be defined in terms of the limits of the use of these devices. The presence of such uses and patterns, whether synchronic or diachronic, whether within ASL or cross-linguistically among sign languages, will then constitute evidence for the correctness and value of this taxonomy; their absence, evidence for its worthlessness. If, for instance, what I have defined as **models** should be found to form a syntactic class within ASL with respect to some feature of discourse, behaving in a particular way not shared by nonmodels, then my class of models is supported, along with the concept of iconicity on which it is based. But if no pattern can be found that selects models from the remainder of sign language, either from the history or present of any one sign language, or after considering the sign languages of the world, then the class of models and the device called modeling will have no provable reality and are, at the very least, useless notions.

Of the underlying images that I will mention in this paper in relation to various gestures, some are quite certain as etymologies or derivations, as in the example 'I looked at my hand'. The shapes of others are justified paradigmatically, either by the recurrence of the same morpheme in other signs (V-legs; V-vision) or by other, perhaps formationally unrelated signs with related meaning (BASEBALL; cf., GOLF, swinging the club, BASKETBALL, shooting the ball with both hands, and FOOTBALL, the line of scrimmage). Other images are supported by tradition and repeated in various printed sources, such as SCHOOL. And some are just guesses with degrees of reliability varying down to zero—probably including a number of those supported by tradition and in print.

Many of these underlying pictures are doubtful, or just plain wrong, **as etymologies**; I have heard two or three proposed for **AMERICA**, which is not likely to have had more than one origin. Some are demonstrably alive and productive in modern ASL (*G*-person in MEET, etc.), some are not (SCHOOL shows no signs of iconic life nowadays, and the image I cite here, though given in Stokoe, Casterline, & Croneberg (1965) as well as Riekehof (1963), is unknown to some native signers).

But the etymology of a sign which signers think of as iconic is irrelevant to its potential iconic use. A sign sometimes seen for BREAD (palm facing forward, middle finger bending down toward thumb as if to make an *8*-hand) is derived from the fingerspelled word b-r-e-a-d by a process of abbreviation (b-d) (Robbin Battison: personal communication via Charlotte Baker). Some signers are aware of this origin, but others etymologize the sign as representative of the softness of bread (a **mime**). If the deaf community in one area accepted the latter explanation and wanted to distinguish lexically between 'soft bread' and 'hard bread' (let us say, rolls baked with a thick, hard crust), they might create a modified version of the sign—e.g., with the thumb and fingers tensely bent at the middle joints rather than lax— to refer to 'hard bread', retaining the present sign for 'soft bread'.[9]

However, I am not proposing etymologies here. I am trying to set up a theoretical framework in which iconicity's historical and synchronic roles can be investigated. In some contexts I have cited evidence for the correctness of an iconic analysis: e.g., the multiplicity of signs in which the *V*-hand behaves spatially like a pair of legs, in shape as well as motion. Where the evidence is not so striking, I have simply described the gesture and the iconic device as I think it operates there. Although I will propose no experiments here to test iconicity, I do have some ideas; I will simply describe the ways and patterns in which I think the principle of iconicity is used in ASL. Let this theoretical structure serve as a basis and stimulus for further research.

1. Basic Iconic Devices of ASL

1.1 Metonymic Versus Direct Transfer of Meaning[10]

Many **REFERENTS**—a term under which I include actions, states, entire events, relationships, and in general all 'meanings', not just those of nominals—which have no visible form—are nevertheless signed iconically in ASL. THINK, for instance, is signed by touching the extended forefinger to the forehead; OLD, by pulling the fist down from the chin (as if stroking one's beard). The forehead, or the brain behind it, stands for **thinking**, the beard for **age**. We can say (following Battison (1971) and I. M. Schlesinger et al. (1970) that these gestures are **METONYMICALLY** iconic with respect to their referents—that they use a picture of one object to denote something else that is associated with that object; and we can call the object directly described by the gesture (forehead/brain, beard) the **BASE** of the sign. The term **base**, so defined, can also be used in speaking of nonmetonymically iconic signs, such as HOUSE (*B*-hands ⌂) and FOLLOW (fist following fist), in which the base is an example of the type of the referent, and the transfer of meaning from referent to sign is not mediated by the relation of metonymy. The iconic gesture itself, whether metonymic or not, can be called an **ICON**. It will also be convenient to use the term **IMAGE** for the pictorial value of the base: e.g., the shape ⋂ that the hands, making the motion ⋂ , describe in the sign HOUSE.

Some other examples of metonymy in lexical signs are as follows. SCHOOL: clap the hands twice (base: a teacher calling the class to attention). HOSPITAL: with right[11] *H*-hand (first and middle fingers extended and touching, thumb holding other fingers down), sketch a cross on upper part of left arm (base: the red cross on a uniform sleeve). BIRD: holding the back of the fist against the mouth, with the knuckles on top and the thumb and index finger extended forward, bring the thumb tip and fingertip together (base: a bird's beak opening and closing).

1.2   Show or Tell: Presentation versus Depiction. Presentation

But the gesture itself may be related to the base in different ways: the signer can either present to the addressee a token of the base object or of the body activity involved in the base action—**PRESENTATION** of the base—or he can make a picture of it—**DEPICTION** of the base. **MIME**, which is probably the best-known of all iconic devices, presents a token of action, as in BASEBALL, 'I looked at my hand', COFFEE (move the fists circularly as if grinding coffee in a hand mill), and WRITE ('write' with a wiggly motion as if holding a pen, on the left palm).[12] Note that the first two examples are metonymic. BASEBALL takes part of the game, the batter's heft, for the whole. COFFEE takes a process for the substance worked upon: grinding coffee in one of the ways in which it is done (but not growing, roasting, or drinking) stands for coffee in any of its forms: beverage, freeze-dried crystals, plant, or ice-cream flavor. The agent whose action is imitated is usually human, but need not be, as in many animal names such as MONKEY (scratch the sides in the classic simian manner); though perhaps the only conventionalized non-human mimes will be, like this one, the name of the agent whose typical action is mimicked.[13]

If the base is a presentable object rather than an action, the signer can point to a token of its type. This device is related to the deictic system of indexing, to be discussed later (see section 2.1.1), and will be called **INDEXICAL PRESENTA-TION**[14]. Examples are NOSE and BODY (move the *B*-hands, palm inward, down the front of the torso), without metonymy, and THINK, with metonymy. Lexical signs of this type must have bases that are always available to the signer; body parts are the outstanding class of such bases.

1.3   Depiction

1.3.0   EXAMPLES AND TYPES OF DEPICTION

But most things that are potentially bases of iconic signs cannot be counted on to be available to the signer when he needs them. To be used as a base, such a thing —whether object, action, relationship—must be, in Battison's (1971) felicitous term, 're-presented' as a picture. Battison calls such re-presentation 'metaphor', but I would prefer to use the term **DEPICTION** for two reasons: first, ASL can use the type of transfer-of-meaning called 'metaphor' in the ordinary sense of the word, as in the sign HELP, whose image is of physical support (right palm underneath left fist, lifting it); and second, it seems that the name 'metaphor', were it to be used as a term in ASL linguistics, would be more aptly applied to a particular class of depiction, **substitutive depiction,** which I describe below.

Some lexical examples of depiction are: HOSPITAL, HOUSE, TREE (rest the right elbow on the left *B*-hand, holding the right forearm upright with its wrist straight and all the fingers extended, spread out, and wiggling slightly), BIRD, and AIRPLANE (hold the right hand in the *thumbspread-horns* shape—thumb, index, and pinky extended, middle and ring folded down—palm downward, about chin level, and move it forward or right-to-left with the index finger pointing in the direction of motion).[15]

There are two classes of depiction, both represented in this list of examples. In one type, the signer pretends that his articulator (i.e., hand, finger, arm) leaves a trace as it moves, and he **draws** the picture with this imaginary trace.[16] This **VIRTUAL DEPICTION** produces a three-dimensional ⬠ in the air for HOUSE and a ✚ on the arm for HOSPITAL. For the other type of depiction, the signer's articulator actually **becomes** the picture: a tree standing in the ground with its leaves fluttering, a bird's beak opening and closing, and an airplane flying. These images depend on a metaphoric relation between the articulator and the base. The relation between fingers and branches in TREE is of the same kind as the relation we allude to in naming the 'head' and 'foot' of a dinner table, a page, or a street: namely, metaphor. But, since metaphor is also used in other ways in ASL, I will call this device **SUBSTITUTIVE DEPICTION.**[17]

In section 1.3.3, I will present a more detailed analysis of virtual depiction. A corresponding analysis of substitutive depiction will follow later since it falls more naturally into section 2, on spatial relationships.

1.3.1 ANALOGUE RULES

Both kinds of depiction depend on **ANALOGUE RULES**, a notion developed in some detail by DeMatteo and discussed also by Battison (1971). DeMatteo defines an analogue rule as a rule which maps a continuous semantic feature continuously onto a continuous code feature. Each point in a depictive icon is analogous to a point in its base, as points of a map are analogous to points on the land. In virtual depiction the analogue rule that relates the icon to the shape of the base must refer to time. For example, the relation of the iconic sign HOUSE to the meaning 'house' might be described roughly as follows: **in the motion of the sign**[18] (which is inseparable from time) the articulators pass through certain points of the signing space and not others. The point through which the articulators pass form a certain shape, which is the shape of the base: a house such as ⌂ , which, in our culture, is in some way the classic or stereotypical house. (Of course, I am not claiming that the signer or addressee consciously thinks this process out, either during signing or at any other time. But such relationships connect the sign HOUSE to its meaning, at some level, coming into play whenever iconicity becomes important.)

In substitutive depiction, however, the image—the shape of the base—is present in its entirety as long as the articulator maintains 'its iconic configuration.[19] The iconic relation of TREE to the meaning 'tree' might be described thus: certain points in the signing space are distinguished from the rest just **by being points in the articulators** (a fact which is independent of motion and time). The articulators in their iconic configuration and orientation form a certain shape, which is approximately the shape of the base: a tree standing in the ground, 🌿 , which in our culture is understood as a typical tree (and which in ASL can stand for a tree of any shape, e.g., even a fir tree). To this shape, motion is added, analogous to motion of the base: the fingers are analogous to the branches, their waving motion indicating the waving of the branches.

1.3.2 TEMPORAL VERSUS ATEMPORAL MOTION

Notice that, though motion is essential to the analogical relationship between a virtually depicted icon and its image, such an icon can also utilize the time-independent type of spatial analogy on which substitutively depictive icons depend. In HOUSE, for instance, the flat hands give the image a depth, in the front-to-back dimension, which does not depend on their motion. The resulting image is three-dimensional,   ⬠ , and not two-dimensional,   ⋀ , although the motion involves only two dimensions,

A substitutive icon like TREE, on the other hand, whose analogical relationship to its image is independent of motion, may involve motion of another sort. The motion of the icons AIRPLANE, BIRD, and TREE—flying, beak opening and shutting, branches waving—corresponds to actual motions of the base; but, although HOUSE requires motion, the walls and roof of a house do not move (except in California). HOUSE can be compared to a drawing or a sculpture, and the signer moves only as the artist in making his motionless creation: for instance, the speed of his motion is immaterial.[20] But AIRPLANE is like an animated cartoon or puppet show: the hand, in *thumbspread-horns* shape with the palm down, looks generally like the wings and fuselage of a plane, and it "flies" through the signing space, above the level usually used for signs that are not associated with some specific part of the head or trunk. The signer's motion in AIRPLANE is a performance whose length and pacing are an integral part of the picture.[21] An analogue rule separate from those already mentioned relates time—and therefore motion—in the icon to time and motion in the base.

In section 2, in the discussion of icons of spatial relationships (constructs), it will be important to distinguish these two types of motion in icons. The kind which can appear in a substitutively depictive icon, such as TREE or AIRPLANE, as part of a moving picture in which time and motion are analogous to time and motion in the base, will be called **TEMPORAL MOTION**. The kind which appears in a virtually depictive icon, such as HOUSE or HOSPITAL, and which merely creates a still picture with no analogical relationship to time or motion of the base, will be called **ATEMPORAL MOTION**.

These two types of motion can also be seen in presentative gestures. Indexical presentation is atemporal: the motion of the pointing finger towards the nose, or the hands down the front of the body, belongs only to the icon, not to the base. Mime is usually temporal, as in COFFEE or BASEBALL, but can be atemporal, in striking a pose, as in a (probably nonlexical) mime I have seen for 'Egypt': hold the arms and head in a way which is reminiscent of ancient Egyptian tomb paintings. (The motion involved here is the motion **to** the pose itself; cf., note 24.)

1.3.3 KINDS OF VIRTUAL DEPICTION

1.3.3.0 Sketching versus Stamping

There are two basic kinds of virtual depiction. In one, the articulator is used as an implement that leaves a trace as it moves, like a pencil on paper or an automobile headlight in a time exposure photograph. A pointed implement (pencil or fingertip) leaves a line as its trace, either straight or curved depending on the motion. A linear implement (piece of chalk held flat, or a straight or bent finger) leaves a surface, whose shape depends on the shape of the implement (straight or curved) and on the motion. A linear implement can also move parallel to itself, e.g., a straight finger moving like an arrow to depict a straight line. A surface implement (trowel or ice-cream scoop, a whole hand held in various flat or curved surface shapes) can leave a trace shaped like itself, when moved parallel to itself—flat hand moved flat, curved hand moved as if along a curved surface—or it can leave a solid trace perpendicular to itself, as if one indicated the height of a stack of papers by putting his hand palm down on the table and then raising it to the height of the stack. This kind of virtual depiction, where a trace is left by the motion, can be called **SKETCHING**. HOUSE and HOSPITAL are sketched icons.

In the other kind of virtual depiction, the implement moves forward and then returns, like a rubber stamp, leaving its trace at the place where it stopped rather than along its course. Here the trace is of the same shape as the front of the implement: a fingertip leaves the trace of a point and the edge of the hand leaves a line. (It is theoretically possible for the flat hand to leave an area trace in this way, but I know of no cases.) This kind of virtual depiction can be called **STAMPING**. It seems to be less common than sketching. The point-based forms of both with the extended forefinger—stamping a point and sketching a line—have much in common with the indexing system (section 2.1.1), and many instances of them are probably best analyzed as belonging to both systems. (These systems of indexing devices are not mutually exclusive, and the analysis of a single gesture may involve one or more.)

The examples of stamping and sketching are grouped according to the hand shapes involved.

1.3.3.1 Fingertip(s)

Clear lexical examples of stamping with the fingertip are hard to find. A possible one is STAR: each hand has the *G*-shape (index finger extended from fist) pointing ahead and upward; the signer alternately moves each hand in the direction it is already pointing. (This can also be analyzed as indexing, pointing to stars overhead.) Another is the decimal point used in numerals, which are made in fingerspelling space, in front and to the right of the throat where the hand can be comfortably held palm out; since in this position it would be uncomfortable to stamp the *G*-hand forward, toward the addressee and onto the imaginary surface in which successive digits of a number are aligned, the signer crooks his index finger (*X*-hand) and stamps the decimal point with a pecking motion. A nonlexical example is 'a field full of flowers', which includes repeated stamping with the *bent-5*-hand (thumb and all fingers spread, bent at the middle knuckles but straight at the base), held palm down, stamping five points at a time all over an imaginary horizontal plane.

When you move a point, the result is a line, and the tip of the extended forefinger of the *G*-hand sketches a line up the back of the left arm, from the back of the hand to the elbow or higher, as in LONG. The shape of a sign or poster can be sketched in the air with both *G*-hands at once: ⌐⌐   . An oval rug on the floor was sketched with a *G*-hand pointing down, moving in an oval shape; indexing combined with sketching, or sketching on the floor with the imaginarily extended forefinger. The cross in HOSPITAL is also sketched; the use of two fingers together may be due to the width of the cross— ⊹ , not + —to initialization[22] with the letter 'H' or to both. The four or five fingertips are used at once, like a rake, with a motion similar to that of HOSPITAL, to sketch a plaid on the arm (SCOTLAND) or a grid in the air (SCHEDULE). Thumb and forefinger are bent into a *C* and the rest of the fingers folded as a fist (*bent-L* hand shape); the extended fingertips then can sketch parallel lines and come together in a common depiction of any formal piece of paper, such as a check, a ticket, or a diploma: ⊏⊐   .

These shapes are fairly simple. But more complex patterns can be sketched. Asked to describe a geometric figure   ◿   , the informant sketched the bottom oblong with *bent-L*s, then the rest with *G*s.

1.3.3.2 Single Finger(s)

Surfaces do not seem to be sketched often with a straight finger, but rather with a flat hand (see next subsection). The only examples I know of are nonlexical. 'Thin dust on top of a table' was depicted with a form of the *bent-L*-hand shape in which the last joints of the thumb and forefinger were held parallel and as far apart as possible; this shape then slid along the 'tabletop' (left forearm held horizontally), depicting the upper and lower surfaces of the dust and the thickness between them. A hollow tube was depicted by making a ring with the thumb and forefinger of each hand, holding the rings together palms forward, and then moving them apart straight out sideways, tracing a long, thin tube.

Forefingers stab down parallel to each other, move toward the signer and stab down again to sketch the four legs of a table (followed, in this sign, by the two

B-hands sketching the top). Pinkies held horizontally tip-to-tip, then pulled in opposite directions, sketch LINE.

I know of no examples of stamping with a whole finger, as opposed to a fingertip (but see section 1.3.3.4).

1.3.3.3 Open Hand

Surfaces are usually sketched with one form or another of the open hand: flat as if to slap (*B*-hand), fingers spread (*5*-hand), fingers together and bent (*bent-B*) or spread and bent (*bent-5*), or *C*-hand (like *bent-B*, but with the thumb forming the lower arm of the *C*). HOUSE uses the *B*-hand, as do one sign for TABLE—like HOUSE, but the motion is ⌐⌐ —and BOX: first, with palms facing each other, move hands straight down to sketch two sides of the box; then, with palms facing you, right hand close to the body and left hand in front of it, repeat the motion to sketch the other two sides. A nonlexical example is 'leg of a table', with *C*-hand, palm facing left: the curvature of the hand represents the roundness of the leg, and the hand moved down along the imiaginary surface. *Bent-5* often sketches the surface of a heap of things or "stuff," a pile of apples or garbage. A *B*-hand, palm down, can move forward (parallel to its fingers) to sketch nonlexically the course of a road: hilly, curving and so on. These surface-sketching open hand shapes are all shaped like the surface they depict, so that they can on occasion depict them substitutively as well.

1.3.3.4 Other Occasional Hand Shapes

I have observed the pinky edge of a *B*-hand used apparently to stamp a straight line, depicting the edges of a tabletop in neutral space with what looked like a wide, shallow articulation of BOX.

Doubtless other hand shapes are possible as the need arises (mostly nonlexically), both in stamping and in sketching.

1.3.4 A POSSIBLE THIRD TYPE OF VIRTUAL DEPICTION

The sign BIG is made with *L*-hands (forefinger and thumb extended at right angles from the fist, both in the plane of the palm), thumb tips together, then sharply separating sideways. The sign RICH starts with the sign MONEY and then has the two *B*-hands, the left palm up and the right palm down above it, move upward. Both of these signs begin by indicating something small—unspecified for BIG, a pile of money for RICH—and end by indicating something large within the same dimension. They can be interpreted as illustrating the growth of something (and so, metonymically, its ultimate size) or as simply tracing its extent with what is, at least for RICH, a solid trace. Or they can be interpreted as a mime, holding the object as it grows; or as a third kind of virtual depiction (alongside sketching and stamping), or a third kind of depiction (alongside substitutive and virtual), which could be called **MEASURING**. Whichever of these possibilities provides the best explanation, or what other one, or combination of the two, is to be decided by further investigation—if indeed this device is used often enough and in enough different ways to yield a workable amount of data.[23]

1.3.5   FUZZY AND AMBIGUOUS CASES

There are borderline cases in which two forms of depiction overlap. A comparison of different-sized articulations of BOX reveals that, as the shape sketched becomes smaller and smaller, two changes occur. The downward motion with which the hands sketch the sides of the box gets shorter and shorter. And the change in orientation that occurs in all forms of BOX, from fingers-pointing-frontwards (to form the left and right sides of the box) to fingers-pointing-to-the-sides (to form the front and back), is made by bending the knuckles rather than the wrists. As a result, the characteristic motion of the smallest form of BOX[24] is not the two "syllables" of downward sketching characteristic of the citation form, but rather the bending of the hands from straight to right-angled. Instead of sketching the sides with his flat hands, the signer depicts them substitutively, with either flat hands or just the fingers of the flat or right-angled hands. But the substitutively depicted left and right sides of the box remain only as traces in memory while the front and back sides are being drawn. It looks as if small BOX is a case of (Heaven help us!) virtual substitutive depiction in which a substitutive icon, namely the left and right sides of the box, is first formed and then removed, thus becoming virtual. The signer then forms another substitutive icon, the front and back of the box, which the addressee combines mentally with his remembered image of the left and right sides.

1.4   Communicating and Maintaining Shapes: Virtual versus Visible Iconicity

So far I have described simple icons according to the devices by which they are produced; they may be presentative or depictive. Types of presentation are mime and indexical presentation; types of depiction are substitutive and virtual depiction, which in turn consists mainly of sketching and stamping.

There is another distinction that overlaps this analysis. When the shape of a base object is at all involved in the image, it may either be visible throughout the duration of the icon, or it may be made atemporally and then have to be remembered. The second case is true of virtual depiction (sketching, stamping, and maybe [depending on the analysis] measuring); the first holds in all other iconic uses of shape: mime, indexical presentation, and substitutive depiction. For mime the shape is more presupposed than asserted: the effectiveness of MONKEY as a mime depends on the constantly visible similarity of shape between a human's body and a monkey's. In indexical presentation the shape of the base object may be irrelevant or a minor consideration (the brain or forehead in THINK), but if it is at all relevant, it is communicated as something that is always visible. In substitutive depiction the shape is the picture.

Such **VISIBLE SHAPES** are less subject to modification than the **VIRTUAL SHAPES** created in virtual depiction. If one wants to communicate iconically the image 'long neck', as in GIRAFFE, it is not sufficient to stretch the neck and point to it (indexically present it). Instead, ASL uses a *C*-hand, curved to fit the throat (thumb to right, fingers to left, palm in), held in front of the throat and then moved up and out to virtually depict a long neck.

The reason for the difference in modifiability between visible and virtual shapes is not hard to find. A particular virtually-depicted shape (especially a sketched one) can easily be rendered differently, subject only to the limitations of the signer's reach and of his own and his addressee's memory. But a visible shape belongs to a physical object—generally part of the signer's body—and is not so readily modified. The signer cannot stretch his neck enough to create the 'long neck' needed for the lexical icon GIRAFFE.[25] This difference in modifiability is implicit in the phonological constraints on ASL as observed by Friedman, among others. She lists as one of the constraints imposed by the manual-visual modality:

> Signs are constrained by the possible movements of the joints and muscles of the hands and arms. For example, no sign may be articulated in which the signer is forced to bend his fingers backwards, even if he is capable of doing so with his other hand. (The important point being that he cannot do so simply with one hand.) [1976b, p. 104]

A visible shape, generally formed by the signer's body or part of it, is directly subject to this constraint (in a form slightly generalized from the above, to include other parts of the body than the hands and arms, e.g., the neck). But a virtual shape is constrained only indirectly, in terms of the signer's atemporal motions as an 'artist'.

1.5   Ad Hoc Modification of Iconic Signs

Iconic lexical signs can be modified to suit the picture more literally to the particular referent. In terms of the two-dimensional iconicity–conventionality continuum (see section 0.1.3), such modification moves a sign south and west, making it less conventional and more iconic. If we examine the basic devices one by one, indexical presentation would not seem to admit of ad hoc iconic modification, since the token of the base object is physically present and usually cannot be modified. The only possible kind of modification I can think of is that in which the token is a physical feature subject to the signer's voluntary control, such as (for some people) cross-eyes, or a convenient modification of a handy token, such as 'He had his shirt rolled up like this' (demonstrated by rolling up one's own shirt in the manner to be described). But this theoretical possibility seems to be little or never used in ASL.

Such modification is closely related to ad hoc modification of mime. But actions are easily modified, so the possibility of ad hoc iconic modification is much greater for mime than for indexical presentation. Many multi-directional verbs can be analyzed as having a mime element that varies in an ad hoc manner: the 'given' handshape in GIVE, for instance, goes from the giver to the receiver.

Iconic modification of substitutive depiction usually depends on analogic use of the joints. In that respect substitutive depiction resembles mime, in which the shape is the signer's whole body itself, which can change only by bending or by depicted 'changes': 'long neck' in GIRAFFE, 'beak' in BIRD. For example, the V-hand form of WALK ('Let your fingers do the walking') has the fingers substitutively depicting the legs, and their changes of shape correspond analogically to the legs' motions at hips and knees. Such modifications are best analyzed as models (section 2). Iconic modification not based on the use of the joints is possible, but I know of only two examples. Both are now lexical and therefore largely conventional, but they must have been ad hoc in origin, and new creations are surely possible. One sign used in reference to obese people is based on a modification of the V-legs as used in WALK$_V$:[26] instead of 'walking' his first and middle fingers, the signer 'walks' his thumb and pinky. And DUCK is the same as BIRD except that the upper part of the 'beak' consists of the first and middle fingers held together rather than the first finger acting alone: 'a bird with a wide bill'. The differences in basic handshape (Y for V, *thumbspread-H* for L) are iconic modifications of substitutively visible shapes.

The most productive ad hoc modification of lexical signs occurs in virtual depiction, where there are almost no physiological constraints imposed on the picture. Some signs, in fact, have almost no meaning aside from the modified element: BIG, SMALL, LONG, HEIGHT (better glossed THIS-TALL). Other signs, though they have meanings apart from their modifiable characteristics, are subject to modification of their precise proportions. Asked to describe a picture of a tall, skinny house, and informant began by signing HOUSE, not in the usual shape ⌂   , but ⌂ . Then he signed DOOR, WINDOW, and other parts in the appropriate places on the remembered sketch, signing the color of each as well (not in place). Similarly. TABLE$_{BB}$ (⊓) can become 'big table' (⊓).

Virtual depiction is probably used in ASL more for (completely or partially) ad hoc description of referents than for **fully conventionalized** lexical items. But consider the sign which Stokoe, Casterline, and Croneberg (1965, p. 52) describe as

$$C_a C_a \overset{p}{\wedge} (\text{imit., hands mold the shape})_N \text{ } bowl, vase.$$

(I.e., C-hands start palm up, then rise while turning the palms to face each other or downward.) Such a sign, while often involving ad hoc depiction, is nonetheless common enough to be considered lexical. This is an instance of the impossibility of classing all gestures as strictly lexical (100% conventional) or strictly ad hoc (0% conventional). Separate tokens depicting bowls or vases of different shapes may form a gradation, such that one token is barely to be distinguished from the tokens most like it, and if two adjacent tokens were the only ones under consideration they would have to be called nondistinctive forms of the same sign; yet the tokens at two extremes of the gradation may refer to a dog's water dish and a spherical vase with a narrow neck, and in a discrete analysis would be called separate signs. See section 2.5.3 on continua of utterances.

Besides shape or proportion modification, there is also modification of movement. (See also sections 2.1.2 'Multidirectional verbs', and 2.5 'Markers'.) So the sign WALK$_{BB}$, using two B-hands 'walking' in substitutive depiction of the feet, can become prolonged and laborious for 'walk for miles and miles, trudge'. It can take on modifications of manner and intonation in ways suggested for other signs by Fant (1972, p. 17–18):

> The sign **work**, like **learn**, is a sign which varies in meaning with the variation in the speed, the size, and number of repetitions. Practice making the sign **work** indicating the following (facial expressions are also extremely important):
> > work long hours
> > work fast
> > work that is boring
> > work that is fascinating
>
> Try the same four attitudes with the signs **learn** and **study**.

(For further discussion, see Friedman, 1974a, 1976b, and Fischer, 1973a.)

There are iconic constraints on ad hoc modification, as well as physiological ones. An icon which is metonymic—whose picture is not of its referent, but of some other thing associated with its referent—should not be modifiable to show a difference in the referent, unless in fact that difference affects the metonymic base. So one cannot sign 'big hospital' by sketching a big cross on the upper arm; but consider the hypothetical sign *HARD-BREAD, involving metonymic use of a mime, in section 0.1.5.

1.6   Deiconization. Iconization

What is presented in a mime is not, in fact, the base action itself; one does not need a bat to sign BASEBALL. The signer presents the same body movements that are utilized in performing the action that constitutes the base of the sign. This motor program (a term suggested by Charles Fillmore) can undergo some modification from its original, the sequence of muscle actions and body attitudes of the base action. In the first place, it is affected by the absence of the 'stage properties': the S-hands in BASEBALL are closed fairly small, as they would not be if the handle of a bat were passing through them. The hands in the mime sign HEAVY are not actually being pressed down by a load, so that their muscular tension and actual shape are different from what they would be in the base situation. Whatever changes and interactions a mime sign may undergo in ASL begin from this "propless" form.

In the second place, any icon, whether formed with mime or with other devices, is at risk of certain changes as it becomes more and more conventional in ASL. It will generally tend to adapt itself to the language's phonology and to ease of articulation, losing some of its iconicity in the process: the sign BE-PATIENT, which once required the signer to "bow the head as if in resignation," has transferred the downward motion to the hand (Frishberg, 1975b, quoting Long, 1918 for the older form). HOUSE, in colloquial signing, often loses the 'walls' present in the citation form: ∠⟍ . What is signed as an icon may be perceived by the addressee in purely formational terms, as a noniconic, purely arbitrary sign (morpheme, etc.), opening the way for that addressee, when he uses the element himself, to modify it (whether consciously or not) in accordance with articulatory and perceptual mechanisms and in disregard of its former iconic value. This process can result in the partial or complete loss of synchronic iconicity: **DEICONIZATION**. (See Frishberg, 1975, for description and analysis of historical change of this sort.)

The hypothetical neologism *HARD-BREAD from BREAD$_8$, discussed in section 0.1.5, would be an example of **ICONIZATION**: an originally noniconic sign coming to be thought of and treated as iconic. In fact, the current folk etymology 'softness of bread, squeezing bread' is itself evidence of iconization. But so far I know of no actual use being made of that icon in ASL.

1.7   Summary of Simple Icon Devices of ASL

The visual image of an iconic gesture can be related to the gesture's referent either **directly**, by being the (kind of) thing referred to, as in HOUSE and NOSE, or **metonymically**, by being something else that is somehow related to the thing referred to, as in THINK (forehead) or COFFEE (grinding coffee). The image may occur in the gesture either as an object or action presented to the addressee, or as a picture that the signer makes of an object which is not present: **presentation** or **depiction**.[27] Presentation is done either with **mime** (COFFEE, BASEBALL) or with **indexing** (NOSE, THINK). Depiction falls (with some borderline cases) into two types: **substitutive**, in which the articulator forms the shape of the object being pictured (BIRD [beak], AIRPLANE), and **virtual**, in which the articulator is used like some sort of artist's implement. Virtual depiction itself has two main types (although there is some evidence that there may be others): **sketching**, in which the articulator leaves its trace as it moves, as in a time exposure photograph (HOSPITAL, HOUSE); and **stamping**, in which the articulator comes up to a point, stops, and retreats leaving its trace, like a rubber stamp (DECIMAL-POINT, 'field of flowers'). Each can be realized with a variety of hand shapes. Iconic signs can be modified ad hoc to make them more highly iconic of the specific referent talked about at the moment (**this** house, as distinguished from houses in general, emphasizing **this** house's individual characteristics). This type of modification is used principally with icons formed by virtual depiction and mime, as opposed to substitutive depiction (but see section 2.5, 'Markers') and indexical presentation, and seems difficult to apply to metonymic icons. Signs can lose iconicity in the course of time (**deiconization**) and perhaps gain it (**iconization**).

2.   Spatial Relationships in ASL

2.0   Introduction

So far I have discussed mainly iconic signs for single referent objects (e.g., HOUSE, COFFEE) and predicates (WRITE, THINK), and since the introduction I have made little mention of the iconic description of spatial relationships in ASL. But this is where ASL differs most, syntactically speaking, from oral languages. There are varieties of English Pidgin ASL that use English syntax and ASL lexical

items (plus some signs coined for the purpose of translating English words or morphemes), and which express spatial relationships, and all others, with English sentences translated word by word, in English order. These systems are in principle no
different from logographic writing of an oral language: they represent spoken English,
but in a manual-visual mode rather than in a vocal-auditory or graphic-visual mode.
It is ASL's use of spatial relationships between its lexical items, as well as temporal
and morphological relationships such as all languages exhibit, that most differentiates its syntax from those of oral languages.

The relationship between the walls and roof of a house, as shown in the icon
HOUSE, is a spatial one, but it is (except for iconic modifiability) a trivial case of
spatial relationship, simple and without much interest—like division by 1. In the
following subsection I will introduce some of the devices of ASL that **use** spatial
relationships existing in the signed discourse. The rest of section 2 will deal with
devices that **describe** spatial relationships existing in the referent—the thing being
talked about—or in the metonymic base by which the referent is described visually.

2.1   Some ASL Uses of Spatial Relationships

2.1.1   DEIXIS: INDEXING

The most obvious case of spatial relationship between objects is deixis: reference to the thing I am talking about as distinct from other things, to the place there
as distinct from here and yonder, to you as distinct from her and me. Oral languages
perform deixis with sound sequences that usually have no analogic relation to the
direction, the distance, or any other feature of the location (individual, etc.) being
referred to. (One exception, though marginal in English, is 'Wa-a-ay over there'.)[28]
In a gestural-visual language, the obvious deictic device is pointing to the referent,
with whatever pointing gesture is culturally appropriate. In ASL linguistics this
pointing is called **INDEXING**. Indexing is iconic insofar as it depends for its meaning on the visual connection between the pointing gesture and its target; but furthermore, it is involved with other iconic devices in ASL. The indexing system of ASL
has been described in detail by Friedman (1975b). A summary of parts of her analysis follows.

2.1.1.1   The Forms of Indexes

INDEXES are gestures that point to a referent, using various hand configurations that will be illustrated with the ASL equivalent of personal pronouns. Simple
reference to physically present referents is made by pointing with the extended
index finger, or G-hand (this is also the hand shape of the numeral 1): I/ME, YOU,
HE/SHE/HIM/HER. For plurals and combinations of these, the signer points in
succession to the people involved, or uses a general sweeping motion across them.[29]
In addition, he also has the option of changing the single finger to the ASL numeral
2 for dual number (same as V-hand, first two fingers extended from fist and separated), 3 for trial (2 plus extended thumb), 4 or 5 for plural (4: all four fingers

separated and extended; 5: same plus extended thumb): WE–2 = $\left\{ {you \atop he/she} \right\}$ and   I, usually with *2-handshape*. The flat hand (*B*-hand), facing and moving toward the referent (for plurals, facing and "sweeping"), marks the possessive index; the fist with thumb extended upward (*thumbspread-A*) marks emphasis. The possessive and emphatic indexes do not distinguish number in the hand configuration. (See also note 43, on Baker's discoveries concerning eye indexing.)

2.1.1.2   Grammatical Locations

Absent referents can also be referred to by indexes. If the signer wants to talk about his friends Asa and Henry, he does not have to keep using their namesigns[30]; he can sign ASA and index a point in the signing space, to his right and in front of him, and thereafter use indexes to refer to that point as though Asa were there (the same hand shape options apply). In the same way he can place Henry on his left and refer to him.[31] Such a point in signing space serves as an anaphoric pronoun. Signers can regularly use three or four of these at once—right, left, right and forward, left and forward—and perhaps even more on occasion.

Setting up an anaphoric point in this way is an instance of **ESTABLISHING** a referent. But, since there are other kinds of establishment, I will refer to this variety, in which these four arbitrarily conventionalized points are used, as **GRAMMATI-CALLY LOCATING** a referent.[32]

In establishing a referent, a signer is referring to the discourse itself. Other types of establishment can communicate something about the referent, but in grammatical location a signer in effect says no more than, 'When I refer to this point in space, I will mean such and such an individual'; and he conversationally implies that he will in fact refer to it. He is defining a conceptual relationship between referent and location, for use later in the discourse.

2.1.2   MULTIDIRECTIONAL VERBS

One of the major uses of grammatically located referents is for **MULTIDIREC-TIONAL VERBS**. These are verbs whose motion and/or orientation indicates their subject and object, or source and goal. The referents can be located or physically present. For instance, the citation form of GIVE is: start with the fingertips and thumb tip of the hand clustered together (*tapered-O* hand shape) and pointing up, at upper chest height; then lower the forearm forward, opening the hand somewhat as if offering something in it. But in use, this means 'I give to you'. For 'you give to me' the motion is reversed; 'Asa gives to me' moves from Asa (present or located) to the signer; 'Henry gives to Asa' from Henry to Asa, and so on, in any combination of persons, either both present, both located (grammatically or in the real world, section 2.2), or mixed. LOOK-AT, another multidirectional verb (*V*-hand, palm down), \ involves less or no directed motion,[33] PITY (*open-8* hand shape, thumb and all fingers are spread, middle finger bent down; palm facing object of pity, and hand moving up and down) is directional only in its orientation. PITY is apparently somewhat "defective" in that either the subject or the object is preferably first person: the examples 'I pity $\left\{\begin{smallmatrix} \text{you} \\ \text{him} \end{smallmatrix}\right\}$' and '$\left\{\begin{smallmatrix} \text{you pity} \\ \text{he pities} \end{smallmatrix}\right\}$ me' give my informants no trouble, but 'he pities $\left\{\begin{smallmatrix} \text{him} \\ \text{you} \end{smallmatrix}\right\}$' and 'you pity him' are ambiguous.

Notice that the motion from source to goal of a multidirectional verb such as GIVE corresponds analogically to motion in the referent event, and as such can be described as temporal motion. The motion with which a referent is established—the indexing motion of grammatical location, or the motion involved in other forms of establishment to be described later—is atemporal, belonging only to the discourse. (Cf., the definitions of temporal and atemporal motion in simple icons in section 1.3.2.)

2.1.3 SPACE TO REPRESENT TIME

Much of time expression in ASL uses space as an analogue of time.

> Time relative to the time of discourse is primarily manifested by a line extending forward and backward from the body. The time line can be divided into three primary areas: (a) the space coincident with and immediately in front of the signer's body, which represents present time . . . (b) the area of space behind the body representing past time . . . (c) the space in front of the body, which represents future time . . . [Friedman, 1975b, p. 951]

Most signs indicating temporal relationship[34] use this standard image, usually only to establish direction as past or future: YESTERDAY/TOMORROW, PAST/FUTURE, -AGO/-HENCE are symmetrical pairs, in each of which the motion (and sometimes orientation) of the first member is backward and that of the second is forward, but the two are otherwise identical or nearly so. Some signs, though, do in fact use specific portions of this time line, or make significant use of distance as well as direction. For example, RECENTLY is formed on the shoulder, PAST waves a hand back over the shoulder: FAR-IN-THE-FUTURE repeats FUTURE and can extend it forwards; UP-TILL-NOW (also called PAST-CONTINUOUS or SINCE) moves forward from below the shoulder and lands in the present, in front of the chest.

There are other analogic uses of space for time in ASL. One of them uses a space-time analogy existing in the real world. The signs for various times of day (MORNING, AFTERNOON, etc.) and DAY itself are based on the apparent daily motion of the sun across the sky—and under the earth, as in NIGHT and ALL-NIGHT. Some other signs, such as OVERSLEEP, also make use of this image. For further details on signs of time, see Friedman (1975b) and Cogen.

2.2 Icons of Spatial Relationships: Construction. Real-World Location

So far I have not discussed the way ASL describes spatial relationships between referent objects. If you, Henry, and I are all in the room together, then our present spatial relationship is obvious, and if I index him, or refer to his location in a multidirectional verb, I am using our spatial relationship, not describing it. If Henry is not present and I locate him grammatically, 'his' point's position relative to my body does not describe any spatial relationship between Henry and me under these circumstances.

But a signer can talk about such relationships, and he will use space analogically to do so. One day I asked an informant to talk about a conversation that had occurred at a party we had both attended. He began by establishing (locating) the people in various places around him, corresponding not to the conventional positions of third person referents in signing space (grammatical locations), but to the people's actual positions at the party, relative to himself. He set up a conceptual model of the room in which the party had occurred, fitting in his signing space, so that his location in the model corresponded to his seat at the party, and he put the other people in their corresponding places: one person on his right, another across the room facing him (established at arm's length), someone else at that person's left, and so on, in various other places easier to specify in ASL than in English.

CONSTRUCTION is my term describing the building of a complex picture (a CONSTRUCT), involving spatial relationships that exist in the base event. In this 'party conversation' construct the referent is the same as the base, and the locations are REAL WORLD LOCATIONS. If, talking about Asa and Henry, I establish them in grammatical locations, I am building a metonymic construct. The fact that Asa is in one place in the construct while Henry is somewhere else is a fact of the metonymic base, corresponding to the referent fact that Asa and Henry are different people.[35] This sounds trivial, but it is, after all, the motivation for grammatically locating them in different places in ASL; just as in oral languages that have this capacity, it is the motivation for using separate third person pronouns ('fourth person' or 'obviative'), or demonstratives, or 'the former . . .the latter'. The conventional, metonymic grammatical locating of Asa and Henry in this example is the same device as the ad hoc, nonmetonymic real-world locating of the people at the party.[36]

The use of these constructs, real world or grammatical, can become quite involved. (The description of the party conversation lasted a number of minutes, including question, answer, and comment flying back and forth across the roomful of "located" people.) Occasionally the identification of a referent (name or brief description) will be repeated to help the signer and addressee remember the identities of the locations. Another device—role-switching, described below—is often used, either by itself or together with the indexing of located referents, to distinguish participants in an event.

2.3   Scales: Staging and Modeling

I have been describing construction in the signing space, built to the scale of the articulators: e.g., people in a room, on a scale on which the people are about the size of the signer's hands. This kind of construction I call MODELING, because of its (usually) reduced scale and because of the way it often uses markers (section 2.5). But constructs may be larger, scaled to the signer's own body size, representing life-size referents. One example of this is the following elicited utterance: (giving someone directions) 'The school is directly in front of you, and way far over on your right is the hospital':

SCHOOL INDEX $^{\text{(forward, straight out)}}$ /

HOSPITAL   INDEX $^{\text{(right, slightly up, arm extended)}}$

Another example occurred in a description of a restaurant scene. The informant and his friends had been signing together; at other tables nearby, other groups of people were speaking various oral languages. The informant described these groups and indexed their locations around him—including behind him, which is an unacceptable location as far as signs are concerned, but perfectly acceptable for real-world indexes.[37] The spatial relationships established here are between the signer's body (which, in the 'school and hospital' example, represents the addressee's body) and the school and hospital or the other groups of diners. Such body-scale construction I call **STAGING**.

Staging and modeling can co-occur, with one element of the referent event being staged and another part being modeled. Although I am getting ahead of myself in introducing markers, I will give an example. An informant was describing a time when he had been sitting in a chair reading and an acquaintance who was drunk had walked over and stood beside him, trying to force his conversation on him. In relating the story, the informant took the role of himself and represented the acquaintance by an upright forefinger, a common marker for a person. He brought the marker in from arm's length at his right, a little above eye level, and winced away from it with his head, grimacing at the acquaintance's "beer-breath." He repeated the close approach and wince several times and signed BOTHER (a multi-directional verb) from the space that was to the right of his head, toward himself: 'He kept coming over and bothering me'. The wince was mime (staging), the marker was modeling, and the verb's directionality referred to both the staged role and the marker.

2.4 Role-Switching

It is common for a signer to take the role of a person being discussed, as in the 'school and hospital' example. When two or more people are being talked about, the signer can shift from one role to another and back; and he usually uses spatial relationships to indicate this **ROLE-SWITCHING**. In talking about a conversation between two people, for instance, a signer may alternate roles to speak each person's lines in turn, taking one role by shifting his stance (or just his head) slightly to the right and facing slightly leftward (thus representing that person as being on the right in the conversation), and taking the other role by the reverse position.[38] He may use the center position, facing straight out, to represent himself, either participating in the action or commenting on it. He may or may not repeat names, as in the 'party conversation' example; whether he does, and how often, probably depends on how well he thinks his audience is remembering who the referents are and which role represents whom. For more details on role-switching see Edge & Herrmann and Friedman (1975b).

Similar role-switching can occur in nonquotative narrative. I have a transcript of a videotaped story about a mother washing an unwilling child. Once the roles in this story are well established—the mother holding the child still with her left hand and washing with her right, looking down and left; the child wincing down and left, and looking up over her right shoulder at the mother—the switches are marked mostly by shift of position, with only an occasional repetition of GIRL or MOTHER.

A signer may describe not only what was done by the person whose role he is playing, but also what happened to that person. Fant (1972, p. 93) has the signer mime hitting himself in the eye, in a context where it is clear that someone else hit him.

Clearly, staging is closely related to mime. If the referent "objects" whose spatial relations are being described are people, then the signer can use mime to describe their actions, which usually will take into account the spatial relations between them. In the example of the mother washing the daughter, much of the interaction was mimed: facial expressions, the mother's washing (with the partially mimic sign WASH), the child's wincing and her attempts to escape. But that example is more mimic than most. Role-switching usually does not involve such drastic shifts of position between the roles. Normally a slight shift of body or head position effects the switch. A signer can use multidirectional verbs between his role positions, and make the roles interact in mimed narrative. In one brief discourse— an elicited narrative of an invented chance meeting of the signer and two other persons—there were about eight interactions between the roles, including one person lighting another's cigarette as well as such lexical multidirectional verbs as GIVE. The changes of role were carried out with slight shifts of body position and some repetition of names. In the 'party conversation' model the informant turned his head and body to play the roles of the various individuals he quoted, as well as indexing their locations in the model and naming them. The role locations were consistent for the model, i.e., a person located at the informant's left in the model would also have a role position at the left. These devices effectively did what signers say should be done in ASL: they created a good picture to communicate the referent event clearly.

2.5   Markers

2.5.0   LOCATIVE ICONICITY AND SHAPE ICONICITY

In the signs FOLLOW (fist following fist) and ON (flat hand on flat hand) the hands represent referent objects, and the spatial relationship between the hands represents the spatial relationship between the referent objects. An analogic relation holds:

                    icon   : referent   ::
    fist following fist : person following person   ::
        hand on hand   : object on object

The spatial analogy is very similar to that which occurs in substitutive depiction; and substitutive depiction is in fact the relationship between each articulator in these models and its referent object. Not in terms of shape—the flat right hand on the back of the flat left hand in ON need not be shaped at all like, for example, the stick on the rock that the signer is talking about—but in terms of location. The iconicity that is chiefly important in these signs is **LOCATIVE ICONICITY**, as opposed to the **SHAPE ICONICITY** that is foremost in the depiction of single referent objects.

Although I described substitutive depiction in terms of shape iconicity (section 1.3.0), the definition will also accommodate these new cases in which the articulator does not assume the shape of the referent object. Here the articulator and its spatial relationships within the signing space constitute the picture. It will be very useful to have a term to denote an articulator which is locatively iconic of a referent object in a construct. I will use the term **MARKER**.

Markers have varying degrees of shape iconicity, from the highly shape-iconic *thumbspread-horns* of AIRPLANE to the potentially zero shape-iconic flat hands of ON (cf., a stick on a rock). The shape can even be irrelevant to the shape of the referent, if the sign's iconicity is metonymic. HELP (right hand, open and palm up, under left fist, lifting it) is iconic of a literal support, which means 'help' by the same metaphor often used in English. But if I say I need help with a math problem, there is no lifting involved; and if any iconic analogy exists between the math problem and the left fist, it is certainly not one of shape.

Frishberg & Gough (1973) speak of morphemes of various sorts in ASL: place of articulation, hand configuration, and motion. Many of the hand-configuration morphemes are markers such as *V*-vision and *V*-legs.

> We can find many . . . examples of distinct signs which use the *V*-hand to represent the idea of eyes or vision. The sign for READ combines the *V* for eyes with the palm up, horizontal surface used in signs denoting book learning [or a sheet of paper in general—MM] . . . READ moves the symbolic eyes up and down over the iconic page several times . . . SIGHTSEEING or WINDOWSHOPPING are made with both hands in the *V*-shape . . .
>
> LOOK-IN-THE-PAST (reminisce) and PROPHECY both use the *V*-hand combined with movement along the "time line" . . . LOOK-AWAY-IN-DISTAIN [sic] moves the *V* sharply by a vertical (index finger) "goal" . . . (p. 17)

> A huge number of signs use this same hand shape to show legs . . . In almost every case the sign is made on the palm, that is, the palm is used as the surface on which the legs stand or lie. This is true in TOSS-AND-TURN, ROLL-IN-THE-AISLES-WITH-LAUGHTER, KNEEL, RESTLESS, DANCE, FLOP-UNDER-THE-COVERS, STAND, WEAKENED, LAY-DOWN [sic], GET-UP, FALL-DOWN, and so on. All the variations on the sign SIT use bent *V*, as in SIT-IN-A-CIRCLE, SIT-ON-A-BENCH. The kinds of variations possible here are discussed in Fischer (1973, p. 19)[39].

(See also Stokoe, Casterline & Croneberg, 1965, pp. 140–143, " $\llcorner V_{\top}^{\perp}$ *see*".) All these signs are lexicalized constructs. They use an articulator in substitutive depiction, in analogical relation to the space around it and/or to another object in that space. In these signs the other object is a motionless marker serving as a ground with respect to which the moving marker's motion is defined.[40] So, for instance, in another sign of the *V*-legs family, JUMP-UP-AND-DOWN, the upturned left palm is not only the surface on which the "legs" are standing, but it also makes it plain that the legs are in fact rising from and returning to a surface: jumping up and down. In transcribing ASL, it has proved useful to refer to a marker that is functioning as the ground of a sign as GROUND.

2.5.1   MARKERS ALONE IN MODELS

A model can show spatial relationships even if there is only one element in it. Motion within the signing space—the spatial relationship of a marker's location at one time to its location at another time—can be perceived with respect to the signer's body, even if he is not part of the model (providing Talmy's 1973 'reference-frame'; see note 40). *V*-legs can 'walk' in various ways within the signing space, which will be understood in context as walking upstairs, climbing over a hill, and so on. Compare AIRPLANE with one of the signs for CAR: this sign for CAR (there are two) uses a *3*-hand shape (first two fingers extended and separated, thumb extended, all radiating in a plane from palm; other two fingers bent down) with the fingers pointing forward and the thumb pointing up. Its lexical and ad hoc use (section 2.5.3) prove it to be a marker. It is made in neutral space, i.e., around lower chest height. But AIRPLANE is articulated around face height, even as a simple nominal (cf., note 21). I know of no other sign articulated in that area which is not either anchored to part of the face, such as the sign ICE-CREAM (anchored to the mouth region), or connected with fingerspelling. AIRPLANE's behavior in models with other elements and in whole-utterance models shows that it is not anchored. Clearly, AIRPLANE is a marker in a model, flying high in signing space, even when it is alone.

2.5.2   THE *G*-PERSON MARKER AND ITS MULTIPLES

The marker consisting of a raised forefinger and representing a person—'*G*-person', because it uses the *G*-hand—was mentioned earlier. Frishberg's argument against the iconicity of the *G*-marker is invalid (section 0.1.4): it seems to be shape-iconic of the general, vertical outline of a standing person and is unquestionably location-iconic. MEET is a right and a left *G*-person coming together, GANG-UP-ON is the right *5*-hand (thumb and all fingers spread wide) moving to and closing on the left *G*-person. LOOK-AWAY-IN-DISDAIN (cf., Frishberg & Gough citation, above) is *V*-vision ignoring *G*-person.

This marker can be multiplied to represent two, three, or many people or individuals of other kinds. The right hand in GANG-UP-ON is one example. Others are QUEUE (two *5*s representing a line of people) and MEETING (*5*s converge from left and right, closing so that all ten fingertips are together). The five fingers spread for 'many individuals' often (as sometimes in TRAFFIC, for instance) have a fast wiggly motion in addition to the motion of the hand as a whole, apparently indicating that each individual is moving rapidly and excitedly, or that the motion of the group in unconcerted and confusing.

Fant (1972, p. 61) translates 'we two went up to him' with a form of MEET in which a *V*-hand 'two people'-marker approaches a *G*-person. I have a record of the *5*-hands, palm in, approaching the signer in a construction of 'lots of policemen coming at me', and of the *5*-hands with palms down converging from the sides toward the center in 'lots of cats running toward something'; in both utterances the markers had the 'unconcerted' wiggly motion. (Note the difference of orientation: a cat's body is long horizontally, not vertically.)

A 'many individuals' *5*-hand marker, whether wiggly or not, bears some phonological resemblance to the *bent-5*s used in stamping a multitude of points ('field of flowers'), in sketching the top surface of a heap ('pile of apples') and in sketching the volume of (or mimically holding, or 'measuring') a large amount (MUCH, RICH), and to the *5* used to mark 'plural' in indexing. Although the exact relations between these devices have yet to be fully clarified, it is plain that the use and iconic value of the 'plural marker' *5*, for example, and the 'surface-sketching implement' *bent-5* are different.

2.5.3 THE AD HOC USE OF MARKERS IN UTTERANCES; CONTINUA OF UTTERANCES

The most important characteristic of markers from the point of view of language typology is their productive use in constructing utterances: namely, establishing their reference to specific referent objects, whose spatial relationships and movements in the referent event can then be accurately described by analogic movements of the markers. Models of this kind often form entire utterances whose analysis poses serious problems for any analytical mechanisms based on those two characteristics common to all oral languages, discreteness of elements and temporal ordering of elements.[41]

Take the English sentence 'The boy met the girl'. It corresponds to part of a continuum of ASL utterances, varying in details of the motion involved in the encounter. The citation form of MEET brings the two *G*-persons (palms facing each other) together from the sides. In this utterance the markers might be established and the verb articulated like this:

$$\left[\begin{array}{l} \text{R} \qquad\qquad\qquad\qquad \text{BOY } G\text{-person}^{\text{(on right)}}\text{------} \\ \text{L GIRL } G\text{-person } \text{---} \\ \qquad\qquad\qquad \text{(on left side of neutral space)} \end{array}\right\} \text{MEET (in center)}$$

But instead of bringing both markers to the center, the signer can keep the 'girl' stationary and move the 'boy' all the way over to her: 'The boy went up to the girl'. Or vice versa. Or he can bring the markers together at any point between their starting positions. 'Manner adverbials' can also be expressed in the same continuum of motion (cf., the quotation from Fant, 1972, section 2.5). The signer can make the style of motion unmarked and casual, or he can move the markers hesitantly, with nervous little motions, adding emphasis with facial expressions and the 'set' of his body. [42] He can, in addition, express a whole range of events extending far beyond the English sentence: the boy or the girl, or both, can turn aside to avoid the encounter, one can follow the other (with various outcomes), they can perform an entire 'dance' before boy finally meets girl.

So the analogic description of motion in ASL can encompass an entire event. ASL's analogic features establish continua not only between different degrees of a predicate such as 'big' (see DeMatteo) and between differently proportioned tokens of a single type of referent (as in section 1.5), but even between propositions, some of which appear to be antonymous. The continuum that includes 'boy meets girl', whose citation form motion is ⟶ ⟵, also includes ⟵•⟶, 'boy and girl separate'.

2.5.4   ESTABLISHMENT OF MARKERS

The real-world and grammatical locations used for third person anaphoric reference (section 2.1.1.2) are established indexically: the signer names the referent and indexes its location. But a marker is visible and does not need to be pointed out, so indexing is optional in the establishment of markers.[43] There is no indexing in the 'boy meets girl' example: name the referent (i.e., sign BOY or GIRL), then make the marker with the same hand. (Note that this involves signing GIRL with the left hand rather than the usual right.) A second method is to name the referent, then set up the marker with one hand and index it with the other. Or a signer may simultaneously name the referent with one hand and set up the marker with the other, not bothering to index. The choice of methods, like the choice of which side a marker will be on in an ad hoc construct or one which represents an entire event, is probably partly dependent on characteristics of the discourse: what is already established in the model, whether the signer prefers to perform much of the action with his dominant hand, etc. The "sidedness" of ASL discourse, and its relation to signers' handedness, remains to be investigated in detail. (Cf., note 31.)

2.5.5   GRAMMATICAL MULTIPLE MARKERS

In addition to representing referent space with signing space, markers have a grammatical function that is similar in one way to that of the third person grammatical locations in signing space, and in another to such oral language constructions as "Now, the first little pig . . ." The signer may extend a number of fingers and establish each one as one of the referents, indexing each of them with his other hand as he identifies them:

$$\begin{bmatrix} \text{R LYNN INDEX}^{\text{(to left thumb)}} & / & \text{ASA INDEX}^{\text{(to left forefinger)}} & / \\ \text{L} \text{--} \end{bmatrix}$$

$$\begin{bmatrix} \text{R HENRY INDEX}^{\text{(to left middle finger)}} \\ \text{L} \text{--} \end{bmatrix}$$

The signer will then index these markers as he would any other referents, whether physically present or grammatically established. Certain multidirectional verbs can also function between them, subject apparently to formational constraints. My guess is that those verbs admissible here are those that involve actual motion of the hand from one marker to the other, such as GIVE or BORROW/LEND (the verbs that Edge & Herrmann call 'multidirectional'); while those which involve only orientation (Edge & Herrmann's 'multiorientational'), such as PITY or LOOK-AT, are not, simply because there is not enough room between the marker-fingers for clear and comfortable articulation of such a sign. But the motion of GIVE, for example, can begin with actual contact between the articulating hand and the giver's marker-finger, proceed in an exaggerated and clear arc to the recipient's finger, and end by touching it.

The transcribed example uses the hand shape *3*, which happens to be the only ASL numeral from *1* to *5* that differs from our hearing culture's gesture for that number: thumb and first two fingers extended, third and fourth fingers bent. (The usual American "hearing" gesture for '3'—thumb holding pinky down, other three fingers extended—is ASL '6'.) ASL appears to use its numeral hand shapes consistently when numbers are being specified, whether in fingerspelling and signing numbers, in indexing, or in the use or markers.[44] (Remember that even the basic and unmarked singular cases, INDEX, *1*, and *G*-person, use the same hand shape.) This phonological equivalence misled Friedman (1975b) into calling the *G*-person marker an index and failing to distinguish it from the deictic indexes of ASL, for which I think the term is best reserved.

2.5.6   MNEMONIC MARKERS AND REMEMBERED ICONIC VALUE

At the boundary between virtual and substitutive depiction there sometimes occurs a special type of marker, exemplified in this utterance, elicited as an ASL version of 'The airplane is over the valley':

$$\begin{bmatrix} R \\ L \end{bmatrix}$$ *B*-hands (palms down) sketch a valley from right to left

----

$$\begin{bmatrix} R \\ L \end{bmatrix}$$ R AIRPLANE ^(flying over remembered location of valley)

(maintain left hand in final position from sketching valley)

The left *B*-hand has the same shape as what it is sketching: it is a flat surface sketching a surface whose curvature is negligible across the width of the hand. Therefore it can become substitutively depictive of a part of the same surface (section 1.3.3.3). At the end of the trace it does so, becoming both shape-iconic and location-iconic of one rim of the valley. The signer and addressee remember the shape of the valley and its relation to this marker. The shape of the valley is important, since the airplane can fly either across it, from right to left, or along it, forward toward the addressee; the informant considered those to be distinct utterances, and insisted on

knowing which direction was meant before choosing either one as an ASL translation of the English sentence. The entire valley cannot be maintained while the airplane flies over, since it is depicted virtually, but the left hand serves substitutively
as a **MNEMONIC MARKER**, depicting a part of the shape. The addressee infers
from its presence and position, as well as its remembered relation to the rest of the
trace, (a) the fact that the valley is still present in the model, and (b) its location
and orientation in the model.

Having to remember this much iconic data about a referent object in a model is
unusual. Most remembered imagery in ASL is purely locative, and the shape of a
virtually depicted icon is usually unimportant in the utterance. When a signer uses
the sign HOUSE, for example, its shape is usually irrelevant to the rest of the utterance.[45] Certainly, in an utterance in which there is no modeling or staging above
the lexical level, such as POSSESSIVE-INDEX HOUSE BUILD YEAR 1876 'Her
house was built in 1876', there is no "picture" of the whole meaning, as there is in
'boy meets girl' once the markers have been established. But even a typical model
like the following one, where the whole utterance is iconically structured, uses
only locative iconicity in the model: ME ADDRESS ASA HOUSE (on left) /
SEARCH+ (to right) HOUSE (on right) SAN-FRANCISCO (on right) / FIND (on
right) TAKE (from left, place of first 'house') PUT (to right, place of second
'house') 'I'm staying with Asa while I look for a house in San Francisco. When I
find one I'll move (out of his house) into it'.[46] Only the location of the 'houses' is
important and must be remembered; their shape is insignificant. "HOUSE (on left)
... HOUSE (on right)" could have been replaced with "a-p-t INDEX (to left) ...
a-p-t INDEX (to right)", the fingerspelled abbreviation for 'apartment' (whose iconic
value is obviously nil), without changing the iconicity of the utterance as a whole.
By contrast, in the 'airplane over valley' example, the signer and addressee must
keep track of the valley's shape—specifically, the location and orientation of the
trough—to communicate the meaning of the model. The mnemonic marker in 'airplane over valley' may function to ease the increased load on visual memory.

2.5.7   THE USE OF MARKERS IN ESTABLISHING LOCATION

Markers can be substituted for indexes in locating referent objects in a model.
In the description of a party referred to in section 2.2, some of the people were
located with the form of *V*-legs used in the lexical sign SIT, i.e., *bent-V* like the legs
of a seated person. The woman sitting across the room from the informant was
established at arm's length in the model with SIT facing the signer. The same marker
appeared in 'The children were sitting around the tree in a circle':

$$\left[\begin{array}{l} \text{R   TREE   SIT+++}^{\text{(around the former place of the tree)}} \\ \text{L   GROUND (of TREE) } \text{-----------------------------------} \end{array}\right.$$

('Children' was not signed.) This SIT marker is also used, interestingly, for non-
human referent objects, especially buildings, apparently with the same metaphor

that appears in many oral languages, including the causative etymon of English 'set.' When it is used of humans it is more informative than an index to a location, because it tells that the person is not just there, but sitting there; cf., note 36.

Another hand shape often used as a locatively establishing marker is *thumbspread-A*: fist with the thumb edge on top and the pinky edge on the bottom, and the thumb pointing up. The referent of this marker is generally inanimate, often a building, as in a construct that could be glossed 'many buildings on the heights': the *thumbspread-A* strikes the back of the palm-down left hand, then goes out and up to the edge of the signing space at about the signer's eye level; then the sequence is repeated, to left, center, and right. (In context this was 'many castles overlooking the river'.) This is a conventional way of establishing a building in a location: the *thumbspread-A*-onto-the-back-of-hand that precedes each establishing motion is very similar to the sign ESTABLISH and closely akin to a family of signs including CHURCH and NATION. Frishberg & Gough (1973) say of this group:

> The back of the hand is used to symbolize external, open space. We can see this in a number of signs conventionally made on the back of the hand and also in contextual variation of signs not normally made on the back of the hand. (p. 22)

It is plain that the *thumbspread-A*-onto-back-of-hand sign, as 'building', includes the notion of 'a thing established outdoors', and the marker of the 'thing outdoors' is then moved to the place in the model where the building is to be located.

I have also seen this marker used to picture rows of medicine bottles on shelves. The marker was moved along horizontally, then down to the next 'shelf', where the motion was repeated. The smooth motion from left to right may have been a phonological reduction of a series of slight downward establishing motions, repeated along the shelf; such an analysis is needed to explain this utterance as a multiple establishment with the *thumbspread-A* marker, and is justified by other instances of the reduction, to a smooth, straight motion, of an underlying series of short parallel motions perpendicular to the line joining the places where they are made: ⟑⟑⟑⟩ becomes   ⟶ .[47]

2.5.8   CONSTRAINTS ON MARKERS

There is no *a priori* reason why the function of locative marking, as seen in ON, 'airplane over valley', and 'boy meets girl', should be limited to substitutive depiction. But there is a perceptual one. Consider HOUSE: it involves atemporal motion, the sketching motion that belongs to the making of the icon but not to the picture that the icon conveys. If you wanted to move the picture—as in 'Jack London's cabin was moved from the Yukon to Oakland'—you would have to sketch HOUSE on your left, say, and then sign CARRY (or a sign of similar meaning) from that place over to the right, labeling the two locations 'Yukon' and 'Oakland'.[48] If you tried to move the sign HOUSE itself, with its virtual (not visible) shape, the atemporal motion of the sign would mix irrecoverably with the temporal motion across the signing space, producing an incomprehensible smear: ⋂   +   ⟶   = ⟨⟨ .

(In contrast, the shape of the 'airplane' marker is visible, and so is not affected by locomotion.) Perhaps some species with different perceptual mechanisms from ours could combine temporal and atemporal motion in such a way, or the potential for combining the might be built into some artificial sign language with conventions to keep the two distinct, but the possibility of using both kinds of motion at once is not part of ASL, and I doubt that any sign language makes use of this combination.

Another logically conceivable way of moving HOUSE is to show several time-lapse photos, or selected sequential frames of a movie: articulate the sign first on the left (in 'the Yukon'), then in the middle, then on the right (in 'Oakland'). But ASL does not have this device; successive articulations of HOUSE in different places would be taken as representing different houses. Consider the two houses in 'moving from Asa's house to a house in San Francisco'. In fact, the sign CITY is a phonological reduction of several successive articulaions of HOUSE.

Within the limits just described, it is still logically possible that a signer might articulate a one-handed, virtually depictive, iconic sign, either once or repeatedly, in one place as a ground, while moving, placing, or creating a figure in another part of the signing space, in a significant spatial relationship to the ground. But that would violate a phonological symmetry constraint of ASL by having the two hands doing very different things, with (probably) separate shapes and motions. (See Friedman, 1974b, 1976b, and Frishberg, 1975b.) In practice, this does not occur. ASL does not seem to use the conceivable device of continuously rearticulating a virtually depictive icon to indicate that its referent is to be thought of as still remaining in the model. That task is left to memory, sometimes with the aid of a mnemonic marker.

In sum, an articulator held in place in the signing space, to show that the refer-ent of a sign is located at an analogous place in the referent space, cannot (continue to) virtually depict the image. The closest it can come to that is to be a mnemonic marker: maintaining the hand shape used for virtual depiction, which is then used substitutively to depict the last-sketched part of the shape (as in 'airplane over valley').

2.6 Establishment and Reference

This subsection is basically a summary of material that appeared scattered through this section, concerning the establishment of various forms and the ways in which those forms are later referred to. I will also include some details that were not mentioned in the preceding text. But, since I have not attempted the extensive study of ASL conversation that would be necessary for an exhaustive analysis of the devices used for establishment and reference, this can only be a brief and general description of them and their place in the iconic systems of ASL.

Establishment is part of construction; it is the process by which a signer says, in effect, 'In what I am about to say, this element of discourse, A (which may be a location, marker, or role-position), will refer to this object of discussion, B.' Refer-ence, as I use the word here, is the use of that A to talk about that B. With a symmetrical predicate, as in 'John and Mary *met*' or 'Hildy and Francesca read for an hour, then they *traded books*' (symmetrical predicates italicized), it may not matter which element of discourse refers to whom: e.g., JOHN MARY MEET (in center) is adequate. But to sign 'John went up to Mary', the signer must communicate to his addressee that the moving marker is 'John' and the stationary one is 'Mary'. Communicating that fact is an instance of establishment.

Locations are usually established simply by naming the referent and indexing the location. Instead of indexing, the signer may move a marker to the location and hold it there for a moment, as was done with SIT in the 'party conversation' example. If the sign naming the referent is not anchored to part of the body and can instead be articulated in space, he may articulate it at the location, as was done with the 'houses' in 'staying at Asa's while house-hunting in San Francisco'. Locations are referred to either by an index, which functions in the utterance as a nominal, or by use in a multidirectional verb. Both kinds of reference appear in YESTERDAY HENRY INDEX $^{(right)}$ VISIT ME / SAY ASA INDEX$^{(left)}$ GIVE $^{(left}$ $^{to\ right)}$ BOOK / INDEX$^{(right)}$ READ ENJOY 'Henry visited me yesterday. He said Asa had given him a book. Henry read it and enjoyed it'.

Markers are established by naming the referent and articulating the marker, either simultaneously or in immediate succession. If the name and marker are not on the same hand, the signer may additionally index the marker with the hand that named it. Whatever the marker does after that refers to the referent.

A signer may establish a role by moving into its position and naming its referent. He may also combine role-switching with modeling, using roles to improve the picture made by indexing locations in a model, as in the 'party conversation'. To refer to the role by entering it, the signer

> can then either orient his body or merely his head in different directions (i.e., to the right, to the left) . . . or he can raise or lower his head or trunk (by bending his knees) to indicate, e.g., two 3P referents of different heights (e.g. mother and child). In either case, the eyes move accordingly. If, for example, the discourse concerns a conversation between a mother and child, the signer will look up (with his head raised) when he assumes the child's role, and will look down (with his head lowered) when he assumes the mother's role. [Friedman, 1975b, p. 950]

He can also refer to another person in the construct, other than the one whose role he is currently occupying, by using the location of that person's role in a multidirectional verb, perhaps by indexing it, or by miming it as though the referent person were there, for example, by lighting that person's cigarette.

2.7   Other Lexical Constructs: Incorporation

FOLLOW, ON, and MEET are lexical constructs in which two markers have the referent relationhsip to each other, i.e., the relation is 'follow', one marker following the other. In WALK-UP, GET-UP, and PROPHECY a marker moves in space, with or without reference to a GROUND marker. In WALK$_{BB}$ (*B*-hands) and its modifications ('trudge', etc.), the basic alternating motion of a pair of markers takes on various modifications of manner. But there are other lexical constructs that are even more evidently models, because an entire separate nominal is incorporated into the verb.

WASH has a citation form: two fists (A-hands) scrubbing each other. But the fists usually scrub whatever is being washed: face, hair, body, etc. In the 'mother washing child' example the signer, as 'mother', leaned down towards the 'child' position and scrubbed, using his right hand in the WASH hand shape and motion and his left hand as a GROUND representing the part of the child being scrubbed. When windows are the objects washed, the signer first articulates WINDOW (in neutral space) and then WASHes the plane of the remembered WINDOW. CHOP-A-TREE forms TREE (minus its GROUND) with the left arm and 'chops' it with the edge of the right hand. In MEAT the signer uses his right thumb and forefinger to grasp the fleshy pad between his left thumb and forefinger; in CHOP-MEAT he 'chops' this pad with the right hand. Note that the incorporated element may be presented (WASH-FACE) or depicted (CHOP-TREE). The sign WINDOW is substitutively depictive (B-hands representing the surface of the window), so the hands act as markers to establish the window in signing space; then WASH is applied to the remembered window.

3. Conclusion

3.1 Once More, Continua

In the Introduction, section 0.1.1, I called it "impossible, as well as undesirable," to draw a sharp line between lexical signs and other gestures, but I had not yet presented any data with which to illustrate that assertion. Now, I think, the data lead clearly to that conclusion.

It would be a mistake to treat SIT, GET-UP, KNEEL, JUMP-UP-AND-DOWN, TOSS-AND-TURN (or RESTLESS), and ROLL-IN-THE-AISLES-WITH-LAUGH-TER as if they were wholly separate lexical items, or even as if they simply shared a morpheme in the same way as English *sit* and *set*, or *inject, reject*, and *project*, as Frishberg & Gough (1973) imply. Most of the elements of movement and orientation that distinguish these *V*-legs signs from one another have no meaning outside the *V*-legs 'family' comparable to their meaning within it. How could they? The knuckle-flexion of KNEEL and JUMP-UP-AND-DOWN, for example, takes its meaning of 'knee-flexion' from the analogy of the *V*-hand to legs. The twisting motion that in TOSS-AND-TURN imitates a person's restless movements in bed occurs also in GREEN, MIRROR, and SENTENCE. In GREEN it appears as a motion common to many initialized signs (of which GREEN is one), and specifically to the names of certain colors; in MIRROR it is part of a conventionalized mime, turning a hand mirror to scan one's face; and in SENTENCE it is a component of a more complex motion that may refer to 'something that is drawn-out' (it occurs also in EXAGGERATE). Only in TOSS-AND-TURN, as part of a construct, does it or can it have the particular meaning it has there. (See also Friedman, 1976b, Chapter 3, "Iconicity and Non-discreteness", p. 79–99.)

Certainly there are morphemes in ASL whose participation in signs cannot be analyzed as part of construction, and whose behavior is entirely comparable to that of wholly arbitrary oral language morphemes. Frishberg & Gough (1973) have listed many of these: place-of-articulation morphemes such as forehead 'masculine', cheek 'feminine', and chin 'negation'; handshape morphemes such as *horns* 'deceit' and *open-8* 'feeling'; and perhaps movement morphemes such as the sharp twist "strong personal characteristics, judgments made by one person of another" (Frishberg & Gough, 1973, p. 8). These appear with a constant meaning in many signs and some of them can be "inserted into" other signs by modifying the sign, with resultant meanings that are just what one would expect to get from adding one morpheme to another:

> In addition, signs normally made with other hand configurations can be made with the horns for special effects, e.g., LAUGH and BORED. These, then, have added information to the ideas expressed by the regular sign. (p. 16)

But *horns* symbolizing 'deceit' and forehead 'masculine' cannot themselves be iconically modified. Yet Frishberg & Gough do not distinguish such morphemes from others that they mention, such as *V*-legs and *V*-vision, which can be adequately and economically explained only in terms of construction.

In fact, most lexical signs which use such markers as *V*-legs and *V*-vision have to be iconically analyzed in exactly the same way as ad hoc constructs do. No formational distinction can be drawn between them. Some constructs are clearly conventional and some clearly ad hoc, but many fall somewhere in the middle of the conventionality scale. It may often be impossible to tell—and unimportant— whether a given construct in a particular utterance is a 'conventional' construct that has been iconically modified ad hoc, or whether it is the result of combining productive elements in a somewhat familiar way. (I say 'construct' here because, although my examples and attention to the continuum of conventionality have been concerned primarily with models using markers, I believe that the continuum between lexical signs and ad hoc constructs exists for stagings as well.)

Iconicity is also a continuum, even for lexical signs, both synchronically and diachronically. HOUSE often appears as just a touching and separation of the two *B*-hands, but it can be as highly iconic as in the example 'tall skinny house'. And the forehead 'masculine' morpheme, now simply a place of articulation for many masculine signs which vary in all other parameters, seems to have originated as the sign BOY, apparently an icon of the brim of a boy's cap in the eighteenth or nineteenth century. (Cf., section 1.6 on deiconization.)

3.2   Summary

Picture-making is a significant part of ASL communication. The pictures made can vary in complexity from conventionalized outlines of single objects (TABLE)

to maps showing the placement of half-a-dozen ('party conversation') and/or the
motion of two and perhaps more ('boy meets girl'); in size from a finger (*G*-person)
to all the space in the signer's vicinity ('restaurant scene', section 2.3) or even at a
distance ('school and hospital', section 2.3); in precision from relationships without
shape (ON) to full-color drawings ('tall skinny house', section 1.5); and in semantic
complexity from simple nominals (COFFEE) to complete stories ('mother washing
child', section 2.4). I have described and classified the devices with which ASL
makes these pictures. There are areas of uncertainty, and the classification may
need to be revised; and there are probably gaps in the description that need to be
filled in; but I do not think that any of these problems are of major proportions.
ME ANALYZE FINISH / GIVE (both hands, signer to addressees).

APPENDIX I: TERMS

AD HOC: (a gesture) Involving at least some productivity, suiting it to the specific referent under discussion and not just to that class of referents. E.g., the ASL sign HOUSE, although it has the shape ⌂ , is used as conventionally as the English word **house**, without regard to the shape of the house referred to. But it can be modified, e.g., to the shape ⌂ to describe a particular tall, skinny house. To the degree that it has been significantly modified from its "normal" shape in this way (section 0.1.3) this token of the sign is ad hoc. Cf. **conventional.**

ANALOGUE RULE: a rule that takes information of a continuous nature (i.e., nondiscrete) and assigns it a linguistic representation that is also continuous, so that variation in the one will be directly mirrored by variation in the other. See DeMatteo. (section 1.3.1)

ARBITRARY: Bearing no intrinsic relation to the referent. Most oral language words are arbitrary, and therefore totally dependent on convention for their meaning; many ASL signs are at least partly iconic and therefore not arbitrary, but are nonetheless conventional. Cf., **conventional.** (section 0.1.4)

ARTICULATOR: A part of the body used to articulate an ASL gesture: usually a hand, sometimes an arm or forearm, occasionally a finger. Also the entire body, the head, and the parts of the face (see Baker, 1976 and in this volume); but those are not treated here.

ATEMPORAL MOTION: Gestural motion that does not refer to motion of the base, but is used only in making the image, which itself is motionless. See **virtual depiction.** Cf., **temporal motion.**

BASE: The thing (action, etc.) which is actually pictured or presented in an icon, not necessarily identical with the referent. E.g., the base of OLD is a beard, but the referent is the meaning 'old'. When the base is not identical with the referent, it represents the referent metonymically. (section 1.1)

CONSTRUCTION: The process of building a complex picture involving spatial relationships, either between two or more objects (including persons) or between an object and itself at different moments as it moves. **CONSTRUCT:** The complex picture so built. Constructs can be metonymic or not. See **staging, modeling, locate.** (section 2.2)

CONVENTIONAL: (a gesture) Depending to some degree on convention for its meaning and use. Cf., **ad hoc, arbitrary.** (section 0.1.3)

DEICONIZATION: The loss (either partial or complete) of synchronic iconicity in an element. Cf., **iconization.** (section 1.6)

DEPICTION: The process of displaying a picture of the base rather than a token of it (its type). Cf., **presentation.** See **virtual depiction, substitutive depiction.** (sections 1.2, 1.3.0)

ESTABLISH: To identify a particular element of discourse with a particular referent, with the possibility of later anaphoric use. For more details than I have given in the text, see Friedman (1975b). See **locate, grammatical location, marker, role-switching**. (section 2.6, and section 2 *passim*)

FIGURE: The object whose location or motion you are concerned with. See note 40. (section 2.5.0)

GESTURE: Any movement of the body, or of a part of the body, that is used meaningfully in ASL discourse. Includes **sign**. (section 0.1.1)

GRAMMATICAL LOCATION: One of the approximately four conventional points in signing space used for third-person anaphoric reference without mention of real-world spatial relationships. See note 32. (section 2.1.1.2)

GRAMMATICAL MULTIPLE MARKER: A **multiple marker** whose spatial value, like that of grammatical locations, is metonymic: the referents of the fingers are not considered to be in any particular spatial relationship. (section 2.5.5)

GROUND: Your reference point for determining the location, path, or motion of the **figure**. See note 40. (section 2.5.0)

GROUND: In a nonsymmetrical two-handed icon, the hand which serves as place of articulation for the other hand. This definition in articulatory terms is equivalent to the one in perceptual terms given in the text. See Friedman, 1974a, and 1976. (section 2.5.0)

ICON: An iconic gesture.

ICONIC: (a gesture) Perceived by signers, or potentially perceived by them, as visually related to its referent. See sections 0.1.1 and 0.1.5 for discussion.

ICONIZATION: The process by which a noniconic sign becomes iconic. (section 1.6)

IMAGE: The picture directly made by an icon. In the icon HOSPITAL, the base is the red cross on a uniform sleeve, and the image is simply 'cross on upper arm' (as sketched in the sign). (section 1.1)

IMITATION: Any linguistic process by which meaningful elements are perceived as similar to their referents or metonymic bases. In oral language, the best-known form of imitation is onomatopoeia; in sign language, iconicity. (sections 0.1.4, 0.1.5)

INDEXICAL PRESENTATION: Presenting a token of the base by pointing to it, as in NOSE or THINK (point to forehead). (section 1.2)

INDEX: Any of the basic deictic gestures of ASL, pointing to an object (person, established location, etc.) with one of a set of significantly differentiated hand shapes. As a verb, to point to (an object, etc.) with an index. (section 2.1.1.1)

LOCATE: To establish (a referent) in some place in the signing space (its **LOCATION**), so that the place can later be indexed or otherwise referred to (as with a multidirectional verb). The location can be either grammatical or real world. See **grammatical location, real-world location**. (section 2.1.1.2)

LOCATIVE ICONICITY: Spatial analogy in which a spatial relationship in the construct represents, via analogue rule, a similar relationship in the base. It can exist independently of shape-iconicity. For a comparison, think of a small map of the U.S.: the dots representing New York, New Orleans, and San Francisco are not shaped at all like those cities' skylines or city limits, but the spatial relationships between them are a good representation of the spatial relationships between the cities. See **marker**. (section 2.5.0)

MARKER: An articulator used in a construct so as to be locatively iconic of an object, so that its behavior and situation in the signing space (whether stationary or moving) represent those of the object. See DeMatteo's observations on the behavior of an icon. See **mnemonic marker, multiple marker**. (section 2.5.0)

MEASURING: An iconic device in which the signer goes from showing a small size in some dimension to a large size in that dimension, with a stative meaning corresponding to the large size. Examples are BIG and RICH, but not GROW-UP (whose movement fits the description, but whose meaning corresponds to the motion itself, not the final large size). I do not know how to classify this device, whether as a third kind of virtual depiction (alongside sketching and stamping), or a third kind of depiction (alongside virtual and substitutive), as a mime-with-metonymy, or as something else. (section 1.3.4)

METONYMY: The relationship existing between an icon and its referent when the icon's picture is not of the referent itself, but of something associated with it (the base). E.g., the picture conveyed by the icon HOUSE is the shape of a house, while the picture conveyed by the icon HOSPITAL is the cross on the upper arm that appears on uniform sleeves. The prototypical house depicted is of the same class of objects as the house being referred to, but the cross on a sleeve is very different from a hospital: the former relationship is one of shared class membership, the latter is a kind of association. HOSPITAL is metonymic, HOUSE is not. (section 1.1)

MIME: A type of presentation in which the signer performs the bodily motions or states of the base, as in COFFEE (grinding coffee in a hand mill), or a (probably nonlexical) gesture for 'Egypt' (striking a pose reminiscent of figures in ancient Egyptian tomb paintings). This definition approximates the word's ordinary colloquial meaning, and is the one I use, but the word 'mime' is commonly used in the teaching of ASL, signed English, etc., with a broader meaning, including also everything that I have classed as **depiction**, and excluding only indexical presentation. Cf., note 12. (section 1.2)

MNEMONIC MARKER: A marker that substitutively depicts a portion of an object just sketched. The marker keeps the object in place and orientation in the signing space, but its shape must be remembered by the signer and addressee. (section 2.5.6)

MODELING: Construction in which the construct (the **model**) is built to a scale on which the articulators can represent referent objects, although the articulators need not do so (i.e., need not be used as markers). The construct is entirely within the signing space and is a (usually) small-scale model of the base event or situation. See **marker, locate**. Cf., **staging**. (section 2.3)

MULTIDIRECTIONAL VERB: A verb whose motion and/or orientation indicates its subject and object, or source and goal. Edge & Herrmann usefully restrict this term to those verbs whose **motion** makes such an incorporation, calling those that mark subject/source and object/goal only in their orientation 'multiorientational'. (section 2.1.2)

MULTIPLE MARKER: A hand shape with two or more extended and spread fingers, each of which represents an individual (usually a person); a plural of the *G*-person markers. The *5*-hand multiple marker usually means not '5 individuals', but 'many individuals'. See **grammatical multiple marker**. (section 2.5.2)

OBJECT: Any physical object, including a person.

PRESENTATION: The general iconic process by which the signer presents an actual token of the base, whether by indexing it (indexical presentation) or by performing it (mime). Cf., **depiction**. (section 1.2)

REAL-WORLD LOCATION: In construction, the locating of objects so that their spatial relationships in the construct are analogous to their spatial relationships in the real world. An example in the text is the 'party conversation' example. Cf., **grammatical location**. (section 2.2)

REFERENT: The meaning of a gesture or entire utterance, or the thing talked about by it. It can be an object (including a person), place, action, state, event, relationship, or what-have-you. Where it has been necessary to distinguish the general meaning that a sign may have in isolation (e.g., 'house') from the specific object (etc.) referred to in the context of a particular utterance (e.g., 'my friend Cathy's house on Virginia Street'), I have generally called the latter 'the particular referent'. Cf., **base**. (section 1.1)

ROLE SWITCHING: Distinguishing the participants in the referent event by assigning to each one a body position and moving from one to another, taking the role of each referent person sequentially. A form of staging. (section 2.4)

SHAPE-ICONICITY: Spatial analogy in which the shape of the image represents, via analogue rule, the shape of the base. Depiction depends on shape-iconicity. The main point of contact between shape-iconicity and locative-iconicity is the concept of depiction: many markers, which are by definition locatively iconic, are also shape-iconic, such as AIRPLANE and *V*-legs. (section 2.5)

SIGN: An ASL gesture that is at least partly conventional and that more or less conforms to certain formational constraints. The reason for these hedges is that no sharp line can be drawn between totally conventional gestures which are unarguably 100% lexical and deserve the name 'signs', and other gestures which are to some degree ad hoc. (sections 0.1.1, 1.5)

SKETCHING: A form of virtual depiction, the process of making a picture by moving the articulators and having them leave an imaginary trace as they move: 'drawing' in the air or on a body surface. Cf., **stamping, measuring**. (section 1.3.3.0)

STAGING: Construction in which the construct (the **staging**) is built to the scale of the signer's body. The signer's body can represent a person; he can be an 'actor' in the construct, which is approximately life size. Cf., **modeling**. (section 2.3)

STAMPING: A form of virtual depiction, in which the articulator moves to a place (in space or on a body surface), stops, and retreats, leaving an imaginary trace in the shape of the surface with which it contacted the (real or imaginary) plane at which it stopped. So a fingertip stamps a point, the edge of the hand stamps a line. Cf., **sketching, measuring**. (section 1.3.3.0)

SUBSTITUTIVE DEPICTION: A form of depiction in which the signer's articulator takes on the shape of the base object. I now prefer the term 'substantive depiction'. Cf., **virtual depiction**. See **marker**. (section 1.3.0)

TEMPORAL MOTION: Motion in the gesture that analogically represents motion in the base. It can occur in substitutive depiction and mime. Cf., **atemporal motion**. (section 1.3.2)

TRACE: The shape resulting from virtual depiction; the mark that signer and addressee pretend remains from movement of the articulator. See **sketching, stamping, measuring**. (section 1.3.0)

VIRTUAL: (an iconic element, either of shape or of location) Not physically present in the icon, existing only in the memory or imagination of the signer and addressee; e.g., a virtually depicted shape or a (grammatical or real-world) location. Cf., **visible**. (section 1.4)

VIRTUAL DEPICTION: A form of depiction in which the signer's articulator, moving atemporally, leaves an imaginary trace in the shape of the base object. See **sketching, stamping, measuring**. Cf., **substitutive depiction**. (section 1.3.0)

VISIBLE: (an iconic element, either of shape or of location) Physically existing in the icon, e.g., a marker or the signer's body. Cf., **virtual**. (section 1.4)

APPENDIX II: TABLES
TABLE 1a
Basic Iconic Devices

PRESENTATION		DEPICTION		
mime	indexical presentation	substitutive depiction	virtual depiction	
			sketching	stamping
TM (AM)	AM	TM	AM	

visible shape   virtual shape

TM and AM denote the character of the motion used with each device: temporal or atemporal. Both kinds are possible with mime, but I know only one example of atemporal mime in ASL: striking a 'tomb-painting' pose for 'Egypt' (probably nonlexical). (I have not included **measuring** here because it is unclear where it belongs in the chart.)

TABLE 1b
Intersections of Some Systems of Iconic Devices

type of construction (scale)*

			STAGING		MODELING
anaphoric elements	visible	currently occupied role**	role-switching		markers
	virtual	currently empty role-positions**			locations
basic iconic devices	visible	mime; indexical presentation			substitutive depiction
	virtual		virtual depiction		

*Staging and modeling can co-occur, either to represent different referents in the same construct ('drunken acquaintance', section 2.3) or to reinforce each other ('party conversation', section 2.4). Virtual depiction can be used with either staging or modeling, but does not seem to belong to either, since the size of the object whose shape is depicted seems to be free: life-size, diminished, or (occasionally) enlarged, specified by other cues if necessary. I place substitutive depiction under modeling because of their close association, via markers (see section 2.5.0).

When the signer is playing any role, even if the utterance has only one role (as in 'school and hospital', section 2.3, where the role is that of the addressee), that role, once established, functions as an anaphoric element. The role the signer is playing at a given moment is **visible, but all other roles are **virtual**, since, though they remain in the staging, they are maintained only in the signer's and addressee's memories.

TABLE 2

The Continuum of Iconicity and Conventionality

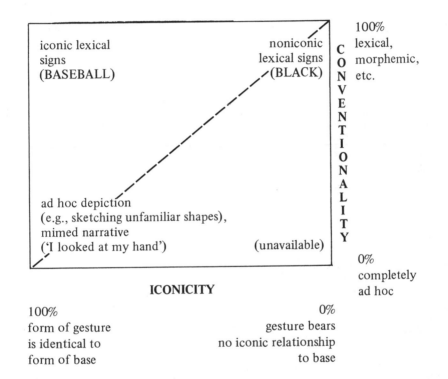

ICONICITY

TABLE 3a

What's What in a Few Selected Simple Icons

Name	Description	Iconic Device	Base	Relation of Base to Referent	Type of Shape
NOSE	point to nose	indexical presentation	nose	direct	visible (nose)
THINK	point to forehead	indexical presentation	forehead or brain	metonymic	(not relevant)
---------	throw a punch	mime	throwing a punch	direct	visible (body)
COFFEE	grind coffee	mime	grinding coffee	metonymic	visible (body)
AIRPLANE	*thumbspread-horns* hand	substitutive depiction	airplane	direct	visible (handshape)
HOUSE	sketch ⌂ with *B*-hands	virtual depiction: sketching	house of traditional shape	direct	virtual (sketched shape)
HOSPITAL	sketch cross on upper arm with *H*-hand	virtual depiction: sketching	cross on hospital uniform sleeve	metonymic	virtual (cross)
HELP	lift left fist with right palm	substitutive depiction	physical support	metonymic	visible (thing lifted & thing lifting

TABLE 3b
What's What in a Few Selected Constructs

Gloss	Description of Element	Iconic Device	Base of Element	Relation of Base to Referent	Referent
'Asa gave Henry a book'	1: points at left and right, previously established as Asa and Henry, respectively	1: grammatical location	1: Asa is on left in model, Henry is on right	1: metonymic	1: A. and H. are being discussed as individuals, not as a group
	2: GIVE (from left to right)	2: multi-directional verb	2: something went from A. to H.	2: direct	2: (same as base)
'Lynn lit Asa's cigarette'	1: role-positions previously established as Asa (left) and Lynn (right)	1: role-switching	1: Asa on signer's left in staging, Lynn on right	1: direct	1: A. was on signer's left, L. on his right
	2: in L.'s role, mime lighting cigarette of A.'s role-position	2: mime	2: L. lights A.'s cigarette	2: direct	2: L. lit A.'s cigarette
'boy meets girl'	left and right G-persons, previously established as girl and boy respectively, come together from sides to center	markers in a model	boy and girl approach each other in a straight line and meet	1: direct	1: boy and girl approached each other in a straight line and met
				2: metonymic	2: boy and girl met, with no assertion made about route

NOTES

*   Besides all the members of the ASL seminar at U.C. Berkeley, without whom this paper would not exist, I would like to thank particularly Carol Padden, for her sound criticism and "informantship," and Louie Fant, Jr., for placing at my service his insights into his native hand. I would also like to thank the National Science Foundation for their Graduate Fellowship, and for the support I received for some of the work on this paper through grant No. NSF SOC 75-03538.

1.   I presume that much of what I say will be applicable to most or all sign languages, but since I am not familiar with any others I will confine this discussion to American Sign Language.

2.   The fuzzy set is a formal structure developed by L. A. Zadeh of the Department of Electrical Engineering and Computer Science at the University of California in Berkeley, as a theoretical mechanism for handling imprecise knowledge. For one attempt to apply the theory of fuzzy sets to a linguistic problem, see Lakoff (1972).

3.   I use the word 'utterance' because I know of no successful attempt to define the notion of an ASL sentence. 'Utterance' ducks the issue.

4.   The descriptions given here of signs (generally in citation form) often are not intended to be phonologically complete, but only to convey the gesture's general shape in sufficient enough detail to show its iconic value or lack thereof.

5.   Pictures have been suggested for this sign: the forehead of a black person, or soot smeared on the forehead (perhaps as on Ash Wednesday). I find neither of these convincing. Folk etymologies abound in the culture of the American deaf, and these seem to be two of them. See also section 0.1.5.

6.   "Signed" = "uttered in the sign medium" (here, in ASL). The gesture is, of course, not considered lexical.

7.   These labels will have to be modified somewhat to take into account the device of metonymy (section 1.1), by reading "base" instead of "referent." Compare Table 2 in Appendix II.

8.   There seems to be a universal tendency in oral languages to a certain phonological patterning in deictic words, but it is not nearly so precise, so systematic, or so pervasive (at least in English) as visual deixis in ASL (see sections 2.1.1–2.1.2). Since this pattern appears to be cross-linguistically general in oral languages (although not without exceptions), it must be attributed to some form of imitation, probably via some synesthetic perceptual mechanism. See Cooper & Ross, 1975, and Ross, 1976.

9.   This possible form of the hypothetical sign HARD-BREAD was suggested to me by Louie Fant, Jr.

10.   Much of the material in this section, and the specific terms 'base' and 'meto-nymy', are due to Battison (1971). He in turn borrows the term 'base' and several of these examples from I. M. Schlesinger et al. (1970).

My fellow linguists at Berkeley, and in the seminars on Alternate Theories of Syntax and Semantics held here in the summer of 1975 by the Mathematics and Social Sciences Board, have showed me how thorny the entire question of metonymic versus direct reference is. I realize now that a simple dichotomy is insufficient; but since a complete solution of this ancient puzzle is beyond me, I will make do for the time being with the admittedly inadequate analysis presented here.

11.   Right and left are not distinctive in ASL, except when the actual directions 'right' and 'left' are involved. A signer will usually favor one hand over the other, though capable of signing with either hand. I will describe gestures as they would be made by a right-handed signer, except when quoting directly from a transcript.

12.   The word 'mime', for want of a better colloquial or standard term, is often used in ASL textbooks for what I call depiction: e.g., Fant (1972), p. 72, virtual depiction of 'coffeepot'; Madsen (1972), p. 29, substitutive depiction of 'oyster'. I will restrict the use of the term 'mime' to the definition given earlier, which approximates its colloquial use outside ASL studies.

13.   In BIRD, another animal mime, the signer must supplement his body with substitutive depiction (section 1.3), having no beak of his own.

14.   Battison uses the name 'presentation' for this device alone. But his nomen-clature misses the similarity of **signification by an actual token** in both mime and indexical presentation (an actual bat-hefting motion, an actual nose; with meto-nymy, an actual forehead to signify the activity performed with the organ behind a forehead), and the opposition of this characteristic to **signification by a picture of a token** in all forms of depiction (described below).

15.   Some signers sign AIRPLANE with the Y-hand (i.e., with only thumb and pinky extended) in this position, orientation, and motion (Judy Kegl, personal communication). This seems to be an instance of partial deiconization (section 1.6) of a substitutive depiction: the fuselage of the plane, or at least the nose, is missing.

16.   This definition will have to be broadened slightly below to include stamping, another kind of virtual depiction. I leave it as it is here for ease of exposition.

17.   I now prefer to call this device 'substantive depiction'.

18.   I will not try to analyze the mechanisms by which signers distinguish between the motion that is part of a sign and the motion of transition from one sign to another. See also note 24.

19.   While the same icon is being maintained; a change of icon is obvious in ordin-ary discourse. For example, the sentence 'I stood up and looked around, and saw

three cars!' might be signed (in context):

STAND-UP LOOK[(side to side)]   SEE THREE CAR THREE

STAND-UP, LOOK and SEE are all made with the V-hand shape ('V-for-Victory'), and THREE and CAR with the 3-hand shape (V, plus extended thumb), but the change of sign would be evident.

20.   Immaterial, that is, to the formation of the image; other constraints can apply. Perhaps the motion can be too slow for the sign to be comprehensible, similarly to spoken or even w   r   i   t   e   n language. If the motion is speeded up, the sign may be perceived as stressed, or as a different sign; see Friedman, 1974a, 1976b.

21.   This is particularly true when AIRPLANE is used in a more complex icon (see section 2.5) and less true in citation form as a nominal, e.g., in

MY UNCLE HE (index) BUY AIRPLANE
'My uncle bought an airplane'.

But the difference between temporal and atemporal motion holds even in a simple icon.

22.   Many signs use the hand shape corresponding to the initial letter of an English word of the same meaning (in some old signs, a French word). Generally this is the result of coining a new sign based on an older one of related meaning: a sign for GROUP or CLASS, made with F-hands, is the sign FAMILY. Or perhaps the entire original sign may have been consciously devised with the English word in mind. Such may be the case with HOSPITAL, and it is certainly true of many modern signs (used primarily for teaching, either English or other subjects).
     Initial-letter hand shapes, like all fingerspelling, are completely noniconic with respect to the referent. The fact that many hand shapes visually resemble the letters that they represent is irrelevant, since the connections between the referent 'family' and the English word /fæmɪli/, and between the initial phoneme /f/ of that word and the letter 'F' and hand shape F, are themselves arbitrary. But 'initialization' may be considered a highly specialized type of metonymy, as it represents the referent of the sign by something associated with it, namely, the English word for it (represented in turn by its inital letter in manual alphabet form).

23.   See also the discussion of GROW-UP in Friedman, 1976b, p. 86–97.

24.   Every sign has four parameters: hand shape, place of articulation, orientation, and movement. Minimal pairs exist for each of these. See Stokoe, 1960, and Friedman, 1974b, and in this volume.
     Some signs may seem at first to have no essential movement, but to consist merely of a contact, and to require incidentally, as it were, only the motion to and from the point of contact: e.g., THINK (forefinger-tip touching forehead),

VAMPIRE (*bent-V*, fingertips touching side of neck). But the manifestation of stress for these signs demonstrates that they do indeed have an intrinsic movement; see Friedman, 1974a, 1976b.

25.   Although in some appropriate context he might use such a device; e.g., telling a story about animals; having introduced a giraffe character, he might indicate that he is taking that role simply by stretching out his neck. See the discussion of role-switching, section 2.4.

26.   The subscript is a nonstandard notation that I am using here to distinguish different signs whose glosses are or might be the same. This WALK ('WALK$_V$') uses a single *V*-hand, while WALK$_{BB}$ uses two *B*-hands.

27.   Lest there be any misunderstanding: even if there is a house present, convenient to point to ('index'), and of the classic ⌂ shape, a signer will not point to it to convey the general meaning 'house'; for that he will use the sign HOUSE. An index to the house could only refer to that house, or, by a transfer of meaning common in ASL, to the person who lives in it, or some other referent that would be clear in context and specifically associated with that one house.

28.   See note 8 and the references cited therein.

29.   "NP conjunction in surface structure is achieved by simply articulating [sequentially—MM] two or more NPs (either lexical items or indices)"–Friedman, 1975b, note 6).

30.   A personal name is either fingerspelled or represented by a namesign, which is usually a well-formed sign referring only to its 'owner'. My namesign, for example, is not a translation of the English name 'Mark'; it means 'Mark Mandel', and it is unrelated to my English name except that, like many namesigns, it is initialized (see note 22). See Stokoe, Casterline, & Croneberg, 1965, section 1.1, p. 291.

31.   According to Friedman (1975b), a right-handed signer's first grammatical location will be on the right, a left-handed signer's on the left. I agree that "handedness" is important, but I suggest that the "sidedness" of grammatical locations can also be influenced by discourse structure. See note 32.

32.   Other arrangements are possible, both real-world (section 2.2) and non-real-world. E.g., the signer may establish the **Three Little Pigs** in a row in front of him. Since the principles of use are the same for all such arrangements, I will refer in detail only to the arrangement described in the text, which is the customary, unmarked arrangement for third person referents.

33.   Edge & Herrmann call such verbs 'multiorientation verbs', reserving the name 'multidirectional' for verbs with directed motion. I agree that this distinction is useful, but in this paper I will group both types together under the name 'multidirectional'.

34. Not all signs of time use the time line. Besides the times of day mentioned immediately below, thefe are names of calendric units such as WEEK, MONTH, and TUESDAY.

35. A signer could, in fact, assign Asa and Henry to the same grammatical location, but only if he were referring to them together, as a 'they' form. To refer to them singly he would have to change his form of reference, just as he would in oral language. He would name them individually, and if he wanted to refer to them anaphorically later on, he would establish separate locations for them.

36. The device is the same, but its use in discourse can be somewhat different. Because the spatial relationships in a real-world construct are part of what the signer is talking about, he can sometimes express them simply for the sake of describing the scene. In the same way, a speaker of any language can say, "Well, Harold was there, and Asa, and Lynn, and Tommie," without mentioning Lynn again or expecting to; and the addressee will not ask "What happened to Lynn?" when her name does not appear again. But grammatical-location establishment has nothing to communicate except that persons X and Y are going to be talked about and may be referred to separately. A signer cannot get away with grammatically-locating someone and then not mentioning him, any more than a speaker could say, "Now, this is something that happened to me and Charlotte," and then not mention Charlotte again.

37. See Friedman, 1974b, 1976b, on well-formedness criteria dictated by the gestural-visual modality, and Friedman, 1975b, on the precedence of real-world location over grammatical convention. In this case, as in the other real-world constructs described in this paper, the real-world locations are determined with respect to the signer's body as ground. (On the term 'ground', see note 40.)

38. Thompson claims that there is no indirect statement or indirect discourse in ASL, but that all reported discourse and sentential complements appear in direct form. Speaking in the role of another person is clearly comparable to direct quotation.

39. Frishberg & Gough's (1973) reference to "Fischer (1973)" is ambiguous in their bibliography, but apparently refers to a working paper, an earlier form of Fischer & Gough (to appear). (The alternative is Fischer, 1973a.)

40. I base my use of the words **FIGURE** and **GROUND** on Talmy's, 1975, definitions:

> The terms have been taken from Gestalt psychology, but are here given the following particular characterization for use in linguistic semantics:
>
> > The *FIGURE* object is a moving or **conceptually** movable point whose path or site is conceived as a variable the particular value of which is the salient issue.
> >
> > The *GROUND* object is a reference-point, having a stationary setting within a reference-frame, with respect to which the *FIGURE*'s path or site receives characterization.

The reference-frame in ASL is generally the signing space, determined by the signer's body.

I extend his definition in two ways, however. To describe ASL, **motion** must be added to **path** and **site** as possible salient variables of the figure. (Motion is not the same as path: motion involves time and speed, path does not.) Furthermore, the ground in the base of an ASL icon, or in the icon itself, need not be stationary. In the sign FOLLOW, the left hand moves and the right hand follows it. The motion of the left hand is crucial to the characterization of the motion of the right hand.

41. See, for instance, Friedman, 1975b, on the simultaneous articulation of the elements of a sign, as opposed to the generally sequential articulation of oral language phonemes. DeMatteo argues persuasively for the necessity of analogic, continuous elements in any analysis of ASL.

42. ASL has a whole world of such "intonation"—some of it morphological (see Fischer, 1973a)—which I will no more than mention in this paper.

43. Baker's research on facial activity in ASL suggests that a marker is always indexed when it is established, if not manually, then with the eyes. See Baker, 1976a, and in this volume.

44. There are secondary hand shapes for '1' (*thumbspread-A*) and '2' (*L*-hand), but their use is restricted to certain environments.

45. The example in section 1.8, 'tall skinny house', is one type of exception: a complex description of a referent object in terms of its outline (which HOUSE uses) and its specific features (added by the signer, as **figures** for which the remembered HOUSE provides the **ground**). Another conceivable type of exception might require the signer to associate other referent objects with specific portions of the first object (e.g., Santa coming down the chimney, which would be in the "roof" area of the house, in the signing space); but I know of no actual examples.

46. The signs glossed TAKE and PUT are both made with a *flat-O* hand, palm down, which is respectively pulled up from and put down into the place referred to.

47. Such as the 'field of flowers', CHILDREN (as sometimes signed), and perhaps the 'sweeping' index to the individuals making up a plural deictic referent. (section 2.1.1.1)

48. By signing or fingerspelling the names in the appropriate parts of the signing space, or by naming and indexing.

VISUAL IMAGERY AND VISUAL ANALOGUES
IN AMERICAN SIGN LANGUAGE

Asa DeMatteo

0. Introduction

For a number of years now, linguists have used the term **grammar** in a systematically ambiguous way. On the one hand, when the linguist uses this term, he is referring to a description of a language, a statement of its structural principles, its regularities, the relationships among its forms, and so forth. On the other hand, he is referring to a coherent system of knowledge, either learned or in many ways innate, which forms the basis for that systematic set of behaviors we call language. In this way, the modern linguist has transcended his earlier role of transcriber and organizer of data and entered the realm of cognitive psychology (see, for example, Chomsky, 1968). That is, when the linguist proposes a particular linguistic description, he is not only making a claim about the organization of linguistic data, but is also making a claim about the organization of the knowledge underlying that data; he is making a claim about the workings of the mind.

While this shift in the role of the linguist has added great excitement and increased significance to the field, it has also placed increased responsibility on the working linguist. No longer can he concentrate on formulating the most technically elegant and theoretically satisfying analysis of a certain body of data; the linguist must constantly be aware of the implications of a particular analysis, concentrating on formulating the analysis that most closely represents the way the data generator, the native speaker, analyzes and organizes that data, the analysis that most closely represents the knowledge the native speaker calls upon to encode and interpret a linguistic event.

I have made this general caveat because some of the notions presented later are theoretically unsatisfying. They do not fit into the generally accepted framework of the structure and behavior of a given language, ultimately reflecting the structure and behavior of the human mind. Nonetheless, the notions presented below appear essentially correct in that they represent most closely the way that speakers of American Sign Language (ASL or Sign) encode their world into linguistic material and interpret that material in the form of linguistic events; these notions, if they are

correct, indicate that the mind can be structured in ways different from those previously supposed.

In this paper, I will concern myself with the role of visual imagery in a language
that exists entirely in a visual mode—American Sign Language, used by the deaf in
the United States. I shall not be concerned with the manner in which the language
describes visual imagery or visual material in general (though such descriptions
constitute interesting data and some are included here); rather, I shall be concerned
with visual imagery as a linguistically significant factor in any proper description of
Sign. I shall argue that the proper understanding of a range of data from Sign requires an appeal to some notion of visual imagery and that, therefore, some representation of visual imagery must be incorporated into the grammar of ASL. I present
five major arguments in this regard: 1) The first concerns certain apparent syntactic
relationships existing among signs that are problematic when viewed in terms of the
sorts of theories proposed for vocal languages. In order to place the discussion of
these phenomena in its proper perspective, I will first discuss the posited structural
nature of sentences in vocal languages. I then apply the general structural principles
of vocal language to ASL in order to test their appropriateness for describing sign
language phenomena. As the reader will see, there remain some residual problems in
such an analysis, problems that are insoluble given the vocal language theories. I
next suggest a way in which visual imagery can account for these phenomena.
Finally, I discuss some related evidence for incorporating visual imagery into syntactic processes. 2) The second argument concerns certain morphological processes
in ASL. I show that there are a number of systematic relationships correlating form
and meaning in ASL, that these relationships for the most part are amenable to
standard morphological analysis, and that we would therefore suspect that ASL is
structured in a way similar to that posited for vocal languages. I will argue, however,
that there is a crucial difference with respect to the basis of this form-meaning
correlation in ASL from the posited relationship in vocal languages. For example, I
present certain paradigms that are inexplicable using the criteria used to account for
similar examples in vocal languages, but that can be explained in terms of viusal
imagery. These cases indicate that some formulation of visual imagery must be
incorporated into the grammar of ASL. I also provide further evidence from morphological processes. 3) The third argument concerns the area of individual sign
semantics. There are cases where groups of signs are apparently quite different in
semantic value (at least in terms of typical English glosses for the signs) but that show
a systematic formational similarity. I argue that a semantic analysis of these signs
based on visual imagery allows one to state a semantic relationship correlated with
their formational relationhsip. As a corollary argument, I present one case where
the semantics and contextual distribution of a sign can only be understood in terms
of the visual imagery associated with the sign. 4) The fourth argument treats what
might be termed productive uses of visual imagery. I present data of different sorts:
the occurrence of certain signs, the forms certain signs take when they occur, some
seemingly pantomimic signs, and one case of a novel creation of a sign—all of which
can be understood only in terms of the visual image presented in each case. 5) The

final argument deals with certain continuous degree phenomena in Sign. There are signs with degrees of movement correlated with the degree semantics of their denotata. While these signs are not based upon or derived from visual images in the same way that the previous examples were, they are nonetheless properly accounted for in terms of visual imagery in that they represent visual analogue representations of degree semantics. These five arguments taken in concert seem to provide overwhelming motivation for the incorporation of a linguistically significant level of visual imagery in any proper model of sign language. It is beyond the scope of this paper to give any detailed presentation of such a model. I do, however, present the outlines of a different, visually based theoretical framework in which to adequately analyze sign phenomena.

One final note: the arguments I present appeal to different factors motivating particular linguistic descriptions. In certain cases, they concern capturing linguistically significant generalizations; in other cases, they reflect the intuitions native signers have regarding their language. These considerations, interacting with the different aspects of Sign grammar, provide many approaches to the argument, all of which lead to the same conclusion: Sign is a language of pictures—a fact that the deaf accept as common sense, but that the vocal-language-biased linguist accepts only after all other conceptualizations of the grammar fail. This paper is an attempt to substantiate my informant's frequent reprimand: "That isn't a good picture."

1. Syntactic Considerations

All natural languages have a set of signs used to denote particular objects, states, and events; however, naming objects will not allow us to communicate much. All natural languages must also have a way of specifying the relationships that exist between and among those objects, states, and events; syntactic patterning constitutes a means for doing this. A natural human language, ASL has signs for objects in the world. These signs take the form of complex structured gestures constructed with attention to certain formational principles and constraints (see, for example, Stokoe, 1960; Stokoe, Casterline, and Croneberg, 1965; Siple, 1973; Frishberg, 1975b; Friedman, 1974b and in this volume). As with any natural language, ASL also has devices for coding the specification of relationships, devices that again are structured along certain principles. In this section of the paper, I will be concerned with syntactic devices in Sign.

Syntactic theories are varied in complex and interesting ways, but those that most American linguists have come to use have two things in common. First, they agree that the surface form of utterances is to be analyzed properly as a molar structure constructed of smaller, molecular units. Second, and possibly more important, they posit some other structure, also composed of a finite set of discrete elements, underlying the surface structures. The motivations for positing such underlying structures are well known and need not concern us here. What I would like to focus on is the elements comprising these underlying structures. Consider,

for example, what has come to be called (extended) standard theory transformational grammar (Chomsky, 1965, 1971). According to this theory, the underlying
elements are taken to be symbols of a formal nature, symbols such as S, NP, VP, N,
and so forth. At a certain point in the derivation of a sentence, some of these symbols are specified for syntactic features that play a crucial role in the semantic
interpretation of the structure, and that in some way account for the nature and
behavior of the elements comprising them. There are also other structural features
such as primitive relationships, but what the reader should keep in mind is that
discrete symbolic elements, which make use of discrete feature markings, govern
the mapping of underlying structures onto surface structures. Now consider a
theory such as the deep case theory proposed by Fillmore (1968). In this sort of
theory, underlying structures are seen to be predicates along with a set of NPs, each
of which is marked, along with other things, for a case, case here being understood
as a functional primitive. The set of case relationships within any underlying structure will predict such derived grammatical relationships as subject and object, and
thus play a crucial role in the mapping of underlying structures onto surface structures. Once again, we find a theory which makes use of a finite set of markings—
here case markings—in order to account for distinctive behavior of surface items.
The last theory I will mention is that which has come to be called generative semantics (G. Lakoff, 1971; McCawley, 1971). According to this theory, underlying
structures are in many ways similar to standard theory structures in that they are
taken to be phrase markers using the same bracketing relationships and labels as
does the "standard" theory. The main difference is that the output of the base
component is in the form of semantic representations (at least in McCawley—Lakoff
leaves the question open). The nature of those semantic representations, which are
still composed of discrete, isolable units, entirely governs the mapping of the underlying semantic structures onto the surface structures of a language.

The point of the discussion thus far should be quite clear. In each of the theories mentioned above, the underlying claim is that discrete units, in the form of
semantic or syntactic markings or features, or semantic primitives, interact with
grammatical mapping rules in order to relate surface structures to underlying structures, semantic structures of a discrete nature, or syntactic structures of a discrete
nature that semantic interpretation rules map onto semantic structures. In short,
the rules in the grammars I have outlined must refer to these elements. This notion
constitutes a strong principle of language structure, and one that essentially seems
correct. That is, as long as we can see vocal language as we do, comprising psycho-
logically isolable elements, it is only reasonable to state its regularities in terms of
rules operating on discrete elements.

Consider now the following sentences of English:

(1)   *The boy met the girl.*

(2)   *The girl met the boy.*

(3)   *The boy and the girl met.*

The same meanings in ASL are signed as described in (4), (5), and (6), respectively.[1]

(4) $\begin{bmatrix} \text{R} \\ \text{L} \end{bmatrix}$ R   BOY *G*-MARKER (R moves)

   L   GIRL *G*-MARKER--

The sign for GIRL (the thumb, extended from the fist, brushes across the cheek toward the mouth, the contact being at the ball of the thumb) is made with the left hand followed by a *G*-MARKER (index finger extending upward from the fist), palm facing right. The left hand holds this configuration throughout the remainder of the utterance. Next, the sign for BOY (fingers and thumb extended, touching, and pointing toward the left, with the hand at the forehead) moves to *G*-MARKER,⟩ palm facing left. The right hand then approaches the left until the thumbs of both hands touch lengthwise.

(5) $\begin{bmatrix} \text{R} \\ \text{L} \end{bmatrix}$ R   GIRL *G*-MARKER (R moves)

   L   BOY *G*-MARKER --

BOY is signed first, then GIRL, which approaches to "meet" the boy as did the boy *G*-MARKER in (4).

(6) $\begin{bmatrix} \text{R} \\ \text{L} \end{bmatrix}$ R   BOY *G*-MARKER --------------------

                                                     (both move)

   L   GIRL *G*-MARKER --

The same as either (4) or (5) except that when the hands both form the *G*-MARKER, both approach and contact.

The importance of this example set lies in the formational changes the sign MEET undergoes. There seems to be a regular, grammatical distinction here. Loosely described, the sign for either BOY or GIRL is made and is then identified with the *G*-MARKER (an anaphoric marker). The same action is then performed with the other hand. The distinctions in (1), (2), and (3) are coded by having the boy *G*-MARKER move toward the girl *G*-MARKER, the girl *G*-MARKER move toward the boy *G*-MARKER, or both *G*-MARKERs move toward each other. Possible analyses of these events within the linguistic theories discussed earlier should be apparent. For instance, the transformational-generative linguist (of both the standard theory and generative semantics persuasions), by referring to some property of the underlying structure of the sentences in question, say, ordering relationships, subject/object relationships, or other, could posit a sign-formation changing rule operating on a class of directional signs like MEET where the configuration, having been specified for one property, moves toward the same configuration having been specified for another property. An analysis of case grammar theory offers another, and to my mind more satisfying, solution. Ignoring ordering relationships, which seem to be irrelevant in these examples, one allows the rule to mention case markings. This is the solution chosen by Friedman (1975b), where she offers a plausible account of these phenomena in her discussion of directional signs (though she does not specifically discuss MEET). She states that

> Each sign of this class, like any well formed sign, must have a movement and an orientation of the hand. The choice of movement and orientation for these verbs is dependent on the location in space of both (a) the AGENT, EXPERIENCEER or SOURCE, and (b) the PATIENT, BENEFICIARY, or GOAL. The direction of the movement (and the orientation of the articulator) is from a point at or near the space established for the agent to that point in space which has the patient as its referent. Thus it is possible, with one core verb, to articulate a great variety of different sentences, merely by a change in direction of movement and orientation. [p. 956]

Either of these solutions is adequate for describing the particular cases in question, though for reasons which need not concern us here one might choose the case approach over the other; however, there are residual problems that turn out to be overwhelming. While we might posit an underlying agent/patient relationship to account for the movement in (4), (5), and (6), there are other related phenomena that do not lend themselves to such an analysis. For example, once both hands are in the upraised *G*-MARKER, there are many sentences that can be signed, all distinguished by movement of the hands toward and away from each other. If they pass each other in space, then the resulting sentence is something like 'The boy and the girl passed each other without stopping' or in the appropriate context, 'The boy and the girl pretended not to see each other'. If the two hands approach each other, and then the one identified with the boy, for example, turns and moves outward again, we have something like 'The boy avoided meeting the girl' or 'The boy saw the girl and then took off before talking to her'. The boy hand can approach the girl hand with a halting, jerking action to mean 'The boy was reluctant to meet the girl, but did so anyway'; the two hands can approach and then both veer away, approach and leap backward in surprise, and so forth, each of these associated with a different meaning. The problems that these phenomena present to any analysis discussed so far should be evident. We would be forced to claim either that with each change in the movement parameter of MEET we have another distinct sign, in which case we give up all hope of placing finite bounds on the number of lexical items, and all hope of accounting for the productivity of the process, or we must claim that the rule specifying the proper movement value of MEET can contain an unlimited number of markings, or be changed by an unlimited number of discrete adjustment rules to account for the indeterminate number of variations in the single sign MEET. This problem is insoluble within the theoretical frameworks outlined earlier.

Given that our theories, and not just our analyses within the confines of those theories, have failed to account for this class of phenomena, we must ask what sort of theory would be necessary to describe them properly. Suppose that we give up the sort of semantic or syntactic representation composed of discrete units, NPs, features, case markings, and so on. It is unclear to me just what the nature of such a visual representation would be; I look to others to argue the nature of visual imagery and visual memory. But we could imagine a visual image possessing all the elements necessary to account for meaning (I will briefly discuss this notion of having all the necessary elements for meaning later). What could the notion of such a visual representation lend to the analysis of the MEET examples? Consider the nature of (4), (5), and (6) once again. Remember that the upraised index fingers were anaphores for the girl and the boy. What each G-MARKER does is trace in the signing space an analogue of the trajectory the actors would take in the real world or some imaginal world. It would seem that the signer must have some visual representation to refer to in order to properly produce the movement associated with the sign MEET. Given that there must be a visual representation of an event, the solution to the problems just discussed seems a bit closer. In each case, the trajectory of the G-MARKERs is a spatial analogue of the movement in the real/imaginal world: the function is to enable the addressee in the signed communication to reconstruct the scene in order to infer the relationships between the two actors in the event.

I would like to expand the notion of the addressee inferring relationships holding between actors in an event. Imagine a case where I am sitting in a room with a woman named Mary. A man named John walks into the room. He walks up to Mary and says something quietly to her that I cannot hear. He then leaves the room, and Mary begins to cry. It is clear that there is no obvious relationship between John's saying something to Mary and Mary's crying other than a temporal one. One event is prior to the other. I am not being unreasonable, however, if I later come to you and report the event with sentence (7).

(7)   *John said something to Mary that made her cry.*

That is, I am allowed, with no stretch of reasoning, to look at a purely temporal relationship between two events and infer a causal relationship. Furthermore, suppose that rather than reporting the whole event to you with sentence (7), I use sentence (8) instead.

(8)   *John said something to Mary, and she started to cry.*

Nowhere in (8) is there any coding of causality; there is no *CAUSE* morpheme, no causal verb. And yet you would not be unreasonable were you to ask me (9).

(9)   *I wonder what John said that made Mary cry?*

In other words, the addressee is allowed to infer relationships from linguistic structures where no such relationship is semantically coded. We might think of (8) as allowing the addressee to construct some image (perhaps a visual image) of the event so that he can infer causality.

We can now return to the problematic MEET examples with a clearer idea of what is taking place. In many of the problem cases, no "meeting" took place at all—that is, in those cases where the G-MARKERs only approach each other but do not contact one another, or where one veers away, or where they pass one another. It may be the case that there is no actual sign MEET at all, just two markers that are spatially related in some way. The notion of meeting may be derivable entirely from the fact that both markers move toward the same location. I suggest that the sequences are analogue reconstructions of the visual aspects of the events which allow the addressee to infer the particular relationship holding between the actors in just the same way that the addressee could infer (7) from (8).[2]

2. Morphological Considerations

It seems fairly clear that any proper understanding of grammatical/semantic relationships among signs in ASL will necessarily incorporate the notion of visual imagery or some similar notion. I now turn to certain semantic relationships in ASL that are in many ways similar to morphological relationships in a vocal language. Here again it turns out that visual imagery is crucial. First, in order to dispel what seems to be a frequently occurring confusion in sign language research, however, I want to draw a firm distinction. As one would expect, any discussion of the relationship of a visual sign to its denotation in terms of visual imagery will almost necessarily include some description of the degree to which that sign resembles its denotation. This question of resemblance turns up repeatedly in the literature, as the issue of the iconicity of signs (see, for example, Frishberg, 1975b; Klima and Bellugi, 1975). A misunderstanding arises from a failure to recognize a crucial fact: the iconicity of a sign can vary along two parameters, namely, 1) the degree to which the form of the sign mimics or resembles its denotation, and 2) the degree to which the behavior of the sign mimics or resembles its denotation. Consider the following case. Suppose I were to attach two sticks together in the form of a cross and then tie a string to them so that I could hold the end of the string and move the sticks around in space. Upon seeing me move these sticks, one might guess that they represent an airplane, both in form (fuselage and wings) and behavior (moving about through the air). Suppose, on the other hand, I attached a button to a string and moved that button around in space. Upon seeing this event, one might find it more difficult to determine that the button represents an airplane, for the form of the presentation (the sign, if you will) is more iconic in the first case than in the second. However, in terms of the behavior of the representations—their moving about—they are equally iconic representations of airplanes, and once the arbitrary translation principle that buttons on strings represent airplanes is established, I am free to represent, in a highly iconic fashion, all sorts of things airplanes can do. This distinction is important not only in the discussion that follows, but also in that most discussions of the iconicity of signs have been concerned with the form of signs rather than their behavior. For example, in Frishberg's description of the historical tendency for signs to become less iconic and more arbitrary over time (Frishberg, 1975b), her discussion was entirely based on the form of signs rather than on their behavior. In fact, I know of no evidence presented to date indicating historical reduction of the iconicity of the behavior of signs.

With this distinction in mind, we can now turn to morphological considerations. To analyze the morphology of vocal languages, one looks for recurrent forms, or classes of forms that exhibit a correlated, recurrent function or semantic value. The notion of form here is crucial; because say /bʊk/, /vɔlyuwm/, and /towm/ in English correspond with respect to a recurrent semantic value, this does not, of course, establish them as a separate morpheme class; there must be a formational similarity. Thus, the forms /s/, /z/, and / əz/ can be isolated as allomorphs of a single *PLURAL* morpheme on two grounds: 1) There is a systematic formational relationship among these allomorphs, a relationship that can be stated purely in terms of their distribution, devoid of any meaning; 2) there is a systematic meaning function associated with these forms. Such analyses are basic, well motivated, and well known. I mention their components only as reference points for a similar analysis of ASL.

The structural units in ASL that immediately seem most analogous to morphemes are signs. Remembering that every sign is a construction of four simultaneous parameters (see Friedman), and noting, furthermore, that there is evidence that this sublexical level of organization has psychological reality (Bellugi and Klima, 1974; Klima and Bellugi, 1975), one can see that it is possible to look for formational similarities in signs and to check any discovered similarities for correlated meaning similarities. In other words, because there is both a lexical and sublexical level of organization in ASL, it is possible to carry out a morphological analysis of that language.

Frishberg and Gough (1973) performed a preliminary analysis of the relationships between the lexical and sublexical levels of Sign; they isolated a number of morphological regularities. For instance, in the place of articulation parameter, they discovered that many signs that have to do with school and book learning are articulated, either in whole or in part, at the open palm facing upwards. Examples include DRAW, WRITE, READ, PENCIL, PAINT, LETTER, PUBLISH, LEARN, STUDENT, STUDY, CRAM, BOOK, SCHOOL, GRADUATE, COLLEGE, LESSON, PARAGRAPH, MAGAZINE, LIST (verb and noun), REGISTER, and PETITION. They then discuss an interesting morphological relationship in the hand configuration parameter. There is another hand configuration made by opening the hand and spreading all the fingers and then bending the middle finger downward; many signs referring to the emotions or the nonvisual, nonauditory senses manifest this hand shape. Examples include TOUCH, TASTE, FEEL (emotionally), and by extension from the latter examples, EMOTION, EXCITED, THRILL, SYMPATHETIC and PITY. In each of these cases, a formational regularity (the open palm place of articulation, the bent-middle-finger hand configuration) exhibits related, if abstract, meaning regularity (things concerned with learning and literate activity, things concerned with the senses or emotions). Rather than describing other such regularities, I will discuss one particular case which provides the basis of further argument. Friedman (1975b) discusses the sign WASH as an example of incorporation of object into the verb in ASL.

Friedman says the following about this sign:

> [It] has as its core structure a double hand configuration AA [that is, fists made with the thumb to the side of the index finger, rather than overlapping the fingers—A.D.] with rotating or alternating movement. The construction **wash-myself** (or **wash-my-body**) is articulated on or near the chest; **wash-hair** is on the head; **wash-windows** is in neutral space—in the area where the sign **window** was articulated, immediately before. The only possible analysis of these verbs seems to be that the object is incorporated in the verb sign. [p. 957]

Friedman has strong motivation for her analysis. The sign BODY is articulated on or near the chest; the sign HAIR is articulated on the head; the sign WINDOW is articulated in neutral space. In short, there seems to be a regular morphological process underlying Friedman's notion of incorporation of object into the verb. Since the sign is transmuted in relation to the place of articulation of the sign incorporated, this process could be stated by a morphological (or perhaps syntactic) rule operating on WASH, which mentions the place of articulation of a sign in the environment, say, as in the following derivation:

(10) HAIR$_u$ WASH$_u$ (both signs in underlying forms)

     HAIR$_u$ WASH$_t$ (WASH transmuted for place of
                              articulation of HAIR)

    ----   WASH$_t$ (HAIR deleted)

Though she does not describe such a process in detail, I imagine that the process described in (10), or some analogous process, is what Friedman had in mind.

I will now consider a few other signs in the semantic domain of 'wash' that also, in a sense, incorporate an object, but that are formationally unrelated to the underlying form of WASH as just given. These include the signs WASH-DISHES, WASH-CLOTHES, and one that appears to be formationally similar to the cases cited, but which cannot be related by the same morphological process, namely, WASH with 'car' as its incorporated object. Descriptions of these signs are given in (11).

(11) a. WASH-DISHES: The hands are open with the fingers extended and touching each other. One hand clasps the other, the palms of the hands facing the signer, the fingers downward at a 45° angle, and the fingers of one hand overlapping the fingers of the other. The hands held in this configuration then move up and down slightly in front of the signer.

    b. WASH-CLOTHES: Both hands are open with the fingers spread and bent slightly like a claw. They are held in front of the signer, one palm up, the other palm down, about one foot of space separating the hands. The hands then rotate slightly back and forth, in an alternating movement.

    c. WASH-CAR: Both hands are in a closed fist, the thumb to the side. They are held in front of the signer, palms down, and moved circularly, one clockwise and the other counterclockwise.

It can be seen that neither (11.a) nor (11.b) is formationally similar to the paradigmatic WASH examples. And while (11.c) is formationally similar to the paradigm case, in that it has the same hand configuration and motion, its orientation, the proper specification of which is necessary for correct formation, cannot be predicted from the formational properties of its incorporated object as could the other examples; there are two signs for 'car', one made with the fists, thumb to the side and palms facing each other, moving up and down in front of the signer as if moving a steering wheel, and the other made with the thumb, index, and middle finger extended and spread, the ring and little finger folded in, touching the palm, and articulated on the palm of the other hand. There is no matching of relevant formational properties in either of the signs for 'car' and the sign WASH-CAR; so WASH-CAR must be counted as an exception to the paradigm.

    It would seem that we have no alternative but to call WASH-DISHES and WASH-CLOTHES independent signs which are completely outside the WASH object-incorporation paradigm, and to call WASH-CAR an exceptional case in the paradigm, if not also an independent sign. On the other hand, all of the signs are related semantically in two senses: 1) They all refer to the same class of events, namely, acts of 'washing', and 2) they all in some sense incorporate their object. We would therefore like to find some way of stating that they are related, and would more highly value the grammar that allows us to make such a statement. One way of doing this has to do with the notion of suppletion. That is, all of the forms can be incorporated into a single paradigm by 1) marking WASH-DISHES and WASH-CLOTHES as suppletive forms in the paradigm, and by 2) marking WASH-CAR as either an exception to the regular processes, or also a suppletive form. We then have a way of relating all the forms simultaneously along with stating their differences. Unfortunately, there is one strong argument against such an analysis.

    When one accounts for exceptional forms in a vocal language in terms of suppletion, there is usually some principled explanation for the suppletive forms, that explanation usually having diachronic relevance. For instance, we can explain the suppletive paradigm of *be* in English as the collapse of three independent and regular verb paradigms in the diachronic development of English; we can explain the suppletive forms of the *PLURAL* morpheme found in the words *children* and *oxen* as remnants of some previous plural formation rule in the history of English. There is no similar explanation available for the exceptional WASH cases I described.

There is another, quite obvious explanation for the exceptional forms which incorporates the notion of visual imagery. This point will become clear on re-examination of the sign descriptions in (11).

It turns out that the hand configuration, place of articulation, movement and orientation in (11.a), WASH-DISHES, represent holding and dipping a dish into a pan of water; (11.b) represents the rotary action of the agitator blades of a washing machine; and the orientation and place of articulation of (11.c) represent those movements that would be made by the signer were he actually washing a car. In short, each of these signs is instrinsically iconic: the form of the sign resembles its denotation in certain ways. As it happens, all of the regular paradigm cases can also be accounted for in terms of their iconicity in a similar fashion. That is, the form of WASH-BODY or WASH-HAIR resembles the action of washing oneself or one's hair. The interesting result of such an analysis is that by invoking visual imagery to account for exceptional cases, we lose all motivation for the formational-similarity analysis of regular cases. The formational similarities can be seen as the fortuitous result of matching iconicity; BODY is iconically made on the body, HAIR iconically at the head, and WINDOW iconically in the space in front of the signer. (See Mandel for a detailed discussion of iconicity in ASL.)

I have been somewhat misleading regarding the iconicity of signs in ASL. It might be imagined from the previous descriptions that sign language is pantomimic in nature, that one codes an event by acting it out. This is far from the case; if the signer actually went through the motions of, for example, washing the body, rubbing the arms, body, neck, and legs with the hands, this would be recognized as an act of mime by both the fluent signer and the individual knowing no ASL. I must stress the point that a sign is a conventionalized gesture, quite specific in the way that it is made. WASH-BODY is made exactly as described, and if it is changed by, say, being made with an open hand rather than a fist, it no longer means WASH-BODY, but ENJOY; if it is made with one hand rather than two, it is the sign SORRY. In short, iconicity and conventionality are in no way polar opposites, and both notions are vital to understanding the nature of a sign. It is important to keep this point in mind not only to understand the nonpantomimic nature of sign, but because it points to a basic confusion in most of the research on ASL in the past; researchers, in stressing the conventionality of signs, have felt it necessary to discount their iconicity.

Early in this discussion I suggested that the linguist must continually evaluate his analyses, asking whether they appropriately represent the way the native speaker analyzes and organizes his language. In my own research, I have tried to find evidence in this regard and was fortunate enough to come across the following two cases. Consider sentences (12) and (13).

(12) *The airplane flew over the valley,*

(13) *I fed the baby.*

When presented with these English sentences for translation into Sign, one deaf informant's first response was to ask how the action was accomplished. In other words, (12) and (13) present a number of possible meanings, some corresponding to the English sentences in (14) and (15), respectively.

(14) a. *The airplane flew across (the width of) the valley.*

b. *The airplane flew through (the length of) the valley.*

c. *The airplane circled the valley.*

(15) a. *I suckled the baby.*

b. *I fed the baby with a spoon.*

c. *I gave the baby a bottle.*

It turns out that to sign the meanings of (12) and (13), the signer must choose a more specific meaning, analogous to those of (14) and (15). To sign the translations of (14), the signer first traces the sides of a valley in the space in front of him with the open palms of both hands; then, while holding the nondominant hand in its final position for VALLEY (to serve as a reference point), the sign AIRPLANE (thumb, index, and little finger extended from the fist) is moved over this imaginary valley with a longitudinal (outward from the signer), latitudinal (from one side of the signer to the other), or circular trajectory, coding (14.a), (14.b), and (14.c), respectively. To sign the translations of (15), the signer signs BABY, which is also an iconic sign in which the two arms fold, palms up, as if cradling a baby; the signer then brings the 'baby' up to his breast (15.a), or, while leaving the nondominant hand and arm cradling the imaginary baby, actually mimes spoon feeding (15.b) or bottle feeding (15.c) the baby. The important fact to keep in mind is that there is a sign OVER and signs for 'feed' (GIVE EAT). However, the signer's first response— his first intuition, if you will—is to choose the more visually based representation, choosing descriptive signs or mimic signs in order to create an icon in the signing space. Apparently, the native signer uses visual imagery to give a sign its appropriate form, to properly distribute the sublexical elements of signs in a way to convey meaning, and to choose appropriate lexical items—which is after all what morphology is all about.

3. Semantic Considerations in Individual Signs

I now turn to the area of individual sign semantics, another area where visual imagery comes into play. Consider the following case. There is a sign that might be glossed as COVET or LUST. It is made by extending all the fingers of the dominant hand, folding the thumb in against the palm, then brushing the outside edge of the index finger downward against the corner of the mouth with the fingers pointing upward. The items in (16) are examples of this sign.

(16) a. HENRY SEE LYNN / LUST

     b. ALWAYS   YOU HUNGRY++ LUST

     c. GIRL ENTER / JOE LUST++

There is nothing particularly iconic in this sign, except that it is usually made with the eyelids slightly lowered, the mouth partly open, and the tongue protruding a bit, the sign looks mildly lascivious. While this sign incorporates the meaning of lust and desire, the informant claims that the "picture" that this sign makes is one of saliva running out of the corner of the mouth. My first reaction to this was that the image of the sign was irrelevant, that it represented no more than a mnemonic or some folk etymology. This reaction was mistaken, for it appears that visual imagery is the most important part of the sign. There are a few superficially unrelated signs that make use of the same hand configuration and that present a similar image. Examples of these signs are:

(17) a. RUNNY-NOSE: The configuration of LUST, palm toward the signer, fingers pointing to the side. The index finger touches the nose and moves slowly downward from the underside. This sign can be made with two hands in the same configuration in alternating motion.

     b. DROOL: Same configuration and orientation as RUNNY-NOSE, but made at the mouth with a fairly slow movement.

     c. PERSPIRE: Same configuration, palm outward from the signer with one or (more often) two hands moving rapidly from the side of the head to the center of the forehead. Often made with wiggling fingers.

     d. BLEED: Same configuration, palm toward signer, fingers pointing downward, made at the point on the body where the bleeding took place if that point is located on the front, upper half of the body, or over the back of the nondominant hand. The same configuration and orientation would hold if the bleeding took place elsewhere. Often made with wiggling fingers.

     e. BLOOD: Both hands in the LUST configuration, palms toward the signer in neutral space, fingers pointing toward the left on the right hand, toward

the right on the left hand. The dominant hand
moves toward the nondominant hand with a sharp
movement until the fingers overlap. Then the
dominant hand moves slowly downward, often
with wiggling fingers.

These signs are related in an obvious way. In each case, the configuration and movement in the sign indicate a liquid exuding from the body, the slower the movement, the more viscous the liquid. This is the visual image attached to that configuration and movement.

Elsewhere in this paper, I have discussed inference from visual imagery. Here
again this notion becomes important, for what seems to be going on here is the
presentation of an icon from which the addressee infers particular meaning in the
same way that he inferred meaning from spatial relationships in the MEET examples. It is noteworthy in this regard that while the LUST and BLOOD examples
may seem highly lexicalized, the other examples are not quite so. PERSPIRE and
especially BLEED require context for a correct interpretation. For instance, with
BLEED, there must be something in the context to indicate that bleeding took
place, such as the signs HURT, CUT, or SURGERY. The addressee appears to
reconstruct an image, here an image of liquid exuding from the body; he infers the
nature of this liquid from contextual facts, such as where the liquid is exuding from,
why the liquid is exuding, and so on.

Thus, we find that there are cases where the form of a sign is not particularly
iconic (the extended finger configuration described above does not much resemble
a flowing liquid), but where the behavior of the sign—here in terms of place of articulation and speed of movement— is quite iconic. This is a different sort of process
from the MEET cases. There, the behavior of the G-MARKERs made use of visual
imagery in order to relate signs to other signs; the markers made an iconic analogue
of an event. And this sort of process differs from the WASH examples. There, a
specific visual image determined the shape of a sign. Here the behavior of the extended finger configuration makes use of visual imagery not in relating it to other signs,
or relating it to different actions, but in assigning a specific semantic interpretation
to a single sign.

There is another interesting group of signs that are superficially unrelated, but
are related by a single visual image—a much more abstract one than in the previous
examples. The following signs all have the same basic hand configuration (both
hands extending the index and middle fingers, spread), orientation (left palm facing
right, right facing left, the dominant hand resting on the nondominant), and place
of articulation (neutral signing space); the signs are distinguished only by the movement associated with each, as described in (18).

> (18) a. CARE: Movement only to the basic configuration.
>
>   b. KEEP: A reduplication by re-formation of CARE
>   at least twice.

c. SUPERVISE: A circular movement of the base
configuration on a horizontal plane.

d. BORROW/LEND: Movement from the location of
the source of the object to the location of the
goal.

The movement types in these examples have been discussed elsewhere in the literature. The noniconic movement in (18.a) is only that movement necessary to form
the sign; movement of the sort found in (18.b) has been analyzed by Fischer
(1973a) as a verbal marking for habitual, durative actions; circular movement of the
sort found in (18.c) is often used as a verbal marking for incorporating plurality of
objects; Friedman (1975b) fully discusses and describes the movement involved in
directional verbs, citing the example of (18.d) specifically; such movement has been
described here as tracing the trajectory of some entity, here the object of BORROW/
LEND. In other words, the movement in each of the cases except for (18.a) (which
seems to represent the unmarked case) has semantic import, and I suggest iconic
value, distinct from the hand configuration, place of articulation, and orientation
constant in all of the examples in (18). With this in mind, consider the following
uses of these signs and the given paraphrases.

(19) a. YOU KEEP (BOOK)
      Paraphrase: You take into your care and keeping
      the book (previously identified).

     b. ME CHILD CARE
      Paraphrase: I habitually over a period of time
      have a child in my care and keeping.

     c. HE SUPERVISE o-f-f-i-c-e
      Paraphrase: As his job, he is responsible for the
      care and keeping of the objects and people in an
      office.

     d PLEASE ONE-DOLLAR YOU-LEND / ME-BORROW
      Paraphrase: Please take a dollar that is in your care
      and keeping and put it in my care and keeping.

I am suggesting that there is an iconic core value for this basic sign, an image involving some animate or inanimate object in the possession, care, and keeping of an
individual; certain manipulations of the basic sign will lend further detail to that
picture so that the result resembles the meanings suggested by the English glosses.

There are numerous examples of superficially unrelated signs that can be seen
to be related on closer examination by a shared scene or image. Examples include
a sign whose visual image involves turning around, and which in the context of a

trip means 'travel' while in the context of a room it means 'look around'; there is a sign, an image of putting a signature on a piece of paper, which in different contexts can mean 'sign a paper', 'register to vote', 'apply for a job', and so forth. In fact, it seems to me that this notion of shared image underlies all of the morphological relationships described by Frishberg and Gough (1973).

There is one more example I will discuss because it demonstrates that not only is the visual imagery of a sign relevant to its distribution, but that it is in fact predominant, taking precedence over the nonvisually based presuppositions of a sign. There is a sign (actually a compound) made by first touching the tips of the index and middle fingers pointed downward, extended and spread from the fist onto the palm of the nondominant hand (if only this much of the sign is made, it is glossed STAND), and then moving the dominant hand (the index and thumb forming a circle and the other fingers extended) from a point below and in front of the nondominant hand to a point above and in front of the nondominant hand. It has been claimed (Bellugi, personal communication) that this sign means 'oversleep', and that it is irrelevant that the first part of this sign suggests an individual coming to a standing position (that is, after sleeping) and that the latter part of this sign suggests that the event takes place when the sun (represented by the configuration of the dominant hand) is well over the horizon (represented by the nondominant hand). As it happens, not only does the first part of the sign surface elsewhere with the meaning 'get out of bed', and the second part of the sign surface with the meaning 'sunrise' (or, with movement from above to below the nondominant hand, 'sunset'), but one informant claims that if it were the case that one was supposed to get up at 4:00 A.M., but failed to get up until 6:00 A.M., the sign could not be used, even though the individual had indeed overslept, the reason being, according to this informant, that the "picture" associated with the sign is of an individual getting up when the sun is high in the sky; and in our world people who get up when the sun is high have usually arisen later than they should have. If the individual did not get up when the sun was high, the image of the sign would not match the imaginal/real-world imagery, and the sign cannot be used.

4. Productive Visual Imagery

I will now consider a group of signs that are used productively to construct visual images in the signing space. In certain cases, these signs have no lexical meaning of their own, but rather serve to trace, outline, and draw shapes, trajectories, and so forth. In other cases, these signs have lexical meaning, but included in the sign is some feature that serves again to trace, outline, and so on. I will refer to these classes of signs as spatially descriptive signs (see Mandel for more detailed discussion of this whole area). Spatially descriptive signs can be punctually, linearly, planarily, or three-dimensionally descriptive; the points these signs describe can lie on a point, a line (which can curve), a plane (which can also be curved), or in three dimensions. I know of only two punctually descriptive signs: the pointed index finger and the extended thumb (movement, place of articulation, and orientation unspecified).

These are used for all-purpose punctual indexing, that is, to describe a point in space where some previously identified object, or some object to be identified, is located. If they come to represent some figure, they then become anaphoric markers, and remain in space at some particular point, or can move, becoming linearly descriptive. While there are only two punctually descriptive signs, there are a number of linearly descriptive signs, including CAR (the version formed by extending the thumb, index finger, and middle finger from the fist), AIRPLANE, EXCHANGE, WALK (the version formed by touching the index finger and the thumb, the other fingers extended, and the version formed by pointing the extended index and middle fingers downward) and all the multidirectional verbs. In each of these signs, the basic configuration has lexical denotation, but the movement in the sign has meaning only in context, for example with WALK, has meaning only in terms of the path of the walking, say, up a hill, around a corner, back and forth and so on. The planarily descriptive signs describe a set of points on an entire plane. These signs most often belong to another sign, a sort of sign radical similar to the radicals of Chinese characters. I have only seen two of these signs: the palms open and flat, and the "claw" hand (fingers and thumb extended and bent), the latter sometimes with a wiggling motion. The palm always faces the plane being described. The open palm sign is much more general than the claw hand sign; it has the effect of only describing a plane while the bent claw hand indicates both a plane along the trajectory of the sign's motion and a great number of objects (people, keys, articles of clothing and so on) crowding that plane. The open palm occurs in the signs MOUNTAIN, OCEAN and FIELD, among others. The claw hand as just defined does not occur in any lexicalized signs that I know of; it occurs rather in ad hoc sign constructions. Our research group has chosen to gloss this sign BEAUCOUP. A good example is given in (20).

(20) *The children were all around me.*

⎡ R   KID CHILDREN ME *G*-MARKER (palm to signer).
⎣ L   BEAUCOUP (palm to signer).

The right hand is a *G*-MARKER whose referent is the signer. Beaucoup, representing a wall of children, rises to contact the *G*-MARKER.

Or

same as above except that the BEAUCOUP circles the *G*-MARKER.

Three-dimensionally descriptive signs are of two types. One type describes the whole figure by enclosing it (usually with the claw hand or a cupped hand) or by tracing two of its three dimensions at a point in space (with an open palm or a bent, open palm, or with the bent, extended index finger and thumb). Examples are given in (21) and (22).

(21) *That city is surrounded by water.*

$$\left[\begin{array}{l} \text{R CITY WATER 'BENT-INDEX/THUMB-HAND'} \\ \text{L} \end{array}\right.$$

The BENT-INDEX/THUMB-HAND describes a body of water in terms of its length and breadth, but not depth, surrounding the nondominant hand in its final position of city.

(22) *The top of the table is dirty.*

$$\left[\begin{array}{l} \text{R TABLE DIRTY 'BENT-INDEX/THUMB-HAND'} \\ \text{L} \qquad\qquad\text{(forearm, palm down, in neutral space)} \end{array}\right.$$

The BENT-INDEX/THUMB-HAND traces the length of a layer on the table top while the relative height of the bent index represents the relative height of the layer of dirt.

These signs demonstrate descriptive productivity that suggests they are based on some visual imagery. They require reference to some visual image for the proper specification of those features manipulated as analogues of pathways, shapes, heights, and so on.

Another type of sign that depends on visual imagery for proper specification is signs that change depending upon the visual aspects of the object or action being described. Examples are given in (23).

(23) a. OPEN: Orientation and exact point of initial contact left unspecified. Two open palms touching at an edge, move away from each other.

b. COPULATE: Orientation unspecified. Two hands with the index and middle fingers extended (representing legs) converge and contact repeatedly.

The signs in (23) will each change orientation, sometimes place of articulation, and even hand configuration, depending upon what is being described. Consider the sign OPEN. With this sign, the orientation depends on what is being opened: wooden case windows will open with both palms facing the signer, initial contact being along the little finger and index finger of the hands; sliding glass doors will open with both palms facing away from the signer, touching at the index finger sides. Given that the extended fingers represent a person's legs in the sign COPULATE, palm-side of the hand representing the front of the body, the possible meanings that can be coded with changes in orientation and contact point are enormous.[3] Both of these signs are visually descriptive in a way that a sign like ENGLISH (the dominant palm covers the top of the wrist of the nondominant hand) is not. And that visual quality is reflected in the signs' ability to change for different imagery, whereas

ENGLISH will be the same in every sentence, except for minor nonmeaningful formational shifts. As is the case with all of the examples given, there is a highly meaningful variability among these signs that cannot be captured by discrete, underlying semantic units. In the case of the signs just mentioned, as well as others described earlier, the signer's hands create an image, adjusting themselves to conform as closely as possible, by way of analogue, to an image in the signer's mind.

There is a final example which clearly shows the visual nature and productivity of signs of the sort already discussed. The example is a coined sign, a spontaneous creation, for the referent 'whale'. The informant first signed BIG FISH and then did an interesting thing: he traced a line over the back of his head from the base of his skull to a point high above his forehead in a giant C-shape. The line was traced with a claw hand, palm facing forward. He then signed FISH again (which is a two-handed sign, the dominant hand in the open palm configuration, fingers pointing directly out from the signer), and then, while holding the dominant hand configuration for FISH, he duplicated in miniature the tracing of the C-shape with the claw hand over the "head" of the fish. Of course, the claw hand represented the water spout from the blow hole on the head of a whale. The signing over the head did not have the proper formational properties of a sign—it was not formed in the signing space—so the signer, having given us a clear idea of what the claw hand represented, moved that claw hand into the signing space in its appropriate location in relation to the fish, and thus, created a sign. Later, the informant demonstrated the same phenomena to two deaf acquaintances without any translation and asked for their meaning. One of the acquaintances has no sign for 'whale'; however, both immediately understood the construction to mean 'whale'.

5.   Degree Analogues

The examples included in the previous sections of this paper argue for the incorporation of visual imagery into a grammar of sign because the signs are representations of some image in the real world or in the mind of the signer. In this section, I will present data in which there does not seem to be the sort of intimate involvement with a particular image as there was in the previous example, but rather underlying degrees of involvement for a particular semantic notion, coded with visual analogues. That is, a more or less abstract, visual image is constructed in the signing space, and that image will vary as an analogue of the degree of whatever semantic notion is being encoded. Examples of these lexical signs of degree are given in (24).

> (24) a. GROW-UP: Open palm hand, palm downward, moves up in neutral space.
>
>   b. HIGH: Dominant open palm hand, palm downward, rises from the back of the nondominant open palm hand.

    c. BIG: The two hands, held with the index fingers and thumbs extended and bent, palms facing each other, move apart in neutral space.

    d. LONG: The dominant hand, held with the index finger and thumb extended, moves up the pronated forearm.

    e. EXTEND: The dominant fist, thumb over fingers, pulls away from the nonthumb side of the non-dominant fist, bending at the wrist.

Each of the signs in this group has movement starting at (approximately) the same point but ending at some point which depends on the degree of the factor coded; each sign will choose the point on its movement continuum where it will stop. For example, (24.a) can start at a point at or below the waist and remain there with the meaning 'child'; it can begin at the same point and end near the bottom of the chest and mean either 'grow to the point of being a preteenager' or just 'preteenager'; it can continue to 'teenager', late teenager', 'adult', 'tall adult', or any point in between. The sign seems to be iconic in a very natural way; the height we choose for the sign could be matched to the actual height of a person, assigning each token of the sign a meaning from child to tall adult. This constitutes a particular kind of iconicity, however.[4] We cannot choose just any way to represent a particular meaning; we must choose a conventional sign. Once the sign has been chosen, manipulations of the sign may be iconic in nature. While the clear arbitrariness of the sign may be difficult to see in (24.a), as we approach (24.e), the truly arbitrary, conventional nature becomes more apparent. The sign in (24.e) means the figurative extension of something as when one tells too many details in a story. It also has the meaning of 'advertise' or 'exaggerate'. To extend a story or to exaggerate is something one can do by degrees; the meaning is a "degree meaning", and the coded representation of that meaning includes a specification of degree. Thus, as we get a relatively higher degree of this meaning factor, we find a higher degree of the coding factor.[5] The addressee judges the coded degree in terms of the visual image created as an analogue to the degree semantics.

    The type of examples presented here are by no means limited. The sign researcher is constantly confronted with cases where visual imagery offers the best, or only, explanation of the data, and it is not at all radical that we would make reference to visual imagery to account for meaning in a language. The sentences of (25) are analogous to the MEET examples in that they rely on visual imagery of some sort but differ from them in that they are nondiscrete in nature.

    (25) a. *John walked across campus.*

        b. *John raced across campus.*

c. *John trudged across campus.*

d. *John bounced across campus.*

e. *John schlepped across campus.*

The choice or verbs (which are rich in visual imagery) can be seen as based on matching the image associated with those verbs and the imaginal world they attempt to convey. Analogous to the 'exuding liquid' examples is (26).

(26)   a. *The baby was drooling all over the girls again.*

b. *Henry was drooling all over the girls again.*

The particular interpretation of the verb is quite different in the two sentences, but here there is a core of visual imagery that holds constant for both.

Thus far the data discussed have included the notion of a visual representation, of a set of lexical signs, manipulated in some way, of a visual/spatial analogue in the signing space corresponding to some visual/spatial aspect of the visual representation, and of some set of inferences drawn from a visual representation. What is lacking is a model in which all of these notions can be related. This model will require some provision for visual representations, some way to map certain aspects of these visual representations onto discrete lexical items, a way to map certain continuous aspects of the visual representations onto visual/spatial analogues, and some provision for inferential processes that will allow semantic elements to be inferred where they are not actually linguistically coded. I have such a model in mind, though many of the details must be left unstated at present. I am not at all sure of the implications of this model; it is not clear what phenomena can or cannot be captured by it. But it seems that a model of these basic outlines will be necessary in order to account for the facts I have presented so far.

The model incorporates, first of all, visual representations. I am not sure what the nature of these representations are, what they might look like, or even if they are linguistic entities at all, though I do suspect that they are distinct from imaginal/ real-world visual imagery. They surely cannot resemble photographs or motion pictures; not all details are available to the signer, nor are they necessary in any sort of visual imagery. I can construct a visual image of, say, the living room in the house where I lived as a child without being able to remember all the details of that living room. I assume these images to be some sort of four-dimensional mental objects where all relevant material is simultaneously available. That is, the fourth dimension is not defined by any real time relationship, but by relating sequences of visual images with notions such as **prior to** and **subsequent to**. I am not concerned with how to represent this image—only with its properties, since we could refer to properties of the representation rather than the visual image itself. Furthermore, it is important to remember that certain images are unique and novel in exactly the way that molar linguistic structures like phrases, sentences, and discourses are novel, while others are quite frozen in exactly the way that lexical items, certain compounds, and idioms tend to be frozen. I take the visual representations to be basic.

The next aspect of the model is a set of lexical mapping rules that map certain aspects of the visual image onto lexical items, or perhaps map certain aspects of imaginal/real-world imagery onto images created in the signing space. These can also be viewed as a set of translation rules that specify the relationship between the image and the coded representation. I imagine these rules will be of the same sort as those that allow the speaker of a vocal language to map certain aspects of an actual event he has witnessed onto lexical items, underlying semantic units, or scenes when he linguistically encodes that event. I would suggest that such rules, which will not be specifically discussed in this paper, will refer to certain truth conditions within a semantic model. Since lexical items have meaning beyond any specific situation where they might apply, this meaning might be captured by some sort of formal language that has meaning only insofar as it implicitly or explicitly denotes individuals, objects, points in time and space, situation, and facts in the world. Dowty (1972) describes semantic models in this way:

> A semantic model might be thought of intuitively as a simplified mathematical abstraction of the world, insofar as individuals, properties, and 'possible worlds' are defined in it. ('Possible worlds' may represent either successive moments in time or possible alternatives to some actual state of affairs or may serve other functions.) [p. 10]

The choice of lexical items may well be affected by conditions other than truth conditions relative to a semantic model. For example, it would seem that lexical mapping rules will have to take codability into account; certain aspects of visual imagery will be coded because they are more relevant to the message intended or because they are more suggestive of other parts of the whole image. Consider a sentence of the type, 'There were all these people in chairs' as opposed to 'There were all these people sitting in this movie theater', where I have referred possibly to the same sort of situation, or even the same image, but the second example of coding conveys more information to the addressee than does the first and thus facilitates his construction of a richer imaginal world. I cannot say how these rules might look in detail, or what their exact nature would be. On the other hand, since rules of this sort will be needed in any language system, it is safe to assume that any model of sign language must have them as well.

The third aspect of the model is a set of analogue rules that map certain continuous or iconic aspects of the scene onto continuous or iconic sign phenomena. There are many areas where analogue rules come into play, such as in the MEET examples, degree phenomena, and in general, all those cases presented where visual analogues are involved. The rules for describing these phenomena are matching rules that take the form of (27):

(27)   Map the points of S onto the points of C. N.B.: S represents some continuous property of the visual representation, C some continuous aspect of the visual code.

It should be noted that these rules do not require the use of any sort of markings in order to account for the behavior of the visual code. They only need to refer to some property of the visual representation. For instance, for the MEET phenomena, the rule might refer to the trajectory of the *G*-MARKERs by referring to the set of points that comprise that trajectory. (It is in this sense that I meant earlier that it may be necessary to refer to properties of the visual image or scene.) Of course, not all points will be relevant; only certain ones will play a part: for example, in (4) and (5), only the beginning and end points. The rest of the points in the code representation could be predicted by a set of redundancy rules or some principles that govern the proper construction of analogues corresponding to visual phenomena. These analogue rules then need some corollary rules or principles that function as redundancy rules, or can be referred to by redundancy rules.

The aspect of the model that includes these principles is a set of analogue formation principles that take the form of general statements in the grammar and tell us how to modify the visual code in representing some analogue rule mapping. A good example comes from Friedman (1975b) where she discusses the indexical reference to location far from the signer.

> When an index for a locative referent refers to the location of a previously indexed and established nominal referent, it is made in the general direction of the nominal referent (i.e., RIGHT, LEFT), but with the superimposition of the feature UP on the index . . . The relative distance of a locative referent from the signer in the real world is indicated by the relative angle of the extended finger in relation to the ground. The greater the angle of the hand in relation to the ground (up to but not including 90°), the higher the arm is raised, and the greater the length of the extension of the arm, the further the distance of the locative referent is from the signer. [p. 949]

As I have shown above, we can not refer to some *n*-ary feature UP in order to properly account for the facts in Friedman's description. The continuum of distance is mapped onto the continuum of hand angle, arm extension, and height. This is the content of an analogue rule, but we must know how the code continuum is to be manipulated in order to map the continuum of distance onto it. Analogue formation principles in the form of (28) will give the proper formal relationship between the coded feature and its coded representation.

(28)   Feature x is represented by code feature y $(y_1, y_2, \ldots y_n)$ (in the context of feature z).

The analogue rule and analogue formational principle relevant to the location index under discussion are given in (29) and (30), respectively.

(29)   Map the points of distance onto the points of a comples function of hand angle, arm extension, and height.

(30) The feature of greater/lesser distance is represented by a complex function of greater/lesser angle of hand from the ground (up to but not including 90°), and greater/lesser extension of the arm from the body, and greater/lesser height of the hand and arm from the ground in punctually descriptive signs.

I do not deal here specifically with inferential processes or with intermorphemic syntactic processes. I feel that the inferential processes will fall out of the semantic model. As explained above, the semantic model is an abstract representation of a world or set of worlds in terms of what holds true in those worlds. We will be allowed to infer the truth value of some semantic notions, for instance *CAUSE*, if a certain truth definitional formula is met. The semantic model should be universal, language-independent, for a subset of units which are abstract semantic primitives, such as case relationships, abstract relational predicates such as *CAUSE, INCHOATE, EXIST*, and so forth; presumably, the semantic model for any particular language will eventually reduce the semantic to these elements. As for syntactic processes in general, they seem to be so intimately involved with the sort of notions outlined above that we must have a better understanding of particular analogue rules and formational principles before we can approach the regular syntactic processes of ASL. These rules and principles seem to substitute for the more familiar syntactic and morphological rules in many cases, making it necessary to investigate the boundaries of the domain of each.

The phenomena I have discussed here all are basically iconic. They represent the areas where ASL loses part of its arbitrariness, in the sense that most linguists have come to understand that term. The relationship between arbitrariness and iconicity, however, is quite confusing. If it were the case that ASL conveyed meaning purely in terms of nonarbitrary images, then there would be no sense in which ASL is learned. But of course this is not the case, and neither do I mean to imply that ASL is nonarbitrary by claiming that it is iconic. The nature of an icon lies in its conventionality; an icon is an image created in a fixed and conventional style. It resembles its denotation, but its import, its meaning, is not purely a function of that similarity; it is dictated by convention. Once a representation of the referent has some specifiable similarity to that referent, there is a very important effect. Consider the following discussion of three design features which Hockett (1966) posited for language.

2.7 Semanticity. Linguistic signals function in correlating and organizing the life of a community because there are associative ties between signal elements and features in the world; in short, some linguistic forms have denotations.

The distension of roe of the belly of the female stickleback is part of an effective signal, but does not 'stand for' something else.

2.8 Arbitrariness. The relation between a meaningful element in language and its denotation is independent of any physical or geometrical resemblance between the two.

Or, as we say, the semantic relation is arbitrary rather than iconic. There are marginal exceptions, including traces of onomatopoeia. In bee-dancing, the way in which the direction toward the target is mapped into a direction of dancing is iconic. The relation between a landscape painting and a landscape is iconic; the relation between the word landscape and a landscape is arbitrary.

2.9   Discreteness. The possible messages in any language constitute a discrete repertory rather than a continuous one.

Any utterance in a language must differ from any other utterance of the same length by at least a whole phonological feature. Utterances cannot be indefinitely similar to one another. Bee dances can be: the repertory of possible dances constitutes a twofold continuum.

In a continuous semantic system (one with property 2.7, but with the converse of 2.9), the semantics must be iconic rather than arbitrary. But in a discrete semantic system there is no necessary implication as to iconicity or arbitrariness; therefore, for language, 2.8 is independent of 2.7 and 2.9. [pp. 10–11]

The important point of Hockett's discussion is that continuity (of semantic system) implies iconicity (of representation) but iconicity does not imply continuity. In the light of the facts described here, this implies a crucial difference between language in the visual modality and auditory modality. Because vocal language is discrete (that is, displays design feature 2.9), it must have a semantic system which is discrete. On the other hand, the real world is full of continuous phenomena (size, loudness, color, movement, intensity, and so on). There must be, then, a mediating system of coding between the real world (or any visual world) and the language coding system; the world must be reduced to a discrete semantic repertory in order to be referred to by the language code. In those areas where ASL is both iconic and continuous in its code representations, there is no such implication of an intervening semantic coding between the visual world and the code representation of the world. In effect, ASL could have visual deep structures.

I have presented various classes of phenomena which suggest that visual imagery is crucial to a proper understanding of ASL. I have also suggested the features of a model seemingly necessary to properly describe sign phenomena. But it is this last point, that sign could derive directly from visual representations, that argues most strongly for the incorporation of visual imagery into the grammar of sign.

NOTES

1.   I am using English glosses of individual signs. For ease of understanding and reconstruction of the signed event, I also provide a written description as well as the glosses. The term marker is used here in the sense of an anaphoric marker as described in Mandel, and in Edge and Herrmann.

2. Actually, Friedman (1975b) has implicitly suggested an analysis of sign sentences where inferences about relationships are made from spatial properties of the sentence (rather than lexical properties). She claims that

> Particularly in respect to discourse concerning spatial relationships, sign language—articulated and perceived in the manual/visual modality—is unique. ASL makes use of the visible area in which articulation is made to convey spatial concepts, by maximizing the use of INDEX, movement and orientation to and from areas of space established for nomimal reference. [p. 958]

The key notion here is 'convey'. That is, there is no need to posit a distinc^t coding of spatial relationships; they can be coded by spatial analogue codings in the signing space. I have merely extended that analysis so that nonspatial relationships can also be conveyed by some sort of spatial analogues without being specifically or distinctly coded.

3. In fact, I was once cornered at a party by a deaf evangelist who proceeded to tell me the entire story of the old testament within the space of two hours. When he finally arrived at the story of Sodom and Gomorrah, he felt it necessary to describe the sexual practices found in the first twin cities. He did this by using the sign COPULATE with many repetitions, moving toward the right, and with an incredible (and interesting) sequence of rapid changes in orientation. This was the only interesting aspect of his entire monologue.

4. There is an interesting co-occurrence restriction in this sign. With movement only to the beginning point of the sign, it has the meaning 'child'. The sign can then reduplicate with a sideward movement to mean 'children'. But when there is upward movement from the beginning point so that, say, 'teenager' is signed, reduplication is blocked. That is, one cannot sign 'teenagers' by reduplication. Clearly the upward movement is iconic, and it would seem that the sideward reduplication is iconic. There may be a restriction on two iconic movements in the same sign.

5. In each of these signs, a difference in degree between any two tokens of the sign when compared necessarily implies a difference in degree of the coded factor (say, "bigness"). Thus, any points P and P' on the continuum of movement in BIG imply a degree D and D' in the coded factor, where $x'>x$. Furthermore, ignoring purely perceptual restrictions, which have no relevance to the formal nature of this coding device, for any pair P and P' mapped onto D and D', there is a P'' which is mapped onto a D'', where $x<x''<x'$. This is a very roundabout way of saying that "bigness" has a continuous degree factor that is represented by a continuous movement factor in the sign. We cannot state a rule which maps one particular P to a particular D; we must allow for some free mapping of a P to a D and then state that no P' such that $P<P'$ can be mapped onto a D' such that $D>D'$. This allows us to map one continuum onto another

continuum. This is very different from mapping the continuum of bigness onto **big** and **very big**. In the latter case, we freely define some P″ such that all P′s where P″< P′ get mapped onto D′ (**very big**) and all Ps such that P″>P get mapped onto D (**big**). Thus, no Ps are distinguishable in terms of D and no P′s are distinguishable in terms of D′. In the first case, we have a continuum of formally discernible messages coded by the continuum of points of D whereas in the latter we have a finite set (here a set of two members) of formally discernible messages coded by the two points of D. In the latter case we can write a rule which maps any particular P onto either D or D′; that rule will refer to some marking for the class of points that are included in **big** and some marking for the class of points that are included in **very big**.

VERBS AND THE DETERMINATION OF SUBJECT
IN AMERICAN SIGN LANGUAGE

VickiLee Edge and Leora Herrmann

0. Introduction

All languages must provide a means by which a speaker can unambiguously indicate the relationships among arguments in a given utterance or discourse. In the oral modality, this is generally accomplished through the determination of case. Languages have two ways of differentiating among cases: either through the use of a fixed word order and prepositional system or through the use of overt inflectional markers. Most languages use some combination of these. English, for example, combines a basic SVO word order with overtly marked accusative and nominative pronouns—he, him; I, me, they, them; etc. Deviations from the standard word order, the passive voice, for example, are indicated by the addition of surface morphemes.

The conclusion that languages have only two ways of indicating case, through fixed word order or case markings, is based on studies of oral languages. Our concern is whether or not this conclusion is supported through the study of ASL, and if not, how ASL accomplishes the task performed by fixed word order or case markings in oral languages.

It has not been claimed that ASL has inflectional case markings, and we have found no evidence to warrant such a claim. It has, however, been claimed that word order plays an important part in differentiating among cases in ASL. Fischer (1975) makes the following statement concerning ASL word order.

> The American Sign Language . . . has a basic word order of SVO. Other orders are allowed under the circumstances that (a) something is topicalized, (b) the subject and object are reversible, and/or (c) the signer uses space to indicate grammatical mechanisms. [p. 21]

In this paper we challenge the claim that word order is relied upon as a grammatical mechanism for differentiating among cases in ASL. We wish to argue that the manipulation of space to indicate cases is the primary grammatical mechanism employed in ASL, rather than simply an exceptional circumstance that allows orders other than SVO.

We will offer counterevidence to Fischer's claim of a basic SVO order, examine the nature of pronominal reference and verbs in ASL as they relate to the manipulation of space, present a method of analyzing ASL discourse that we call Listing, and discuss the ways in which this type of analysis can be used to disambiguate subject-verb relations. Finally, we will present two examples of entire discourses analyzed by this method.

1.   Counterevidence

In citing the use of space to indicate grammatical mechanisms as one of the circumstances under which orders other than SVO are allowed, Fischer is referring explicitly to the use of real or grammatically established referents, as opposed to true nominals, in signing verbs. She describes this use of space as follows:

> What verbs in ASL can do is, once the location of referents has been established, to move or orient the hands between them, thus indicating clearly and unambiguously the grammatical relations involved. [p. 16]

Viewing this circumstance as exceptional fails to account for an important feature of ASL discourse. Friedman (1976a) points out:

> ... it is the case that in discourse the locations of referents are almost always established prior to the occurrence of the verb... [p. 129]

Friedman's observation points out that it is important to use ASL discourse rather than isolated sentences as the corpus of data. She has further observed that elicitations of isolated sentences show a marked resemblance to English. Thus it appears that in ASL discourse the occurrence of true nominals, and thus an SVO order, is the exceptional circumstance and that the use of established locations for referents dominates (see section 2 for further discussion).

Fischer's discussion of the use of space is limited also, in that it acutally describes only one type of verb in ASL: multidirectional verbs. Using Fillmore's concepts of Source and Goal (Fillmore, 1968), Friedman (1975b) has described multidirectional verbs as follows:

> Each verb has a core meaning and corresponding physical structure consisting of (a) hand configuration and (b) place of articulation. The movement and the orientation of each verb in surface structure is determined by the location (in space), real or grammatically established, of the source and the goal of the action. [p. 955]

For example, GIVE consists of a hand configuration in which the tips of the fingers (including the thumb) come together with the palm facing up, and a place of articulation in neutral space. The signer will move his hand from the location of the source (the person giving) to the location of the goal (the person receiving). 'I give you' would thus be signed with the signer's hand moving away from his chest area toward the addressee. 'You give me' would be signed with the signer's hand moving away from the addressee's location toward his own body. The flexibility of the movement of multidirectional verbs allows the signer to employ space to indicate grammatical relationships unambiguously, without relying on an SVO word order. This fact is accounted for by Fischer's description of the circumstances under which orders other than SVO are allowed.

Not all verbs in ASL have this flexibility of movement. For example, SUR-PRISE is signed by holding both hands at the sides of the eyes and flicking the index fingers up from a fist (accompanied by a surprised facial expression), and LOVE is signed by folding the arms over the chest with fists in a self-hug. As all signs do, these verbs have some sort of movement, yet they cannot move off the body nor manifest directional movement. For the time being we will refer to these verbs as non-multidirectional. Fischer's claim concerning word order in ASL predicts that sequences containing non-multidirectional verbs and reversible arguments will be signed in SVO order.

When we began our study, our principle focus was testing this prediction and if found incorrect, discovering the method of disambiguation for non-multidirectional verbs occurring with reversible arguments. Because we were looking at a grammatical feature that is definitely a feature of English, we had to devise elicitation procedures that would rule out an English bias to our data (see below for further discussion of biases).

Rather than give our informant English sentences to sign, we either acted out sequences of events and asked him to describe what happened using a set of specified verbs, gave him a set of verbs and asked him to make up a story using them or, in four cases, wrote a brief outline of a sequence of events and asked him to sign a description of what happened using a specified set of verbs. It should be noted that all the written outlines were based on actual sequences of events in which our informant had participated, and thus functioned as reminders of those events rather than as English sentences to be signed.

The data corpus we elicited constituted discourse rather than isolated sentences and was not based on English input. We have already discussed the importance of the first fact and will return to it again in sections 2 and 3. The importance of the second fact has been discussed by Friedman (1975b), who has pointed out that ASL is one extreme on a visual language continuum ranging from Signed English or another visual code for English to ASL. Which "language" a signer uses is determined by the sociological and sociolinguistic circumstances of the discourse situation. Thus, data can be biased due to the signer's linguistic competence in English and his choice to use one of the visual codes for English, or due to elicitation procedures based on English. Our informant was trained to control the first factor, and we elicited in such a way as to control for the second factor. The most important feature of our corpus is that it is as true a reflection of ASL as is possible to obtain given that our informant is linguistically competent in English and that it is composed of elicited data.

The first non-multidirectional verbs we looked at were ANGER, BOTHER, FRIGHTEN, OBEY, and SURPRISE. We approached these verbs with the assumption that they might be used as transitive verbs appearing on the surface as two-place predicates, as is often the case in English. We expected, for example, to find something analogous to 'Alice frightened Donald' appearing in ASL. We found, however, that this is not the case. With the exception of BOTHER (see section 3), they appeared as one-place predicates in discourses where indexing and body movement[1] were used to differentiate between two people interacting.

Upon further investigation we found that ANGER, EMBARRASS, FEEL, FRIGHTEN, LOVE, OBEY, RELIEVE, SICK-OF, and SURPRISE all appear as one-place surface predicates anchored to the experiencer (see section 3 for a discussion of anchoring).

(1) Vicki established on right.[2]
    Leora established on left.

⌈   body right and looks left   body center
|
⌊   SURPRISE

⌈   body moves side to side
|
⌊   TALK (side to side)

Vicki sees Leora and is surprised to see her. Vicki and Leora talk to each other.

(2) Child established on right and down.
    Mother established on left and up.

⌈   body slightly right
|
⌊   GIRL   HIDE jumps out (toward left)[3]

⌈   body center   body left
|
⌊   INDEX (to left and up)   FRIGHTEN

⌈   jumps back in fright body left   angry expression
|
⌊   ANGER GO (from right to left)

⌈   body right   head faces up and left
|
⌊   CHILD   looks at mother[4]   OBEY GO (right to left)

A child hides under something and jumps out at her mother. The mother is frightened. She is angry and tells the child to leave. The child obeys and leaves.

(3) Tom established on right.
Cathy and Leora established on left.
Signer established as himself in center.

$$\left[\quad \text{MARKER}^5 \text{ (representing Tom) (moves from right to signer's face)}\right.$$

$$\left[\begin{array}{l} \text{head turns away from marker} \\ \qquad\qquad\qquad \text{ME SICK-OF ME TALK (to left)} \end{array}\right.$$

Tom came up to me. I turned away because I was sick of him. I talked with Cathy and Leora.

These examples are not isolated cases, but reflect the way the preceding verbs systematically appear. Thus, one cannot sign:

(4) ME FRIGHTEN

and mean 'I frightened someone'. The only meaning possible is 'I am frightened'.

Further evidence for this comes from our very first elicitation in which we asked our informant to sign only the verbs and names of the people involved in a series of actions. In describing a situation in which Leora angered Vicki, he signed:

(5) VICKI ANGER LEORA

He signed first the experiencer (Vicki), then the verb and then the cause of the anger (Leora). Similarly he signed:

(6) VICKI SURPRISE VICKI

to describe a situation in which Leora surprised Vicki. The significance of these examples is that in a situation where we forced our informant to use true nominals and word order to disambiguate, we got an NVN order in which the verbs mentioned above appeared as surface one-place predicates anchored to the experiencer.

The conclusion to draw from the data presented thus far is that none of these verbs (ANGER, EMBARRASS, FEEL, FRIGHTEN, LOVE, OBEY, RELIEVE, SICK-OF, and SURPRISE) function as surface transitive verbs in ASL. When they appear in NVN sequences, the sequences are not interpreted as SVO.

When it is taken into consideration that 1) true nominals infrequently occur, and locations for referents are almost always established in discourse; 2) not all verbs have the freedom of movement that multidirectional verbs have; and 3) there is at least one class of verbs for which neither the directional use of space to indicate grammatical mechanisms nor an SVO order apply, we are forced to the conclusion that the reliance on word order applies to at best a marginal part of ASL. The task before us is to discover and describe the mechanisms by which ASL indicates who is being talked about and what his relationship is to other arguments of a given verb. In the following sections we attempt to describe these mechanisms.

2. Pronominal Reference

In the following discussion we will analyze only pronominal reference for people. It should be noted, however, that pronominal reference for objects, time, and locations can be made in much the same way, employing the same basic principles.[6] The systems for pronominal reference are based on representation and/or the manipulation of space. An analysis of the components comprising pronominal reference will make this point clearer.

We define **proforms** as those entities that represent referents. These include locations in space that are established as the hypothetical locations of referents, and markers which are understood or explicitly labeled to take on the identity of referents.[7] Markers have two forms: the signer's hand(s) (articulated markers) or the signer's body (body markers).[8] We have defined proforms very narrowly and explicitly as either locations in space or markers. There are a variety of ways in which proforms can be referred to and employed in ASL discourse.

Indexing is one form of pronominal reference that can be accomplished by pointing to a proform (either a marker or a location) or to a person who is present at the time of the discourse. Indexing is also a means by which a proform can be established. Thus a signer can point to a marker or location in space while simultaneously signing a nominal or name;[9] from then on in a given discourse that proform is understood to represent the referent indicated by the nominal or name. The sole purpose of indexing is to establish a proform or make pronominal reference. For this reason we refer to indexing as overt pronominal reference.

Body movement is an interesting and complex form of pronominal reference in that it consists of both types of proforms. Body movement can be used to establish the location of referents. Thus, for example, the signer can turn his body to face left and sign a nominal or name in that position; from then on that location (whether occupied by the signer or not) is understood to represent the referent indicated by the name or nominal. In addition, the signer's body is used as a marker, as it is understood that the signer assumes the identity of the referent for that location when he occupies that location. This is true whether the location was established as a proform through body movement or indexing. Thus, whenever a signer assumes an established location, he is both making pronominal reference to a referent and assuming the identity of the referent.

We distinguish between the act of moving the body into a location which is the act of pronominal reference and remaining in the location that then becomes a means of employing the proform (see section 3). Thus, body movement is a means of making overt pronominal reference, though, as opposed to indexing, this is not its only function.

Pronominal reference in ASL has two basic components: proforms and the mechanisms for making reference to a proform or a referent actually present. Proforms take two forms: either locations in space or markers. As discussed thus far, there are two mechanisms for making overt pronominal reference: indexing and movement into a local proform. None of these forms and mechanisms involve lexical items, but rather involve spatial representation. Rather than being lexical items, proforms consist of at most one of the four formational parameters of which ASL signs are composed. Locations consist of a place of articulation and markers consist of a hand configuration (articulated marker) or a place of articulation (body marker). Because proforms consist of only one formational parameter they can be incorporated into other signs; the proform becomes one of the parameters of the sign while maintaining its function of representing a referent (examples of this will be given in the following section). It is through the incorporation of proforms into signs that proforms are employed rather than simply referred to in signing. Through the employment of proforms, pronominal reference is made, however it is not an overt pronominal reference.

This system is an integral part of ASL discourse. It is not found, however, in elicitations of isolated sentences. When examining the nature of pronominal reference in ASL it is necessary to use discourse as a corpus of data.

3.   Verbs

As indicated in section 1 of this paper, all verbs in ASL cannot be described by a single set of features. In this section we will offer a preliminary classification of verbs in ASL based on the verbs examined. Since a means for classifying verbs has not been our primary focus, the classification system we propose is in no way exhaustive nor does it include all types of ASL verbs, but it is intended as an example of the type of analysis we see as crucial to an understanding of the grammatical mechanisms in ASL.

The following classes are based on the spatial characteristics of ASL verbs: multidirectional, multiorientational, and bodily anchored.

Multidirectional verbs have been described in section 1 of this paper. They are characterized by directional movement along an approximate horizontal plane in neutral space. As indicated, multidirectional verbs always move from the location (either a proform location, a marker, or an actual person) of the source to the location of the goal; that is, the movement of the verbs traces a path between source and goal. Furthermore, there is something which actually traces the path: an object for GIVE and LEND/BORROW, information for TEACH and TELL, and people for MEET and FOLLOW.

Another way of analyzing these verbs is that they consist of a marker(s) and a movement which have specific semantic features associated with them. As such, the marker represents the entity tracing the path defined by the movement of the verb. The movement of multidirectional verbs establishes a spatial beginning and ending point of action, which denote the semantic concepts of source and goal. For example, GIVE can be viewed as a marker (in this case a proform for an object) that represents the thing being given (the patient) moving from the person giving (the source) to the person receiving (the goal).

Semantically, these verbs incorporate the notion of something or someone (patient) being transferred from one person or place (source) to another (goal). Formationally and spatially they incorporate source, goal, patient, and path of transference. The phonological design of these verbs allows the optimal manipulation of space to visually depict the notion of transference.

Friedman (1976a) has argued that this class of verbs is defined by the semantic distinction of action versus nonaction (non-multidirectional verbs). However, this class includes seemingly nonaction verbs such as TELL and TEACH which are characterized by the same syntactic and formational features as other verbs in the class which are clearly action verbs (GIVE, MEET, BRING/TAKE, and so on). It seems to us that the semantic feature of action is actually a subclass of the semantic feature of transference. Action entails movement through space with a spatial beginning and ending point of action. As such, action can be viewed as transference from one spatial location to another.

That these verbs incorporate source, goal, and patient is borne out by the fact that none of these arguments need overtly appear. A result of this is that these verbs are not syntactically anchored[10] to either source or goal. The most extreme example of this is a sequence in which the signer signs a verb moving between two previously established locations in neutral space (proforms) without indexing either location. Examples provided in the data we looked at were cases in which a multidirectional verb was signed while the signer assumed the goal's location, as in

(7) ⎡ body right[11]

   MOTHER   GRAB (from left to right) GIRL

   ⎣ INDEX (to right) GRAB   CHILD (on left)

   The mother grabs the child.

cases in which a multidirectional verb was signed while the signer assumed the source's location, as in,

(8) Leora established on right.
    Vicki established on left.

   ⎡ body left

   ⎣   GIVE (from body to right) MONEY

   Vicki gives Leora money.

cases in which the goal's name appears first, as in,

(9) ⎡ ASA LEND/BORROW (from left to right) LYNN

　　 ⎣　　　　　　　　　　　　　　　　　　INDEX (to left)

Asa borrows money from Lynn.

cases in which the goal's name is signed while the verb is signed, as in,

(10) Lynn established on left.
　　　Signer established as himself.

　　⎡ LYNN (name held at chest)

　　⎣　　　GIVE (moves from body to left)

I give it to Lynn.

We also found cases in which the source's name preceded the verb, in which an index to the source was held while the verb was signed, and cases in which an index to the goal was held while the verb was signed.

These cases demonstrate free syntactic anchoring for multidirectional verbs. They also provide examples of the ways in which proforms can be employed. Markers or locations can be used as the beginning or ending point of the verb's movement (place of articulation) and markers can be used as the verb's hand configuration, without overtly referring to the proforms in either case. When this is the case, pronominal reference is made through incorporation of proforms into the verb.

Bodily anchored verbs are characterized by nondirectional movement or articulation along an approximate vertical plane directly in front of the signer's body, and in some cases, including the body. The verbs we looked at which fall into this class are the verbs we discussed in section 1 (with the exception of BOTHER, see below): ANGER, EMBARRASS, FEEL, FRIGHTEN, LOVE, OBEY, RELIEVE, SICK-OF, and SURPRISE (OBEY is exceptional and will be discussed later). These verbs are articulated on or at the body; their movements cannot be reversed; and the movements are not directional as far as indicating arguments is concerned. As pointed out in section 1, these verbs appear as one-place predicates and do not function as surface transitives. Semantically these verbs denote the experiencing of an internal state of being or feeling.

The verbs in question can be analyzed along the same lines as the analysis proposed for multidirectional verbs. They consist of a marker (the signer's body, which is the place of articulation) for a person and a combination of hand configuration and movement which describes an experience (state of being). Some verbs visually describe the experience they denote more directly than others. For example, RELIEVE is signed by holding the arms at the sides of the body and then moving the forearms, one above the other, from the upper chest to the abdomen across the front of the body. In addition, almost all of these verbs are accompanied by an appropriate facial and bodily expression, which is further indication that the signer's body is functioning as a marker. Because these verbs are always articulated on or at the body, they formationally incorporate the experiencer in addition to the experience. The phonological design of these verbs allows optimal manipulation of space to visually depict their semantic content.

Not surprisingly, the form of pronominal reference most often used in conjunction with bodily anchored verbs is body movement. It is this form of reference that establishes both a location and a marker in the form of the signer's body. This second proform can then be incorporated into the verbs of this class as their place of articulation.

Bodily anchored verbs are similar to multidirectional verbs in that they both semantically, spatially, and formationally incorporate the arguments associated with the verbs (the experiencer for bodily anchored verbs; source, goal, and patient for multidirectional verbs). Even though this incorporation is a feature of both classes, bodily anchored verbs are syntactically anchored (multidirectional verbs are not) to the experiencer and this argument must appear overtly. This fact does not constitute counterevidence to the claim that the experiencer is incorporated into the verbs of this class, but rather it is the result of the formational properties of these verbs and the means by which the argument is syntactically incorporated into the verbs. Bodily anchored verbs are articulated on or at the body and the body functions as a marker for the experiencer. If the signer has moved into an established location for a referent, the signer has made overt pronominal reference to the referent and has established his own body as a marker for the referent. When he signs a bodily anchored verb in that location, the referent will be understood to be the experiencer. If the signer signs the verb in his natural signing position, the signer will be understood to be the experiencer and his body is viewed as a marker for himself, for first person is the unmarked form and no overt pronominal reference need be made. Therefore, when the signer is signing from his natural signing position and this location has not been established as the location for any other referent, he must either index an established location or use a nominal for the referent if he wishes to communicate that someone other than himself is the experiencer of a bodily anchored verb. Consequently, whenever body movement is not used as a means of pronominal reference, the signer must indicate the experiencer (other than first person) either through indexical reference or the use of a nominal sign.

As already mentioned, OBEY is exceptional in that it has two places of articulation, one of which is at the body and the other in neutral space. It is not exceptional, however, in that the movement between the places of articulation is not directional and cannot be reversed, and it demonstrates the same syntactic anchoring of the other bodily anchored verbs. The question arises as to whether or not OBEY denotes an internal experience. It is possible that OBEY denotes a willingness or decision to obey and that the phonological design denotes that this decision entails some kind of action. On the other hand, OBEY may belong to an entirely different class. The answers to these questions can only be found by looking at the ways in which OBEY is used and at other verbs in ASL that may have similar characteristics.

The final class of verbs we will describe is multiorientational verbs. It includes four verbs that we examined: BOTHER, PITY, QUESTION, and TEASE. These verbs are characterized by directional orientation along an approximate horizontal plane at a static point in neutral space. Each of these verbs has a core meaning, hand configuration, movement, and place or articulation. Their orientation establishes the relationship between arguments in a way analogous to the movement of multidirectional verbs. The location defined by the direction of orientation of the backside of the hands always represents one argument and the location defined by the direction of orientation of the front of the hands always represents the other argument.

This class is the most difficult to characterize semantically because we have very little data in which its members are used. It is clear that these verbs are two-place predicates, which is a feature that separates this class from the other two discussed earlier (multidirectional verbs being three-place, bodily anchored verbs being one-place). Further it is clear that the argument represented by the location behind the hands is always that of the agent of the verb. And it appears that the second argument is the patient as it is the one being acted upon; i.e., the one being bothered, pitied, questioned, or teased.

As with the two classes previously discussed, the arguments of this class are incorporated into the verb. This class differs, however, in that incorporation of proforms takes place within the parameter of orientation rather than place of articulation or hand configuration. The arguments are defined within the parameter of orientation for each multiorientational verb. Local proforms and body markers can be incorporated into the verbs by orienting the verb between the proforms so that the locations of the proforms correspond to the locations of the arguments as defined for each verb through its orientation.

We do not have enough data to determine whether or not these verbs are syntactically anchored, but suspect that they are either similar to multidirectional verbs and are not anchored, or are anchored to the agent.

Finally, there is a dangerous pitfall into which those who attempt to semantically classify ASL verbs can easily fall: imposing the semantic content of the English glosses used for signs on the signs themselves. Glosses are only translations or labels and may not correspond exactly to the meanings of signs in ASL. To determine what something means in an oral language, one must look at the way it is used by native speakers of the language and the syntactic environment in which it appears. The same is true for ASL, but in addition, one must examine the phonological structure of a sign. Because ASL is a visual language, it can use the modality within which it is used to communicate to represent semantic notions somewhat more directly. As non-native speakers of ASL we must be careful to use a sign only in ways we have seen illustrated, to preserve the syntactic environment in which it appears, and to examine the visual representation it phonologically creates in order to determine its meaning and thus its semantic classification. We will learn nothing about ASL by imposing the semantic content of our glosses upon the signs they label.

In this section and in the preceding we have demonstrated that the system of pronominal reference is spatially based and that verbs are formed in such a way as to incorporate proforms and thus spatially establish grammatical relationships. Once again we wish to point out that proforms, especially locations, are almost always established at the beginning of discourse. Thus given the nature of pronominal reference and verbs in ASL, the signer almost always has the option of using space to indicate grammatical mechanisms. There is powerful motivation in ASL to use this option, which is based upon incorporation of spatially defined proforms. As Bellugi and Fischer (1972) have demonstrated, the fact that a sign takes longer to produce than a spoken word creates the motivation for using communication time efficiently by packing a great deal of information into a single sign. They have pointed out and discussed incorporation as one of the ways that this can be accomplished. It seems clear to us that rather than being an exceptional circumstance, the use of space is a primary feature of ASL grammar.

4. Listing

We have described proforms, overt pronominal reference, pronominal reference through proform incorporation, and the forms of ASL verbs. We know the identity of the arguments for three classes of verbs: bodily anchored verbs are experiencer anchored, multidirectional verbs move the patient from source to goal, and multiorientational verbs are oriented between agent and patient. The task before us now is to describe how the three types function together in discourse to indicate which referent is the experiencer, source, goal, patient, or agent.

ASL is structured in a way that we analyze as **lists**. This structure provides us with knowledge of which referent is being discussed; that is, the subject. We will later give six specific types of lists with examples of each. At this point, however, we will discuss listing in general terms. It is easiest to approach listing by looking at a simple description of the activities of two people. Take, for example, the following sequence:

(11) LEORA SIT VICKI SIT READ BOOK

In this sequence, Leora and Vicki are explicity named and their names followed by descriptions of their activities. Thus, we can rewrite the sequence in terms of two lists each headed by one person's name:

(12) LEORA: SIT
      VICKI: SIT
              READ BOOK

This list is headed by an overtly signed name; that is, the signer gives us the subject's name following it with a set of signs. We will later discuss ways of indicating the subject without explicitly naming him or her—each of these ways being different mechanisms for heading a list. We will see that these other ways also operate by first giving the subject, followed by the signs to be connected with that subject, or by relying on context to disambiguate, and either not mentioning the subject altogether or giving us the identity of the subject only after the list of verbs has begun.

Without going into detail now, we would like to introduce a second way of heading a list, namely by indexing a real world referent. As described by Friedman (1975b), such indexing takes precedence over grammatical indexing (indexing a proform). The purpose of mentioning real world indexing now is to allow us to cite, as an example, an entire story in transcription and then show how it can be analyzed into lists. The indexes found in this story serve the same function as the overtly mentioned names.

First, let us look at the transcription of this story. It is an account of an event that we staged for our informant and then asked him to describe.

(13) [ONE TIME MY CLASS I TEACH SIGN CLASS

[INDEX (to actual class) STUDY READ BOOK STUDY VICKI

[ENTER gestures guns with extended index fingers pointed at class

[INDEX (to actual class) FRIGHTEN

[gesture hands-up INDEX (to actual class)

[glazed facial expression
  SPECIAL FILM PERSON LOOK SLEEP DREAM

One time my class. . .I teach a sign class. . .was studying. They were reading their books when Vicki entered and pointed two guns at them. The class was frightened. They put their hands up. Everyone did, except the film person who gazed into space daydreaming.

This story can be analyzed as an introduction and four lists:

(14) introduction[12]: ONE TIME MY CLASS I: TEACH SIGN CLASS

  class, indexed: STUDY
         READ BOOK
         STUDY

  VICKI, named: ENTER
         points gun at class

  class, indexed: FRIGHTEN
         put hands up

SPECIAL FILM PERSON, named: LOOK
                               SLEEP
                               DREAM

Thus an entire sequence can be broken down into a series of lists. The verbs within each of these lists carry within their meanings an indication of what type of argument the head of that list is.

When analyzing a discourse into lists, one must keep in mind the following general principle:

> The last mentioned or otherwise indicated grammatical subject remains subject unless the signer indicates otherwise.

As with all rules, this one has exceptions and these will be discussed later, but for our present discussion, we can look at the rule as binding. We can see the importance of this principle in the following sequence:

(15) LEORA STAND BORED WALK MEET FRIEND HI

   GIVE BOOK LAUGH

If we apply our principle to this transcript, we can rewrite (15) as the following list:

(16)   LEORA: STAND
                BORED
                WALK
                MEET FRIEND
                HI
                GIVE BOOK
                LAUGH

If we do not apply our principle, we might conclude falsely that the friend laughed rather than that Leora laughed. Our means of determining that FRIEND does not begin a new list will be discussed later.

Our claim is that all ASL descriptions of people and their actions or attributes will take the form of lists. These lists can be headed in a number of different ways. Each of the heading mechanisms uses space in order to create a proform for reference to an entity. As we will see, names are thrown in in order to identify these proforms. Following is a list of all the ways we have isolated that a signer can head a list. Brief descriptions and one example of each method are given.

A. NAMING

As a list heading device (as opposed to a device used to clarify the identity of an already established heading) naming is used when the signer does not employ any form of pronominal reference and occupies his natural signing position (center). In this circumstance, when the signer signs a name, he indicates that he is not discussing himself and that the following signs are not to be associated with him. In doing so, he establishes his body as a body marker for the referent and establishes this proform as the heading of the following list of signs.

Example:

LEORA HUNGRY VICKI STAY[13]

Leora's hungry. Vicki says "gotcha".

Lists:

> *LEORA*, naming: HUNGRY
>
> *VICKI*, naming: STAY

B. MARKING

This form of heading employs an articulated marker (not a body marker). A marker is most often introduced while depicting the movement of a referent. If the identity of the referent represented by the marker has not been indicated, this is done and then the verbs to be associated with the referent are signed. For our purposes we break down the marker's use to represent a referent and its use to represent the movement of the referent.

Example:

⌈ INDEX (to signer) LOOK HI
⌊

⌈ LYNN (name held at chest)   SMILE
⌊   MARKER (moves from left to center)

⌈ MARKER (moves from left to center) DANCE SECRET DANCE
⌊

I looked, and seeing Lynn, said "hi" to her. She came up to me smiling. She was dancing and had a secret.

Lists:

> *me*, real-world index: LOOK
>   HI LYNN
>
> *LYNN*, marking: movement from left to signer
>   SMILE

(*Lynn*, marking): movement from left to signer
          DANCE
          SECRET
          DANCE

C. GRAMMATICAL INDEXING

As previously described, a signer may point to a location in space in order to establish and/or refer to a local proform for a person. As described by Friedman (1975b) this system is conventionalized and bears no relationship to the real world locations of the referents. The system which Friedman describes involves indexing to the left, upper left, right, and upper right of the signer. In addition we include in this class indexing to markers and indexing to *3*-markers.[14] A list can be headed by such grammatical indexing when the index is followed by a set of verbs.

Example:

The *3*-marker has been established as representing three children.

$$\begin{bmatrix} 3 & \text{EMBARRASS} \\ \text{INDEX (to finger no. 2)} \end{bmatrix}$$
The center child was embarrassed.

Lists:

    center child, grammatical index: EMBARRASS

D. REAL-WORLD INDEXING

In addition to the above type of indexing, a signer may point to a real-world entity in order to refer to it. Thus the signer is locating the actual spatial location of the topic of discussion. Such indexing can be followed by a set of verbs which will then be understood as referring to the entity previously pointed to.

Example:

INDEX (to class) STUDY READ BOOK STUDY VICKI ENTER
The class was studying and reading their books when Vicki entered.

Lists:

    class, real-world index: STUDY
                              READ BOOK
                              STUDY

VICKI, naming: ENTER

E. BODY MOVEMENT

Body movement has been described in section 2. It is a conventionalized system in which two local proforms are usually established in any given discourse, although signers claim they can establish three. We will use the term body position to refer to a local proform (and the body marker when that location is occupied by the signer) when body movement is used in a discourse. As pointed out above, the signer also establishes a body marker for a referent when he moves into a body position. Within this system, the use of a body marker differs from its usage in conjunction with naming. The possibility of confusion between first and third person reference always exists when the signer is using naming because he is signing from his natural signing position. Body movement, however, is a conventionalized system and there is no confusion possible between first and third person reference, so the signer need not constantly rename the proform. To establish the proforms (both local and body marker) the signer moves his body into a location (facing left, for example) and assigns an identity to the proform. From that point on, unless the position is renamed with a new nominal, movement into that position indicates that a list is beginning and that the referent represented by the position is the head of that list.

Example:

Vicki established on left.
Leora established on right.

⌈ body left   questioning facial expression   body right
⌊   LEND/BORROW

⌈   body left
⌊ GIVE (to left)   TAKE (from right)

Vicki asks to borrow (some money). Leora gives it to her and she takes it.

Lists:

   Vicki, body movement: LEND/BORROW ?

   Leora, body movement: GIVE (to Vicki)

   Vicki, body movement: TAKE (from Leora)

F.   HEADLESS LISTS[15]

A headless list is a series of verbs which are not explicitly labeled (either through overt pronominal reference or the employment of a nominal) as belonging to a given referent. They can be headless for one of the following reasons:

(1)   context indicates who is doing what
(2)   the first person unmarked form is used
(3)   the verb has directional movement or orientation that clearly indicates its subject

Example of (1):

[LEORA SIT VICKI SIT READ BOOK TIME

[
        FOLLOW (to left)

  MARKER (to left) ----------------------------

Leora is sitting. Vicki is sitting and reading a book. She looks at the time and leaves. Leora follows.

Lists:

   LEORA, naming: SIT

   VICKI, naming: SIT
                       READ BOOK
                       TIME
                       leaves (MARKER to left)

   Leora, headless (1):   FOLLOW

Example of (2):

[TIRED DEPRESSED

I'm tired and depressed.

Lists:

   me, headless (2):   TIRED
                          DEPRESSED

Example of (3):

Lynn established on left.
Signer established as himself.

⌈ body center

FINISH GRAB (from center to extended left)
⌊

I thought the whole matter was finished, but she grabbed it from me.

Lists:

me, body movement: FINISH[16]

Lynn, headless (3): GRAB

We have described six heading mechanisms all of which establish and/or employ a spatial proform(s). Naming indicates that the signer is temporarily establishing his body as the proform for a referent and that this proform heads the following list. Marking indicates that the articulated marker used to represent the movement of a referent heads the following list. Grammatical indexing indicates that the proform indexed heads the following list. Body movement indicates that the body marker representing the referent associated with a given location heads the following list. The head of a headless list is indicated through context, unmarked first person reference, or the directional movement or orientation of a given verb.

These heading mechanisms correspond to the types of reference described in section 2. Naming involves reference through the use of a nominal. Body movement, grammatical and real-world indexing involve overt pronominal reference. Headless lists involve unmarked pronominal reference or pronominal reference through incorporation. Marking also involves pronominal reference through incorporation due to the double function of articulated markers of representing a referent and representing the movement through space of the referent.

The system outlined thus far is not as simple and neat as it appears. There is a complex interplay between the types of pronominal reference, the functions and relative salience of the various proforms, and the characteristics of the various classes of verbs. In the remainder of this section we will use examples from the data we have examined to describe and clarify this interplay.

The heading mechanisms just described may be used in conjunction with one another. For example, a nominal and an index are used to indicate that the signer is referring to the child when he signs OBEY in (17):

(17) Mother established on left.
       Child established as down.

⌈   looks up and left

⌊ INDEX (down) CHILD   OBEY

The child obeys her mother.

Lists:

CHILD, index, naming: OBEY

In our data we find no instances of heading by grammatical indexing to a body position not occupied by the signer that is not immediately followed by a body movement into that position. This occurs, for example, in (18) where the mother has been established on the right and up, and the child on the left and down:

(18) ⎡   body left
     ⎢ GIRL   STUBBORN   hits at mother's location
     ⎣ INDEX (down)

The girl is stubborn and hits at her mother.

Lists:

GIRL, naming, index: STUBBORN

(**girl**, body movement): hits at mother

This makes sense if looked at in the following manner. If the signer remains in a body position and indexes another body position as in the hypothetical sequence:

(19) ⎡ body left
     ⎣   INDEX (to right) SURPRISE

we would most likely interpret the index as indicating the source of the surprising rather than the experiencer of SURPRISE. In other words (19) means not that the right referent is surprised, but rather that the left referent is surprised and the right referent is somehow related to the fact that the left referent is surprised. Similarly, in a discourse in which body movement is not being used, a sequence like (20)

(20) ⎡ body center   ANGER
     ⎣   INDEX (to left)

could be interpreted as meaning that the signer is made angry by whatever the left referent is doing or saying, but if the signer has indicated that this discourse is not about himself, (20) will be interpreted as meaning that the left referent is angry.

This phenomenon is the result of two facts. First, it should be noted that the verbs in these examples are bodily anchored verbs. As discussed in section 3, bodily anchored verbs use the signer's body as marker for the experiencer. Body movement creates a body marker proform that can then be incorporated into the verb. Clearly then, in this circumstance, the body marker will take precedence over the local proform indexed and the referent associated with the body marker will be viewed as the experiencer of the verb. This fact makes sense when it is remembered that the signer's body has more real-world salience than a location in space in the discourse situation. That these examples do not involve multidirectional and multiorientational verbs results from the fact that there would be no need to employ an index; the direction of movement or orientation of these verbs would establish the identity of the arguments. Second, the difference between indexing in a sequence where body movement is being used and where it is not, is that in the former case the position of the body is viewed as crucial to the heading of a list. Thus, body movement is the strongest mechanism available for the heading of lists. Whenever a signer takes a body position, he will be understood to be establishing that entity affiliated with that position as the head of the following list.

This discussion leads directly to another observation based on our data. Friedman (1975b) points out that real-world referents take precedence over the grammatical indexing systems available to signers. We find that this is true in our data as well. Whenever our informant knew what the real-world spatial relationships between the characters in the skits were, he would set up his body positions, indexes, etc., to correspond to those relationships.

There are two exceptions to this in our data, the first of which is relevant to the previous discussion. First, if the real world referents moved around a substantial amount in a manner unrelated to the central point of the story, our informant chose to simply fix one person on the left and the other on the right for purposes of reference. Here, ease of articulation serves as a constraint on the desire to portray things as they really were. Second, signers seem to show a preference for using their own body as a proform, rather than an articulated marker, index or unoccupied body position when they are describing themselves. For example, the following description was given of Lynn elaborately giving our informant a video tape box. We elicited this sequence in order to see if our informant would move into Lynn's position and imitate the complicated manner in which she had given him the box, thus leaving himself, as the recipient of the tapes, as an empty body position. The verb GIVE is multidirectional, and as such, moves from the location of the source to the location of the goal. If our informant were to sign GIVE from Lynn's position, he would use his body to represent Lynn and leave himself, as referent and goal of GIVE, as a location in space. The transcript of the description that our informant gave of this event is as follows:

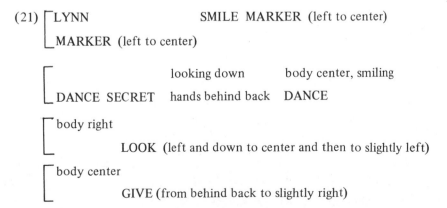

(21) ⌈LYNN   SMILE MARKER (left to center)
     ⌊MARKER (left to center)

     ⌈   looking down   body center, smiling
     ⌊DANCE SECRET   hands behind back   DANCE

     ⌈ body right
     ⌊   LOOK (left and down to center and then to slightly left)

     ⌈ body center
     ⌊   GIVE (from behind back to slightly right)

> ⌈ body right
>
> ⌊   TAKE (left to body)

Lynn is smiling as she comes up to me. She dances. She has a secret.
Her hands are behind her back and she's looking down. She dances.
I look at her. Lynn gives me something and I take it.

In the skit described in (21), Lynn actually danced and smiled at the same time that she gave our informant the box. As can be seen, our informant broke down Lynn's actions rather than moving into a body position and miming her entire action from that position. A more accurate picture of Lynn's actions would have required our informant to set himself up as an unoccupied body position (the recipient of the gift) and mimed or signed Lynn's giving. Our informant did not do this. By shortening the portion of the action in which he was involved, namely that portion where GIVE was being signed, he maintained the primacy of his own body as referent for itself. Our claim is that the signer will use his own body as the vehicle for discussion of himself even if to do this results in a deviation from the real-world occurrence. By doing this, the signer is conforming to a more dominant real-world fact—that he is in fact himself.

A more striking example of the priority of using the signer's own body as referent for itself rather than using another form of reference is given below:

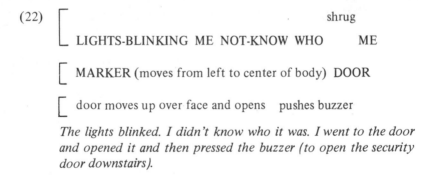

(22) ⌈   shrug
      ⌊ LIGHTS-BLINKING ME NOT-KNOW WHO   ME

      ⌈ MARKER (moves from left to center of body) DOOR
      ⌊

      ⌈ door moves up over face and opens   pushes buzzer
      ⌊

The lights blinked. I didn't know who it was. I went to the door
and opened it and then pressed the buzzer (to open the security
door downstairs).

The line that our informant traced of himself going to the door (see marker in (22) above) is not a reflection of the real world. A truer depiction would be a marker in the left hand moving from the left close to or behind the signer's body to the center of neutral space. However, tracing that line would force the signer to separate himself as signer and himself as referent. In (22), our informant is trying to communicate that he ended up in front of the door. Because he is both signer and referent, he wants his body to represent itself and therefore, the marker's movement deviates from real-world movement in a manner that allows him to do this. Thus the signer's desire to use his body as a proform representing himself when he **is** the referent rather than using an articulated marker or unoccupied local proform, overpowers the desire to represent things precisely as they occurred in the real world.

Thus we have seen two phenomena: 1) A body marker dominates over other proforms. Because body movement employs a body marker, it dominates over other forms of reference (except naming) so that if body positions have been established, one cannot index to the left, standing in the right body position, and sign a verb meaning its subject to be the left referent. In particular, when body movement is being used a sequence like,

> body center
>
> INDEX (to right) VERB

would be interpreted as the signer being the subject of the verb. 2) The signer's body will be used as a referent to itself whenever reference to the signer is needed. In order to avoid, or at least minimize, any split between the signer's real-world self and the method of reference used when referring to the signer's role in the events being discussed, the signer may manipulate his portrayal of another aspect of the real world, namely the action portrayed by the sign that forces the split to occur.

There seems to be a relationship between 1 and 2 above; namely that the signer as communicator and the signer as a referent are the same entity. Therefore, any signs that might be associated with the signer (either as referent or body marker), **will** be; and any indexical system or markers set up by the signer when discussing himself will allow him to base signs on his own body. This is supported by the fact the first person reference is the unmarked form.

We have discussed six ways of heading lists. The question of how signers choose the particular method to use is interesting. The most important factors that determine this are the nature of the visual image the signer wants to create and how this image can be communicated using different methods. Signers vary in their choice of methods, some relying heavily on indexing while others rely more heavily on body movement.

We found that our informant tended to use body movement when two entities (individuals or groups) were interacting. For example, in (23) where body movement is used, Cathy and Leora are located to the signer's left, Tom is located as the right body position, and the signer is in the center. Cathy and Leora, however, are only tangentially involved in the story. The left body position is never assumed by our informant; he only signs TALK in that direction. Thus, there are only two body positions utilized, and two actively involved entities in the story.

(23) [MY r-o-o-m-m-a-t-e BRING FRIEND t-o-m NAME t-o-m,

                                                    head facing left

  [HAPPEN SAME (to right) NAME t-o-m TALK (to left)

  [MARKER (from right) ENTER (from right)

  [MARKER (from right to face) DRUNK FAT DRUNK

$$\left[\begin{array}{l} \qquad\qquad\qquad\qquad\qquad\text{winces \quad body slightly right} \\ \text{MARKER (from right to face)} \end{array}\right.$$

$$\left[\begin{array}{l} \qquad\qquad\qquad\qquad\text{body center} \\ \text{BOTHER (slightly toward left)} \qquad\qquad \text{ME SICK-OF} \end{array}\right.$$

$$\left[\begin{array}{l} \qquad\qquad\qquad\text{body slightly right} \\ \text{ME TALK (to left)} \qquad\qquad\qquad \text{BOTHER} \end{array}\right.$$

$$\left[\begin{array}{l} \qquad\qquad\qquad\text{shrug} \\ \text{MINUTES BOTHER} \end{array}\right.$$

My roommate brought a friend named Tom who it turns out has the same name as me. I was talking to Cathy and Leora and he entered from the right. He bugged me. He was fat and drunk and bugged me. He bothered me. I was sick of him and talked to Cathy and Leora. He bothered me and he kept on bothering me.

Indexing to real-world referents,[17] grammatical indexing, or naming are used when a lot of people are involved in activities:

(24) $\left[\begin{array}{l}\text{ONE TIME MY CLASS LEORA BRING (left to center)}\end{array}\right.$

$\left[\begin{array}{l} \qquad\qquad\qquad\text{faces left \quad body center} \\ \text{VICKI CLASS SURPRISE} \qquad\qquad \text{VICKI} \end{array}\right.$

$\left[\begin{array}{l}\text{COME-HERE HERE SURPRISE}\end{array}\right.$

One time in my sign class the following happened. Leora brought Vicki to class and the class was surprised that Vicki came.

(25) $\left[\begin{array}{l}\text{ONE LATE-AFTERNOON CLASS ENTER all sitting in a circle}\end{array}\right.$

$\left[\begin{array}{l}\text{WAIT LYNN ENTER THINK INDEX (to class) COME-HERE}\end{array}\right.$

$\left[\begin{array}{l}\text{LATE ANGER ARGUE ANGER INDEX (to class) ANGER}\end{array}\right.$

$\left[\begin{array}{l}\text{CLASS ANGER ANGER INSULTS ANGER HENRY}\end{array}\right.$

$\left[\begin{array}{l}\text{SPECIAL MARK SILENT}\end{array}\right.$

One late afternoon the class entered, sat in a circle, and waited. Lynn entered. Thought the class, "she came late." They were

angry and argued. They were all angry. The class was angry
and there were insults. Mark and Henry were the exceptions,
they were silent.

When discussing the pros and cons of vegetarianism, our informant set up two local proforms in front of his body slightly off center in each direction. One location represented animals who eat meat, and the other represented animals who eat vegetables. His choice of a more central location for his reference points (rather than extreme right or left, as is the standard form) was probably related to the fact that the two groups were being described, compared, juxtaposed, and interacting with each other in ways that were easier to represent if the two were placed close together and side by side. In addition, the fact that groups were being referred to may have influenced his method of reference.

Thus far, we have seen that our informant tended to use body movement when there were two entities actively involved in the story and that he used grammatical indexing or, of course, real-world indexing when referring to a group experiencing one action, emotion, and so on. We also found that he tended to use a *3*-marker or indexing a local proform when talking about three participating entities (including or not including himself). Our informant claims that three distinct body positions can be used when describing three actively involved participants, although he never produced an example of this when we elicited stories about three people. Perhaps this is because these elicitations were based on financial transactions among three people in which the verbs most often used were multidirectional. Ease of articulation and the desire to be clear, as well as the quality of the visual image produced, all influence the signer to use indexing in stories of this type. Perhaps certain other situations involving three people would better be described using body movement.

Though we found examples in our data of an articulated marker used to head a list, it occurred rarely and only in a context in which neither body movement or indexing was used. The following is an example where both an articulated marker and body movement are being used. Notice that it is the body movement which is used to head the lists and grammatically establish the referent, rather than the marker.

(26) ⌈ body center   looks left
     | VICKI AND LEORA
     ⌊

     ⌈   body right
     | MARKER (left to center) VICKI   HUNGRY EAT
     ⌊   MARKER (left to center) ---

     ⌈ body left
     | LEORA o-k o-k
     ⌊

Vicki and Leora were walking along over on my left. Vicki said
she was hungry and wanted to eat. Leora said ok.

The body positions in (26) are used throughout the rest of the discourse. They clearly seem to be the listing mechanism at work. A list analysis of (26) would be as follows:

(27) ***LEORA AND VICKI***, marking: walk along

      VICKI, body movement: HUNGRY
                                    EAT

    LEORA, body movement: o-k o-k

It seems that in (26) the upheld articulated marker is used to communicate that the signer is now establishing body positions for the two people he had previously (through use of the two articulated markers which began the example) placed in a spatial relationship to himself and that he is no longer part of the discourse.

The principle use of articulated markers is to depict the movement of referents in space. This fact places a constraint on the use of marking as a heading mechanism. In using an articulated marker as the primary list heading device in a discourse, the signer denies himself the possibility of using that marker for its primary function. If articulated markers were viewed as a crucial form of list heading, any use of an articulated marker would be seen as the beginning of a new list, yet as we have seen most uses of articulated markers occur within lists and do not head them. We feel that this is so because markers are needed throughout a discourse to perform their primary function. In addition, a grammatical referent must be fixed in space or, as is true of real-world referents, fixed to some easily identifiable referent. Marking as a heading mechanism differs from the other five in that the others all assign an identity to a spatially located referent that can have some permanence. Marking is not used as the main way of heading lists in any discourse we have seen; rather, it occurs seldom in discourse and each usage is unrelated to those which precede it.

For most of the examples presented in this paper, there are redundancies in the heading processes. Many of these redundant reassertions of the head of a list take the form of names or nominals. We found, in general, that naming as a list-heading device rarely occurred by itself, rather, names or nominals occurred as part of another heading mechanism. They appear to occur in free variation with their nonoccurrence. As we have seen, the setting up of a list does not necessarily require the overt mention of a name when context indicates who is being discussed.

We believe that the observations discussed above are the result of two factors. First, it appears that the principle function of names and nominals for people is to assign an identity to proforms. As already mentioned, each heading mechanism establishes and/or employs a proform. As such, the proform is the principle referring device for people in ASL and is a primary component of the grammatical structure of ASL. Proforms must, of course, be tied to a referent in order to perform their referring function. Thus, the only predictable occurrence of names or nominals (for people) is at the time a proform is originally established near the beginning of a given discourse. Secondly, while signing, the signer seems to be monitoring his own utterance, doing without names when context makes the identity of the subject obvious and inserting them at intervals in order to remind the addressee of the identity of the entity being discussed. The signer reminds his or her addressee whose body position is whose, who an index to the left refers to, etc. In short, the signer continues to remind the addressee of the referent of the proform heading the current list. The same monitoring goes on in oral language. In both modalities, the speaker (or signer) occasionally errs, prompting the addressee to ask for clarification.

In the preceding discussion, we have pointed out some of the factors that determine the choice of one particular heading mechanism over another. These include: 1) the nature of the visual image the signer wants to create and how this image can be communicated using different methods; 2) the type of referents and interactions between them being described; 3) the primary function of some types of proforms; 4) the particular class of verbs predominantly used in a given discourse; and 5) the ways in which all of these interact with and influence one another. In addition, we have alluded to a sixth factor by pointing out that some heading mechanisms dominate over others. This last factor needs further discussion and clarification.

It will be remembered that near the beginning of this section, we stated the following general principle, which is part of the listing structure:

> The last mentioned or otherwise indicated grammatical subject remains subject unless the signer indicates otherwise.

Given that the same proforms that function as the basis of the heading processes are also used in discourse for reference outside of the heading process (that is, they are used within lists and do not indicate the head of a new list) the addressee must have some way of knowing when the signer is or is not indicating a new grammatical subject through his use of a proform. It appears that one of the ways in which ASL accomplishes this is through the following hierarchy of heading mechanisms within the listing structure, which establishes the dominance of one heading mechanism over another. By dominance we mean that in a stiuation where two types of reference are made which conflict with one another, the one both intended to head a list and understood to do so dominates over the other (or is stronger than the other).

BODY MOVEMENT
REAL-WORLD INDEXING
GRAMMATICAL INDEXING
MARKING
NAMING
HEADLESS LISTS

Superimposed over this hierarchy is the use of names and nominals (not the heading mechanism, naming) to establish and/or reassert the identity of the head of a list.

We feel that the organization of the hierarchy above is motivated by the following factors: 1) body movement and indexing are two conventionalized forms of overt pronominal reference, and thus, allow the least ambiguity; 2) the signer's body used as a proform in body movement has more real-world salience in the discourse situation than the location in space used in indexing, even though the location represents a referent; 3) real-world referents dominate over grammatical indexing; 4) the primary function of articulated markers is to depict the movement of referents; 5) by definition, naming is used only in a context in which other forms of reference are not used, and 6) headless lists permit the most ambiguity.

If this hierarchy of heading mechanisms did not exist, any use of a proform could be viewed as the head of a new list. As we have pointed out in the discussion of several of the examples used in this paper, this is not the case. This hierarchy, in combination with the general principle mentioned earlier, is the sixth factor that comes into play in the signer's chioce of a heading mechanism. Further, this hierarchy allows the signer to employ a variety of proforms in a given discourse, which in turn, provides the signer with a choice between several methods in creating the best visual image of that which he wishes to communicate in a given discourse.

The grammatical structure of ASL, which we have analyzed as listing, is basically a process in which the signer indicates who he is talking about and then lists the signs that are to be associated with that referent. The topic of discussion (the grammatical subject) is indicated through the use of one or more heading mechanisms, which have as their basis spatially defined proforms. The manner in which the referent is to be related to the verbs in the following list and to the other referents in a discourse, is indicated through the manner of articulation characteristic of the various classes of verbs. The surface manifestation of a given verb indicates the semantic identity of the referent with respect to the verb. In other words, the verb carries in its semantic content and surface manifestation, the indication of which argument of the verb the referent is. One of the chief ways in which this is accomplished is through the incorporation of the proform, which represents the referent and heads the list, into the verb.

The listing structure is related to other phenomena in ASL. Namely, as Friedman (1976a) has pointed out, a discourse usually begins with the setting (where, when, and/or who) of the information to be communicated in the discourse, followed by the information that is the actual topic of discussion. This setting remains constant until the signer indicates otherwise.

We find a similar pattern in the creation of descriptive visual images or representations. For example, if a signer were to sign an ASL equivalent of 'The bird flew out of the tree', we would expect something like,

(28) ⌈ TREE ---
     ⌊ BIRD MARKER (representing bird, placed on tree)

followed by some type of movement of the marker to depict the bird's flying. We find that in creating descriptive visual images, one sets up the locations and actors first and then depicts the action that took place.

Listing appears to be consistent with other aspects of **ASL** in that it takes the form of giving first the actor, topic of discussion, or grammatical subject followed by a depiction or description of that entity's actions, attributes, role in an event, etc. Further, the structure of listing is consistent with the principle governing the creation of a visual representation. Namely, one sets up the components of the representation and then establishes the relationships and ways of interacting between them.

The listing structure, which incorporates and systematizes the use of spatially based proforms for people and the spatial characteristics of the various classes of verbs used to indicate which referent is which argument, has as its basis the use of space to indicate grammatical mechanisms.

5. Ambiguity and Disambiguation of Subject-Verb Relations

Our notion of listing in itself does not explain how every subject-verb relationship is established. In this section we will discuss some ambiguities in our data showing how the addressee interprets the N–V relations the signer intends to express.

In section 4 we saw that certain lists were headless. This category was broken down into three subcategories:

1. context indicates who is doing what
2. the first person unmarked form is used
3. the verb has directional movement or orientation that makes clear who is its subject

We would like to discuss (1) and (3) in depth, citing relevant examples from our data.

The following is the example used above to illustrate headless lists (1):

(29) ⎡ LEORA SIT VICKI SIT READ BOOK TIME
　　　⎢
　　　⎢　　　　　　　　FOLLOW (to left)
　　　⎣ MARKER (to left) ----------------------------

(29) is unclear because the follower is not explicitly identified. We know, however, that there are two people involved in this sequence and that the marker in the dominant hand represents Vicki's leaving. Further, this marker is upheld while FOLLOW is signed with the nondominant hand. The contextual information above allows us to conclude that Leora followed Vicki. Notice the structure of the list for (29):

(30)　　*LEORA*, naming:　SIT

> *VICKI*, naming: SIT
>   READ BOOK
>   TIME
>   leaves (MARKER to left)
>
> *Leora*, context: FOLLOW

The following is another example of a headless list, the head of which can be identified through context:

(31) ⌈ ONE DAY ME SEE ASA VICKI INDEX (to marker) ASA
      ⌊   MARKER --------------------

      ⌈ VICKI MARKER (moves to left passing left hand marker)
      ⌊ --

      ⌈ ASA   WOW LIKE VICKI LOOK WALK
      ⌊ LOOK

      ⌈ MARKER (moves to left) LOOK MARKER (to left)

      ⌈   body right and looks left
      ⌊ taps shoulder (on left)   SURPRISE

      ⌈ body center   body left   body center
      ⌊   TALK   LOVE   TALK

      ⌈ body left   body right
      ⌊   KISS (left hand kisses right hand)   slaps (to left)

In this example, body movement is used for the first time just before SURPRISE is signed, and we have been given no explicit indication of who the referent of the right body position is. We do know, however, that Vicki has walked past Asa and is standing somewhere over on the left. Further, we know that Asa has walked over in that direction and tapped someone on the shoulder. We can conclude from context that Vicki is surprised and that the right body position represents her. Because we know that there are only two participants in the discourse, we know that another body position will represent Asa. This is supported by what happens in the rest of the discourse in which the body positions are used. A breakdown of (31) into lists and its translation would be as follows:

(32) introduction: ONE DAY ME SEE ASA VICKI

      ASA, marking: stands around (MARKER in left hand)

VICKI, marking: walks past Asa
                 (MARKER to left and past other marker)

ASA, naming: LOOK
                 WOW
                 LIKE VICKI
                 LOOK
                 WALK
                 goes over to Vicki (MARKER to left)
                 LOOK
                 goes over to Vicki (MARKER to left)
                 taps shoulder

Vicki, context: SURPRISE

Asa and Vicki, headless (3): TALK

Asa, body movement: LOVE

Asa and Vicki, headless (3): TALK

Asa, body movement: KISS (Vicki)

Vicki, body movement: slaps (Asa)

One day I saw the following event involving Asa and Vicki. Asa was standing around when Vicki walked past him. He looked at her and thought, "wow." He liked Vicki. He looked at her and started walking over to her. He kept on looking at her as he walked up to her. He tapped her on the shoulder. She turned around and was surprised. They talked to each other. Asa loved Vicki. They talked to each other and then Asa kissed Vicki. Vicki slapped Asa.

We have already seen one example of a headless list for which disambiguation takes place because of the direction of movement and semantics of the verb (see example (3), p. 154). In this example, Lynn gives the signer a gift. The signer is holding it in his right hand, but it is snatched away with the left hand which moves left to an extended position. If we rewrite the sequence given in section 4 as a series of lists, it is easy to disambiguate:

(33)   *me*, body movement: FINISH

        _____: GRAB (center to extended left)

We have three alternatives in deciphering this sequence. First, the signer could be the agent and doing something to the gift himself. This is unlikely given that the visual image created by the verb's movement does not portray any action the signer could expect us to associate with the recipient and holder of the gift. A second possibility is that some new person could be performing the action. To sign this, however, would violate a basic principle of ASL, namely that one lays all one's cards out on the table and then discusses the relationships between the people involved. The third, and last, possibility is that Lynn is grabbing the gift. Like all multidirectional verbs, this one goes from source to goal. Since the verb moves to the extreme left, Lynn's position, it is safe to assume that she is the agent and is grabbing the gift back (this was actually the case in the skit being described). Like other multidirectional verbs, GRAB can be used without overt mention of the referents because it incorporates both source and goal into its movement.

In the preceding discussions we have encountered several sequences in which a noun is mentioned where that noun is not intended to signal that the previous list has ended and a new one is beginning. These nouns either appear as direct or indirect objects:

> (16) *LEORA*, naming: STAND
> BORED
> WALK
> MEET VICKI
> HI
> GIVE BOOK
> LAUGH

or can head a subordinate list within another list (the transcription for (33) is given in example (24), p. 160):

> (33)   *LEORA*, naming: BRING (left to center) VICKI
>
> *CLASS*, naming: (looking and facing left where Vicki entered)
> SURPRISE *VICKI*, naming: COME-HERE
> SURPRISE

Obviously, in many cases it is impossible in context to interpret such nouns as the head of a new dominant[18] list. However, nouns such as VICKI in (16) and VICKI in (33) could be looked at as heads of new lists which control the rest of the verbs listed in the examples. Thus one might misinterpret these sequences leading to lists like the following (examples 34 and 36 refer to 16 and 33 respectively):

> (34)   *LEORA*, naming: STAND
> BORED
> WALK
> MEET *VICKI*, naming: HI
> GIVE BOOK
> LAUGH

(35) *LEORA*, naming: BRING VICKI

     CLASS, naming: SURPRISE

     VICKI, naming: COME-HERE
                         SURPRISE

Clearly, ambiguity of this nature would place a strain on communication. We find, not surprisingly, that sequences like (16) and (33) are not really ambiguous. In addition to the mechanisms discussed in section 4, ASL relies on context (or the likelihood of a given noun being associated with the verbs that follow it) to disambiguate such sequences. In (16), for example, we may ask what the primary function of VICKI must be. The answer is to tell us who Leora met. In ASL, and we imagine in most languages, one does not find 'meet' occurring without a direct object. In fact, ASL is structured so that MEET is often signed in an $N_1 N_2 V$ sequence where the manipulation of space can indicate who is being emphasized (i.e., N_1 met N_2 versus N_2 met N_1) or that neither is being emphasized and the sequence means 'N_1 and N_2 met or ran into each other'. Thus the mention of VICKI in (16) serves to inform us of whom Leora met. If the signer wished the following verbs to be connected with Vicki, he would make a second reference to Vicki that would serve to head the new list. The following list would result if the second reference was made by indexing:

(36) *LEORA*, naming: STAND
                         BORED
                         WALK
                         MEET VICKI

     Vicki, indexing: HI
                         GIVE BOOK
                         LAUGH

In (33), VICKI COME-HERE serves to tell us the cause of the class's surprise. We find many occurrences in ASL of such a structure where the cause follows the verb. We have seen that VICKI SURPRISE LEORA translates into English as 'Leora surprised Vicki' or more in the flavor of the original, as 'Vicki was surprised. Why? Because of Leora'. In the story in which (33) appeared, we were told that Leora brought Vicki to class. It makes most sense, then, to interpret (33) as is rather than as was done in (35).

We found another interesting example of subordinate lists:

(37) *CHILD*, body movement: THINK *mother*, indexing: BOTHER
                                                   TEACH

     (*child*, indexing): WASH (mother)

The child thought about the fact that her mother had bothered her and tried to teach her. She washes her mother.

Here our informant was obviously aware of the potential for confusion. The story (which is transcribed in section 6) involves a mother trying to wash her child's face while the child struggles with her. The child finally grabs the wash cloth and washes the mother's face. In the sequence listed in (37), the child is established by movement into a body position. Remember that body movement is the strongest form of list heading. The signer wishes to describe the child's thoughts and since these involve the mother's actions, he must insert one list in another. The verbs in this subordinate list, BOTHER and TEACH, are multiorientational and multidirectional respectively. Their articulation is such that they indicate that the mother is bothering and teaching, but their directionality is muted and slight as if to mark that at the time discussed, the mother is not doing these things, but rather the child is remembering them being done. When our informant finishes describing the child's thoughts, he re-establishes the child through indexing and signs WASH in the direction of the mother's location. The strategy here is revealing. WASH has hitherto been associated with the mother, not the child. The informant has just been describing the mother's actions, although this was in the context of the child thinking about them. These two facts make confusion possible if the sequence were simply to be followed by WASH. Perhaps the addressee would assume that the signer had confused body positions and was talking about the mother washing the child again. To avoid such confusion, the child is indexed as a reminder. Thus, whenever context makes confusion possible, the signer is especially careful and will put effort into making clear which referent heads which list and which verbs belong in which list.

We have shown how headless lists can be disambiguated. In the process, we have seen that the general principle stated in section 4 is not correct as stated there. The principle could be better phrased as follows:

Principle of Subject Determination in ASL: The last indicated subject is associated with all verbs until a new subject is indicated. If the method of heading is dropped and no new head is given, or if in context a verb seems incongruent with the last mentioned subject, the new subject is that entity who in context is the most logical one to be associated with that verb.

6. Examples of Analyzed Discourses

Below we present two transcripts of discourses based on real occurrences or skits. As with all the transcripts in this paper, these have been simplified to enable nonsigners to understand the sequences. Nothing crucial to the list analysis has been deleted or simplified, however. Following each transcript is a rough translation into English and an analysis of it into lists.

(38)

```
                              body right
     ME  SEE (to left)  HAPPEN          MOTHER
                                        INDEX (to right)
```

```
     GRAB (from left to right)  GIRL          GRAB  WASH
                                CHILD (on left)
```

```
    WASH-FACE  WASH
                   holding child   jerks child  INDEX (to left and down)
```

```
          body left   winces
     GIRL               leave me alone   struggles
```

```
    body right
                WASH   shakes child  INDEX (to left and down)
```

```
    body left              looks to right (at mother)
                GIRL  struggles
```

```
    body right
                WASH  WASH  INDEX (to left and down)
```

```
    body left
                struggles  HIT (to right and up at mother)
```

```
    body center
                WASH  WASH  now what?
```

```
    TEACH  WASH  GIRL
                    INDEX (to left and down)
```

```
              body left
     STUBBORN          HIT (right and up at mother)
```

```
    body center
                WASH  jerk child  WASH  BOTHER  BOTHER
```

```
    body left
                CHILD  THINK  INDEX (right and up to mother)
```

[BOTHER TEACH INDEX (left and down to child)

[
                                        body center
  WASH (right and up at mother)   SEE (to left)

[WOW FORGET-IT

*I saw this event. A mother grabbed her child, a girl, and washed
her face. She jerked the child towards her. The child winced
and wanted to be left alone. She struggled to get away. The
mother washes the child, shaking her. The child struggles more,
and the mother washes. The child struggles and hits at her
mother. The mother washes, thinks about what to do, and
then teaches the child to wash herself. The child is stubborn
and hits at her mother. The mother washes the child, jerking
her. The mother bothers the child. The child thinks about the
fact that her mother bothered her and tried to teach her. The
child washes the mother. I saw that. Wow! Forget them!*

Analysis into lists:

    introduction: ME SEE (over there on the left) HAPPEN

    MOTHER, body movement[19] : GRAB GIRL/CHILD (over there on the left[20])
                                 GRAB
                                 WASH
                                 WASH-FACE
                                 WASH while holding child
                                 jerks child

    GIRL, indexing; body movement: winces
                               leave me alone
                               struggles

    mother, body movement: WASH
                         shakes child

    GIRL, indexing; body movement: struggles
                               looks at mother

    mother, body movement: WASH
                         WASH

    girl, indexing; body movement: struggles
                               HIT mother

mother, body movement[21]:   WASH
                                 WASH
                                 now what?
                                 TEACH WASH

GIRL, indexing: STUBBORN

(girl, body movement[22]):   HIT at mother

mother, body movement: WASH
                             jerks child
                             WASH
                             BOTHER
                             BOTHER

CHILD, body movement: THINK   *mother*, indexing: BOTHER
                                                        TEACH

(child, indexing):   WASH mother

me, headless (2):   SEE
                      WOW
                      FORGET-IT

(39) ⎡ ONE DAY ME SEE ASA VICKI INDEX (to marker)
     ⎣   MARKER --------------

     ⎡ ASA VICKI MARKER (moves to left passing left hand marker)
     ⎣ ---

     ⎡ ASA   WOW LIKE VICKI LOOK WALK
     ⎣ LOOK

     ⎡ MARKER (moves to left) LOOK MARKER (to left)

     ⎡   body right and looks left
     ⎣ taps shoulder (on left)   SURPRISE

     ⎡ body center   body left   body center
     ⎣   TALK   LOVE   TALK

     ⎡ body left   body right
     ⎣   KISS (left hand kisses right hand)   slaps (to left)

$\lceil$ body center

         CONFLICT-BETWEEN-THEM
$\lfloor$

$\lceil$ nose in air, snobby facial expression

$\lfloor$ MARKER (to right)   ASA MARKER (to right)

One day I saw the following event involving Asa and Vicki. Asa was standing around when Vicki walked past him. He looked at her and thought, "wow." He liked Vicki. He looked at her and started walking over to her. He kept on looking at her as he walked up to her. He tapped her on the shoulder. She turned around and was surprised. They talked to each other. Asa loved Vicki. They talked to each other and then Asa kissed Vicki. Vicki slapped him. There was conflict between them. Vicki walked off with her nose in the air. Then Asa walked away too.

Analysis into lists:

     introduction: ONE DAY ME SEE ASA VICKI

     ASA, marking: stands around (MARKER in left hand)

     VICKI, marking: walks past Asa (MARKER to left and past other marker)

     ASA, naming: LOOK
                      WOW
                      LIKE VICKI
                      LOOK
                      WALK
                      goes over to Vicki (MARKER to left)
                      LOOK
                      goes over to Vicki (MARKER to left)
                      taps shoulder

   Vicki, headless (1); body movement[23]:   looks left
                                       SURPRISE

   they, headless (3)[24]:   TALK

   Asa, body movement: LOVE

   they, headless (3): TALK

   Asa, body movement: KISS Vicki

   Vicki, body movement: slaps Asa

they, headless (3)[24] : CONFLICT

Vicki, headless (1); marking: walks off with nose in air
                                    (MARKER to right)

ASA, marking: walks away (MARKER to right)

7. Conclusion

In this paper we have been concerned with the grammatical mechanisms used in ASL to indicate the relationships among arguments with respect to a given verb. We have offered counterevidence to a description of ASL grammar as having a basic SVO word order by citing phenomena (the establishment of locations for referents in almost every ASL discourse and a class of verbs for which neither the directional use of space nor an SVO order apply) not accounted for by a word order description of the grammatical structure of ASL.

The spatially based proforms and forms of pronominal reference for people in ASL, three classes of verbs in ASL, and the ways in which the various proforms and classes of verbs interact to indicate grammatical mechanisms through the use of space have been defined and discussed as part of the description of the grammatical mechanisms in ASL.

An analysis of the grammatical structure of ASL consisting of lists has been offered. These lists take the general form of the topic of discussion (grammatical subject) followed by a set of signs that communicate information about that topic. Specifically, each list is headed by one (or more) of six heading mechanisms that establishes and/or refers to a proform. This proform functions as the grammatical subject and indicates the referent under discussion. The verbs following the head of the list indicate through their semantic content and surface manifestations what type of argument the head of that list is with respect to a particular verb and its relationship to other arguments in the discourse. This is accomplished primarily through the interaction of the proform and the verbs; the interaction has as its basis the use of space.

Circumstances, restrictions, and principles governing the choice of one heading mechanism over another have been described and discussed. In addition, ambiguities found in the data we examined have been described, and methods for their disambiguation have been proposed.

The listing structure described in this paper accounts for: the various forms of pronominal reference and their highly frequent use in ASL discourses; the surface manifestations of three classes of ASL verbs, including one that could not be accounted for by a word order description of the grammatical structure of ASL; the various methods by which space is used to indicate grammatical mechanisms; and the occurrence of names or nominals in free variation with their nonoccurrence;

The analysis of ASL discourse into lists is a systematic approach to the use of space to indicate grammatical mechanisms. It allows us to view the use of space to indicate grammatical mechanisms and create visual representations as a conventionalized system. As we have indicated, this analysis in consistent with other phenomena found in ASL.

Once again, we must point out that the grammatical structure we have described applies to the discussion of people and their interactions with each other. We have been led to the conclusion that the use of space to indicate grammatical mechanisms is the basis of the grammatical structure of ASL. Whether or not this conclusion applies to all aspects of the grammatical structure of ASL can only be determined through examining discourses involving referents other than people.

Finally, one could easily examine the structure we have described and argue that we have basically described an SVO, or at least SV, structure. While this may be true on a very superficial level, a description of the grammatical structure of ASL that stops at the level of word order fails to describe many of the basic mechanisms employed in ASL—mechanisms that optimally exploit the manual/visual modality through the use of space to indicate grammatical relationships and create visual representations of those relationships.

NOTES

1. We give the following rough definitions for indexing and body movement which will be discussed in greater detail in section 2. Indexing and body movement are two of the mechanisms used to refer to established locations for referents. With indexing, the signer will point to the location of a real or nonpresent referent. With body movement, the signer will move into the location for a nonpresent referent.

2. Directions for reading transcripts: where relevant, we will give the established locations for referents prior to the transcript. **Right** and **left** refer to the signer's right and left, **center** to the signer's body or to his natural signing position. Indications of body movement and facial expressions will be given in lower case letters on the top line. English glosses for standard signs will be given in upper case letters. Glosses for nonstandard signs will be given in lower case letters. Signs will be given on the second line. When direction of movement is relevant, this will be given in lower case letters in parenthesis immediately following the sign. When the two signs are simultaneously signed, the sign articulated by the nondominant hand will be given on a third line. Translations will follow the transcripts.

3. For HIDE and "jumps out" the signer places his right hand in a fist representing the child under his flat left hand, palm down, representing the table, and then rapidly moves his right hand out from under his left hand toward the left.

4. For "looks at mother," the signer moves his hand in the shape of a pointing index finger from the level of the child on the right to face level, pointing left and up.

5. Again we give the following rough definition for marker, which will be discussed in greater detail in section 2. A marker is a handshape (usually an extended index finger pointing upward) used to represent a referent.

6. See Friedman, 1975b.

7. We are drawing a distinction between representation alone and assuming an identity in discussing locations and markers simply because it is difficult to think about empty space assuming an identity. Clearly, representation is an integral part of taking on an identity.

8. Markers have been defined and discussed by Mandel as part of a larger description of the structure of ASL. We believe that the narrower definition of markers we are using is in agreement with Mandel's more general definition, but is naturally restricted to the scope of this paper. We feel, however, that it is important to include the signer's body as one of the forms of markers, rather than restricting markers to articulators only. Functionally, an articulator and the signer's body used as markers are the same: they both represent and take on the identity of a referent. Beyond this basic function, however, the two forms differ in the ways they can be employed to communicate something about the referent they represent. The primary difference is that articulated markers can be used to depict movement (movement of the entire referent from one location to another as opposed to movement taking place in a static location, i.e., swaying back and forth or moving a single body part) of the referent by tracing a path in space while body markers cannot. The source of this restriction is obvious: if the signer used his own body to depict movement through space, communication would become difficult or impossible, and the communication would move out of the realm of language.

9. The simultaneous signing of a name or nominal is only one means by which the signer can indexically establish a proform. For others, see Friedman, 1975b.

10. A verb is syntactically anchored to an argument if that argument must be overtly referred to in connection with the verb whenever it is signed, either through indexing or body movement.

11. It should be noted that this example occurred at the beginning of a discourse and that the right location was being established as the mother's location, rather than simply referred to.

12. Our notation for lists works as follows: first the name of the referent is given in boldface italics, followed by the type of heading mechanism(s) used. A colon separates this from the verbs, etc. which make up the list. When a heading

ing mechanism appears for the purpose of reminding the addressee of the identity of the proform used, it is placed in parentheses.

13. STAY means roughly 'gotcha' in this type of context.

14. The number three is made with the thumb and fingers one and two extended while three and four are folded. A three-marker is made by holding a *3*-hand in front of the body, palm up, fingers away from the signer. The signer can index each finger in order to refer to each of three entities. Thus, the fingers are each markers of a sort (see Mandel). The signer can also index the relative positions of the fingers and thumb (right, left, and center) and the addressee will know that their identities correspond to the identities of the three fingers similarly situated.

15. This type of list will be discussed in greater detail in section 5.

16. Perhaps FINISH serves as a comment on the entire interaction just described and is not, strictly speaking, part of a list of verbs associated with the signer, the recipient of the gift.

17. As Friedman (1975b) points out, referring to real-world beings or places takes precedence over other types of reference. We usually asked our informant not to use real-world indexing precisely in order to investigate how he would discuss someone who was not present. We found that he tended to set up his body positions or indexic references so that they in some way corresponded to the real world at the time the event being related occurred.

18. I.e., a list that erases the head of the previous list.

19. In the transcription several forms of reference are used, but it should be clear from the rest of the discourse that the body position is being established as the head of the list.

20. This establishes the left as the location of the child. The sign CHILD is formed by putting an open, flat hand at about thigh height with the palm down (as if marking the height of a child). The sign, in this instance was signed on the signer's left, and functions as an indication of where the child is to be located for grammatical purposes.

21. The mother is usually discussed as being on the right with the head looking down and left, the child on the left with the head looking up and right. Here, although the signer has moved out of the left position but not all the way into the right position, it is clear from context and from the direction of his head, that he is discussing the mother. Thus, a center position can indicate reference to the mother as long as context and other indicators such as head turning are consistent with that of the mother.

22. HIT, here is signed quite as one would mime it—with fists hitting in the direction where the mother has been located. Using body position enables the signer to make a good visual representation here, since he can take on the identity of the child and hit at the mother's now empty position. Thus, we find a body shift within a list. It seems clear that in addition to conforming to the conditions discussed in section 4, this shift is performed in order to make a better visual representation of the action.

23. Context tells us that Vicki is the subject of this list and therefore, that the right body position refers to Vicki. This leaves the left position as referring to Asa.

24. In both of these cases, the verbs go from side to side—from Asa's location to Vicki's and back. Their directions indicate that something is going on between these two people; their meanings indicate just what is going on.

THE LACK OF SUBORDINATION
IN AMERICAN SIGN LANGUAGE [1]

Henry Thompson

Most oral languages have many subordinating constructions of one sort or another. Early in our investigation of ASL we began to suspect that at least one of the most common of subordinating constructions, relativization, was not present in the language. The subsequent clear establishment of relativization as at least one case where ASL eschewed subordination in favor of polysentential coordination provided the stimulus to re-examine other subordinating constructions in English, together with their counterparts in ASL, to see whether in fact ASL **ever** used syntactic subordination. It is clear that this is an important question, as the assumption that subordination occurred has been implicit in prior work on ASL syntax (c.f., the analysis of word order restrictions in Fischer, 1973b and also Liddell, 1975 on which more will follow).

The tentative conclusion, as presented in this paper, is that there is **no** syntactic subordination in ASL. In order to establish this thesis, this paper examines manifestations of various constructions in ASL that might be expected to be subordinating. All of the associated argumentation is essentially based on the failure of some subordinating phenomenon to appear in samples of ASL which are either direct translations of English subordinate constructions or, in the case of narrative or dialogue, ASL that would clearly be translated into English using a subordinate construction. Such failure to appear does not of course constitute proof of the claim as such. Instead, the point of this paper is to make the claim seem reasonable by weight of examples and to encourage its further examination.

Since our principal concern in this paper is syntactic, a fairly simple transcription scheme is used in the presentation of examples. Data was obtained in two different ways. In the first, the informant was given written English sentences with instructions to sign as close a translation of the meaning of the sentences as possible. The responses were either transcribed immediately, usually by several people simultaneously, with several repetitions often necessary, or else they were videotaped for later transcription. In the second, the informant was videotaped signing a longer narrative, either while describing some real or imagined event or in discourse with another signer. In examples of the first sort, the English sentence is cited first,

1. The research reported in this paper was partially supported by a Graduate Fellowship from the National Science Foundation.

followed on the next line by the ASL response. For examples of the second sort, the ASL is cited first, followed by a contextually plausible English translation.

Lexical signs are given in caps, modeling (see Mandel for a definition of this term) in lower case, fingerspelling by lower case letters separated by dashes. Vertical juxtaposition indicates simultaneity, either two-handed signing or expression and intonation. '/' indicates a gross pause (greater than one second); shorter pauses are indicated by the length of the pause in videotape fields (60 per second; 1 field = approximately 0.016 sec.) inside parentheses, thus: (16). 'dur' stands for durative marking on a verb, 'ext' for an unusually slow or extended articulation. 'IND' (index) and 'G-IND' (genitive index) refer to the normal deictic 3rd person references, simple and possessive respectively. 'M' refers to a marker (again, see Mandel). A dashed line extending from a sign indicates the length of time the sign is maintained. Transcriptions from videotape are marked with the notation 'vt'.

Much of the discussion in this paper is critically dependent on establishing and locating sentence boundaries in a segment of ASL discourse. When transcribing directly, only the grossest pauses can be effectively noted. The use of videotape makes possible some greater degree of precision, but establishing the exact duration of a pause by examining a tape, field by field, is still quite a subjective procedure. The figures given in this paper represent the best estimate of the number of fields between the end of a sign, which I take to be immediately after the cessation of the motion associated with the last part of the sign, and the first indication that a new sign is underway, which is typically indicated by one of three things: the beginning of a shift in hand configuration, the beginning of a new motion by the dominant articulator, or the beginning of a new motion by the nondominant articulator. This is clearly a subjective and fuzzily defined procedure, but after a period of self-training, focused on the idea that the answer should be zero (or close to it) for many many potential juncture locations, I feel I have reached a level of consistency sufficient to make the data obtained reliable and useful. It is my experience that pauses of less than 10–15 fields (0.15–0.25 sec.) are not usually perceptible to me, that pauses of greater than 25–30 fields (0.4–0.5 sec.) are easily perceptible and interpretable almost exclusively as sentence boundaries or performance difficulties (the equivalent of spoken 'uh'), and that pauses of an intermediate duration between those extremes are usually perceptible, but that no single fixed interpretation is possible. Just as in oral languages however, although pauses of varying duration **may** occur between sentences in a discourse, a pause is not necessary. Oral languages use suprasegmental features such as pitch and stress to indicate sentence boundaries. Baker has suggested that the suprasegmental feature of eye contact may serve the same purpose in ASL. Unfortunately, the utility of eye contact information for determining sentence boundaries in the examples given here is rather limited. The accuracy and relevance of eye contact data seem to be at least partially dependent on the presence of a signing interlocutor. Most of the data in this paper is drawn from situations where the informant was signing directly to the camera, or alternating between signing at the camera and at the other people in the room. It is therefore often extremely difficult to determine what constitutes eye contact and what does not. Even in those cases where reasonably reliable data can be obtained (transcribed herein with a raised + indicating the beginning of eye contact and a raised ⁻ indicating the end), not enough is known yet about exactly how eye contact marks sentence boundaries to permit an unequivocal interpretation of the data. Much experimentation remains to be done before we can determine an effective procedure for locating sentence boundaries in an ASL discourse.

The first phenomenon we will examine is that of relativization, both restrictive and nonrestrictive. In English, both types of relative clauses are clearly marked syntactically: by the use of a 'WH-word' at the beginning of the clause, by the placement of the clause after the noun or noun phrase it modifies (hereafter the head), usually immediately after, and by the absence from the relative clause of the noun or noun phrase which is coreferential with the head. Other oral languages use similar syntactic markings.

In English, restrictive relative clauses usually serve to refine the reference of the head; nonrestrictives, to comment on it. Similarly in ASL, some clauses serve to refine or comment on references in other clauses. But there does not appear to be any syntactic marking which is used to indicate that a clause is serving in that capacity. 'WH-words' exist in ASL for use in questions, and they also appear in Signed English translations of English sentences with relative clauses. But they do not occur in ASL to indicate relativization. Insofar as it is possible to isolate segments of discourse which would probably have been expressed using a relative clause in English, no regularities in clause order, word order, or deletion can be observed which might signal some syntactic paradigm similar to relativization in English. Unfortunately, in the transcribed corpus of undirected, continuous discourse and dialogue we have obtained to date, no clear and unambiguous examples of what would have to be expressed in English as a relative clause occur. This is in itself interesting, but without a much larger corpus and some method for identifying potential examples that is not totally subjective, it is probably wise to refrain from speculation.

Thus, most of the hard evidence comes from a much more artificial source: an informant's translations into ASL of English sentences containing relative clauses.

Examples (1)-(5) below are among the first elicited using English sentences containing relatives, and should give the reader an idea of the sort of ASL responses such sentences provoke. Unfortunately, no pause data was transcribed.

(1) *The girl who will give a speech tomorrow met Lynn.*

    GIRL THAT GIRL GIVE SPEECH TOMORROW GIRL MEET

    LYNN FINISH PAST

(2) *The book that's on the table is red.*

    BOOK ON TABLE RED

            IND

(3) *The girl Asa gave the dog to is pretty.*

ASA GIVE DOG GIRL IND PRETTY
                                       IND

(4) *Asa, who likes ice cream, went to McCallum's yesterday.*

ASA LIKE ICE-CREAM GO m-c-c- YESTERDAY

(5) *Lynn, who was sitting on a chair, suddenly fell over.*

LYNN SIT FALL
          dur

There is no evidence here for syntactic marking of subordination. No WH-words occur. In examples (1)–(3) there are no deletions at all. If we assume sentence breaks after ICE-CREAM in (4) and SIT in (5), the deletions that occur in these examples occur in the sentences translating the main clause of the English sentences (hereinafter the M sentence. Similarly we will call the sentence which translates the English relative clause the R sentence.) Nothing prevents us from placing such a sentence break there. In later examples where pause and eye contact data are available to determine sentence boundaries more clearly, sentences where the subject or object have been elided frequently occur. Such elision of a repeated noun phrase occurs quite frequently in connected narrative discourse (for discussion see Friedman, 1976a). In fact, I claim that all five of these examples should reasonably be considered to consist of two complete sentences. In the examples above, the R sentence comes first, followed by the M sentence. In examples (6)–(9) below, obtained in the same session as (1)–(5), that order is reversed.

(6) *Asa met the girl standing near the store.*

ASA MEET GIRL STAND NEAR STORE
                   IND   dur

(7) *Lynn saw the math teacher whom she admires.*

LYNN MEET MATH TEACHER SHE LIKE

(8) *Lynn met the man who won the Mr. America contest.*

LYNN MEET BOY IND WIN EXERCISE PHYSICAL

(9) *Lynn talked to Asa, who is interested in sign language.*

LYNN TALK-TO ASA ASA INTEREST SIGN KNOW YOU KNOW

Once again we have no WH-words, and reasonable divisions into two sentences, with all deletions occurring in the second sentence. This is consistent with the suggestion made earlier that such deletion as does occur stems from some sentence-to-sentence discourse rule eliminating repetitions of previously established referents. In the total corpus of 26 examples of ASL translations of English sentences with relatives, there are twelve deletions, all from the second sentence, whether derived from the English main or relative clause. The table below gives the breakdown of sentence order versus deletion. MR denotes examples where the M sentence preceded the R sentence as in (1)–(5), and RM denotes the opposite, as in (6)–(9).

	Deletion from R	Deletion from M	No Deletion
MR	4	0	8
RM	0	8	6

It is impossible to support any claim that deletion marks a relative clause in ASL after considering this table. Having by now eliminated WH-words and deletion as possible syntactic markers, all that remains is sentence order and word order within sentences. In all the previous examples, and indeed in the whole corpus from which they are taken, such a constraint seems to exist. We have shown that there is no syntactic marking of subordination, and that both the main and relative clauses of an English sentence are rendered as distinct sentences when translated into ASL. If we consider the data presented so far, it seems necessary that the R sentence must be next to the site of the head in the M sentence, whether or not the head is deleted. Thus in all the RM type sentences, the head occurs in intital position in the M sentence, while in all the MR type sentences, the head occurs in final position in the M sentence. The English sentences that provided this corpus were not constructed with word order in mind, however, and so not all combinations of relative positions of the head in the main and relative clause were represented. More data were gathered in an attempt to explore the word and sentence order problem with a more carefully constructed set of English stimuli. Nine sentences were constructed, representing all possible combinations of locations for a head in a three-place main clause with a three-place relative. The results are given below.

(10) *The man who gave Asa the book gave Henry a copy.*

IND MAN GIVE ASA BOOK / IND GIVE HENRY COPY   vt
　M　　　　　　　　　　　　　　　M

(11) *The book which Asa gave to Henry was written by Lynn.*

BOOK ASA GIVE HENRY / BOOK WRITE b-y LYNN   vt

(12) *The man who gave the book to Asa sent it to Henry.* *

IND MAN IND GIVE BOOK ASA / IND SEND BOOK TO HENRY vt
M------------　　　　　　　IND　　IND　　　　　　IND

* The informant misunderstood the original sentence, which was 'The man who Asa gave the book to sent it to Henry'. This introduced a hole in the paradigm, as the sentence he actually signed has the head in the same location as (10).

(13)*Asa sent the man who gave Henry the book to school.*

ASA GET SEND MAN TO SCHOOL / MAN GIVE BOOK TO HENRY vt

(14)*Asa gave the book which Henry got from Lynn to his mother.*

ASA GIVE BOOK TO MOTHER / THAT BOOK LYNN GIVE HENRY vt

(15)*Asa sent the man to whom Henry gave the book to school.*

ASA GET SEND MAN TO SCHOOL / IND HENRY GIVE BOOK MAN vt
                                              M

(16)*Asa gave the book to the man who met Henry at school.*

ASA GIVE BOOK TO MAN / THAT MAN MEET HENRY IND SCHOOL
   M   M   IND   vt

(17)*Asa sent the book to the man who Henry met in school.*

ASA BOOK SEND TO MAN IND / HENRY IND MEET IND SCHOOL vt
           M----------------------------------

(18)*Asa got the book from the man who Henry gave the book to.*

HENRY   MEET BOOK GIVE / GIVE ASA   vt
     M   M---   M-------------

All these examples represent complicated relationships, and the English sentences are not simple. Although it sometimes required several readings, the informant was always able to convey in ASL the situation described in the English. Examples (13)-(15) are especially interesting. The head is located in the middle of the main clause in the English sentence, with other noun phrases at both beginning and end. The fact that the M sentence of the resulting ASL did not have to rearrange the word order indicates that the constraint that the site of the head in the M sentence must be next to the R sentence suggested above was wrong. But note that in these examples, the R sentence has been rearranged to put the head first in all cases. In fact, in all 26 examples which make up the relevant corpus, there is only one example, (7) above, where the site of the head is not at the beginning of the second sentence, whether M or R. But as for the deletion case, there is no reason to suppose this is due to any fact relating to relativization. First position is the preferred location for the topic in ASL, and clearly that which is common to both sentences, namely, the head, is a likely candidate for the role of topic in the second sentence, so we would expect to see it in first position (see Friedman, 1976a).

The simplest explanation for all the examples above now becomes quite clear. There is no such thing as a relative clause in ASL. Independently motivated deletion and topic placement rules account for such regularities as might appear to exist in the data, independent of their origin as translations of English sentences containing relatives. There is no apparent distinction between the translations of restrictive and nonrestrictive clauses. If there is any indication of subordination, it is determined semantically and/or contextually, not syntactically. ASL simply uses two or more coordinate, syntactically equal sentences where English uses a single sentence containing two clauses, one syntactically subordinate to the other.

Before leaving the topic of relative clauses, some comments are in order on a recent paper on the subject by Liddell (1976). Liddell describes an intonation contour which he says signals relative clauses in ASL. I feel that although the paper convincingly demonstrates the existence of a previously unremarked contour as well as its relevance to questions of ASL grammar, it does not contain any convincing evidence that relative clauses exist as a syntactic device in ASL, or that this contour serves to mark them. This paper is not the place for a detailed critique of Liddell's work, but as he does at one point briefly consider and explicitly reject a polysentential analysis similar to the one presented here, I think it only fair to point out the ways in which I find his arguments less than compelling.

Liddell's theoretical perspective on ASL is clearly very different from my own. He assumes, for instance, that ASL has preferential word order, and that a transformational analysis—including rules of topicalization and question formation—is appropriate to ASL. In contrast, I would say that ASL does not have preferential word order, and is best analyzed by a nontransformational discourse level grammar (c.f., Friedman, 1976a, and DeMatteo for more detail). It is therefore not surprising that I interpret the data he presents differently than he does.

It is unfortunate that more details on elicitation procedures and transcription methods were not included, since these can easily have subtle but important effects when investigating complex phenomena subject to more than one interpretation. This is especially true for ASL, because of its position at one end of the Sign Language Continuum (see Friedman's introduction to this volume for discussion). Disturbance of data by influences from the rest of the continuum is difficult to detect, difficult to guard against, and potentially seriously misleading. It is also unfortunate that no data on pause length and location is included in the paper. Given the difficulty of establishing sentence boundaries in ASL, some discussion of the basis on which such decisions were made seems in order, especially since the issue of polysentential coordination versus relativization is raised.

Liddell presents four arguments against a polysentential analysis. The first is that there are two different ways to sign the same sequence of lexical signs; one with a distinguished contour over part of the utterence, and one without the contour. The construction where the contour is absent is easily interpretable as two sentences. The one where it is present is most naturally translated into English using a relative clause. But this in itself says nothing one way or the other about whether the ASL construction is in fact one sentence with a relative clause, or two sentences, one with a marked intonation contour. An alternative explanation for the presence of such a contour, which in many contexts is suggestive of the function of relativization in English, will be offered below.

The second argument Liddell makes is that the two different versions already mentioned mean different things. It is hard to see what is meant by this: of course the data with the contour means something different from the data without it, but once again this implies nothing one way or the other about where the sentence boundaries fall.

His third argument is that if the contoured data is to be interpreted as two separate sentences, then other, explicit conjunctions should be permitted to intervene, e.g., BUT. He asserts that the fact that such intervening conjunctions are judged unacceptable stems from a syntactic constraint; but these judgements can be interpreted equally well as stemming from a pragmatic or functional constraint at the discourse level (see below).

His final argument is that a relative clause but not a sentence can appear as the object of a preposition, and he offers one example in which a clause with the marked contour appears as the object of a preposition. This is the only example given, and it does not contain plausible data. My feeling is that the example cited contains a correction, and is not interpretable as a single sentence. The sentence was uttered through the preposition, the speaker realized that his intended coding of the object of the preposition as a simple noun was insufficient to identify it for the addressee, paused, and produced a new sentence identifying it more fully. This is of course unlicensed speculation that I cannot substantiate without more examples along with pause data. No such examples occur anywhere in my data.

I would suggest that the correct analysis of the contour Liddell has discussed is that it is a discourse level marker of material either mentioned earlier in the discourse or present in the common speaker-hearer context, which material the speaker wishes to return to prominence. Liddell himself points out that many of the sentences he analyzes as relative clauses are sometimes preceded by verbs such as REMEMBER, KNOW, and SEE. To me, this is a clear indication that a discourse level referential meaning for the contour such as I have proposed is in fact correct. It is hard for me to see how any analysis of data such as ASA INTEREST SIGN KNOW (from (9) above) as a relative clause is possible.

Given the analysis I propose, the nonoccurrence of an intervening BUT, as discussed above, clearly follows. The function of the initial sentence is not assertion, but "foregrounding" reference, and so it is not a suitable basis for contrast. The presence of BUT in such a context makes no more sense than it does in the somewhat parallel English case:

There was a dog chasing a cat, remember? (*But) it came home.

In summary, I have tried to point out that Liddell's data, although certainly valuable for its presentation of a hitherto unremarked intonation contour of obvious importance to ASL grammar, nevertheless in no way establishes the existence in ASL of relative clauses as a syntactic form.

Indirect questions are closely related to relative clauses in English, as complement clauses introduced by a WH-word. With the exception of sentences with the verb KNOW, discussed below, ASL analogues of indirect questions fall into two categories as exemplified by the following.

(19) *He was still angry so he refused to tell me whether or not they had called.*
ANGRY NOT TELL-ME FINISH CALL o-r NOT-YET CALL

(20) *The child must do whatever the mother says.*
CHILD MUST FOLLOW MOTHER TELL CHILD

(21) ⁻ME⁺ ASK⁻ ME BORROW BOOK   vt
                 ?--------------------? (question intonation, brow furrowed,
                                                          eyebrows raised)
I asked if I could borrow the book.

(22) *You mustn't ask Mary how old she is.*
YOU MUST NOT ASK OLD
                        IND
                   ? (question intonation)

(23) MARK WANT KNOW / WHAT ASA GIVE HENRY WHAT   vt
Mark wanted to know what Asa gave Henry.

(19) and *(20)* are fairly far removed from the sense of questions in the English, and in ASL they are rendered by polysentential paraphrase, with sentence breaks presumably occurring after ANGRY and TELL-ME in (19) and after FOLLOW in (20). The others are much closer to the sense of questions, and appear to be rendered in ASL as some sort of direct speech. Thus in (21) the eye contact data suggests a sentence break after ASK and what follows, ME BORROW BOOK with question intonation throughout, is the normal rendering into ASL of the question 'Can I borrow that book?' Similarly in (22), pointing at someone while making the sign OLD with question intonation is one way to ask 'How old are you?', and in (23) the pause data clearly suggests two sentences, with the second being in standard direct question form. Once again in these cases we find no overt syntactic marker of subordination, and plausible analyses that do not involve any subordination at all. The verb KNOW, along with its lexicalized negative NOT-KNOW, has presented several examples which are resistant to this analysis, however. Several occurrences of KNOW HOW . . . or KNOW WHY . . . were observed, where there was at least some suggestion that the HOW or WHY had been combined with the KNOW to form a compound verb. Further investigation is clearly needed before claiming that these compounds are conceptually a single verb, although as long as no examples of KNOW WHAT. . . or KNOW WHO. . . turn up, such an analysis seems intuitively plausible. One further problem, about which I have nothing to suggest but feel obligated to mention, is the occurrence in discourse, on two separate occasions, of

the utterence ME NOT-KNOW WHO as a complete sentence.

In English a distinction is made between direct and indirect speech. There is a straightforward grammatical difference between *John said that he saw Bill* and *John said "I saw Bill"*, or between *I saw a man run across the street* and *I saw the following thing: a man ran across the street*. This distinction does not seem to exist in ASL. Consider the following examples.

(24) ME TELL [+]FRIEND[−] ME DOUBT GO   vt

   I told my friend that I doubted I would go.

(25) *He told me that there will be nice weather until Sunday.*

   IND [+]TELL-ME[−] [26] PRETTY DAY WILL CONTINUE UNTIL SUNDAY   vt

(26) *I saw Leora teaching Vicki to dance.*

   ME SEE [20] LEORA TEACH VICKI   vt

(27) [+]HAPPEN[−] [30] MOTHER CHILD FIND . . .   vt

   It happened that a mother found her child . . .

Many other examples fall into this pattern, including many with TELL and SEE. Certainly there is no grammatical marking of any subordination evident. I would suggest that in fact what we see here is really direct speech, that there is no distinction between direct and indirect speech in ASL. Support for this idea comes from the following additional facts: the narration of reported speech or thought is often accompanied by a slight change in body orientation, indicating adoption of the role of the reported speaker; first person pronouns often replace third person ones; and the verb of saying or thinking sometimes occurs both at the beginning and end, like quotation marks, delimiting the reported speech from the speaker's own. If this is the case, one can hardly talk of grammatical subordination. The so-called main verb is merely a context establishing comment on the important part, the reported act, speech, or thought which follows. The frequent presence of pauses or eye contact cues separating the comment from the report, as in all the examples above, also lends support to this idea. Now consider the following examples.

(28) *I expect Henry to write a good paper.*

   ME FEEL [20] HENRY GOOD WRITE PAPER   vt

(29) ME THINK / IND BETTER STOP EAT MEAT   vt

   I think you ought to stop eating meat.

I would like to suggest that an analysis similar to the one proposed above for verbs that report external perceptions such as SEE and TELL is also appropriate for verbs which report introspection of some sort, such as FEEL and THINK. I think examples (28) and (29) support this suggestion, but more data along this line are needed.

Nominalized sentences occur in English in many environments besides indirect speech, with many different grammatical markings such as **for-to, that, possessive-ing**, and so forth. The question of the existence and nature of nominalization in ASL is extremely complex. There are certainly no overt grammatical markers of nominalization, but a plausible analysis of all the various sorts of nominalization constructions in ASL purely in terms of coordinate structures is much harder to construct and motivate than it was for the other phenomena discussed above. The available data can be divided into three basic classes, depending on the verb involved. The first group consists largely of verbs which report emotional states.

(30) *I regret that Asa had to leave.*

MUST ASA MUST GO / SORRY   vt

(31) ASA ⁺RELIEVE⁻ / GIVE   TOM LYNN   vt
                              MONEY

Asa was relieved that Tom gave the money back to Lynn.

(32) ME SURPRISE YOU COME HERE   vt

I'm surprised you came here.

This type of response to an English nominalization was quite common. The nominalized proposition is expressed as an independent sentence, either preceded or followed by another sentence consisting of what were the higher verbs in the English. At least the following verbs fall in this class: HAPPY, ANGRY, SURPRISE, RELIEVE, SORRY, and PROMISE. English has two place predicates for most of these, but ASL predicates are one-place, experiencer-based (see Edge & Herrmann). Thus the English sentence *A irritated B* might be translated into ASL as B ANGRY FAULT A. Given this pattern of expressing the experiencer and the emotion in one sentence and the cause in another, no special device is needed to nominalize the causing event. In line with this, it is interesting to note that when given the sentence 'It bothers me that Amy didn't come to class today', the informant responded that he could not translate it into ASL using the verb BOTHER, which is a two-place predicate in ASL. If nominalization was possible, the result would be something like AMY NOT COME BOTHER ME. The evidence definitely places PROMISE in this class, which suggests that a better gloss might be *cross my heart* or *I am sworn.*

The next group of examples all involve the verb KNOW.

(33) *It is obvious that Mark hates cigarettes.*

YOU KNOW / MARK HATE CIGARETTE   vt

(34) *Lynn knew that nothing had happened.*

LYNN KNOW FOR-SURE NOTHING HAPPEN

These examples represent a more problematical type. Some sentences containing the verbs DOUBT and BELIEVE exhibit the same pattern. We have a pattern which looks very much like the English construction, only missing the *that*. Sometimes, as in (33), there is a pause, sometimes, as in (34), not. I frankly do not know whether to say that there is subordination here or not, or even how to tell. All the sentences of this type were obtained as translations of English sentences; none occurred in discourse. I can see three possible analyses: (1) These sentences are not ASL but rather Signed English, (2) they are ASL, but susceptible to the same kind of comment-report coordinate analysis as proposed earlier for THINK and FEEL; or (3) they are ASL, and they are a simple subordinate construction that occurs only with these verbs. The available data do not in my opinion provide conclusive support for any one of these three theories, although the lack of subordination elsewhere in the language suggests that of the three, the third is the least likely.

The last group contains three oddballs—WANT, STOP, and FORGET.

(35) *I want to go eat some ice cream.*

ME WANT GO ICE-CREAM   vt

(36) *. . .I'm quitting today.*

ME TODAY STOP WORK   vt

(37) LYNN FORGET TELL CLASS . . .   vt

Lynn forgot to tell the class that . . .

(38) ME WANT IND TEACH-ME VIDEOTAPE   vt

I wanted him to teach me to videotape.

(39) *I forgot that I was supposed to . . .*

ME FORGET [16] ME MUST . . .   vt

(35)–(37) are part of a large class of examples with those verbs. In contradistinction to the cases discussed for KNOW, there are never any significant pauses or eye contact markings in these sentences, and they occur both in discourses and translations. One possible analysis that suggests itself on the basis of both syntax and meaning is that these three are auxiliaries or modals like CAN, MUST, FINISH, etc. (see Fischer, 1973b). But what does this say about (38) and (39)? (39) is pretty much okay; other modals like SUCCEED and FINISH exhibit similar behavior, standing alone with a subject as an independent sentence. (38) is definitely a problem, however. No self-respecting modal allows two **different** subjects. I will return to this and the other possible counterexamples to the claim, but first a little more positive evidence.

The amount of grammatical interactions possible is much greater between a main clause and a subordinate clause than between two sentences. The examples given below, where in English a morpheme can be said to have crossed a clause boundary, but where it cannot make the equivalent move in the ASL translation, can thus be interpreted as evidence that the ASL translations are in fact two sentences.

(40) *Who do you think likes Cathy?*

    YOU ⁺THINK⁻ [10] WHO LIKE CATHY   vt
                 ?-----------------------------?

(41) *When do you expect to arrive in L.A.?*

    YOU FEEL [25] WHICH DAY ARRIVE l-a   vt
                ?------------------------------------?

Another possible test along the same lines would be to see whether NEG-raising can occur in ASL. Unfortunately, all attempts at obtaining ASL translations of NEG-raised English sentences produced some distress on the part of the informant, followed either by what was quite clearly a word-for-word Signed English translation, or else by a paraphrase in ASL that accurately conveyed the sense of the English, but that lacked sufficient grammatical relation to the English to permit conclusions to be drawn. No NEG-raised utterances were ever observed, either in discourse or in translation. The issue is further complicated by the fact that ASL appears to lack NEG-transportation as well, as evidenced by the examples below.

(42) *None of your friends is intelligent.*

    YOUR FRIENDS ALL STUPID
also   YOUR FRIENDS ALL ZERO SMART ZERO

(43) *Not one of my friends eats vegetables.*

    ALL MY FRIEND NOT-YET EAT v-e-g-e-

If, as these examples seem to indicate, the NEG morpheme is not particularly free to move around in ASL, it may be that NEG-raising is not possible for that reason, rather than because of any sentence boundary effects. Before returning to the main issue, I want to present two more examples which seem to be related to this whole question, but for which I have no analysis to offer.

(44) *Asa saw someone.*

(45) *All of your friends are not intelligent.*

   NOT ALL YOUR FRIEND / SMART
                                   NEG (headshake)

When presented with sentences like (44), the informant consistently refused the (normal in English) opaque reading of *someone* and insisted on the transparent reading. Something similar seems to be involved in (45), where the informant has picked a reading of the English sentence, ungrammatical for some speakers and much less favored by the rest, namely 'Not all of your friends are intelligent'. The Generative Semantics treatment of transparency-opacity and quantifier scope phenomena is based on questions of subordination, which is why I think these small problems may be related to the larger concern of this paper, but my intuition is no more detailed than that.

The last set of examples, which involve final clauses of various types, is only tangentially germane to my principal claim, since the constructions are coordinate in the original English as well as in ASL, but I include them nevertheless because I think they illustrate in a very subtle manner the way ASL uses sequentiality, juxtaposition, and space to communicate things for which English uses a lexical item.

(46) *I went to the store because Asa asked me to go.*

                    body turn
   ASA ASK ME   GO STORE

(47) *I went to the store because I was hungry.*

   ME GO STORE ME HUNGRY

(48) *Asa smashed the mirror.*

   MIRROR BREAK ASA THROW

(49) *Since she left him, he has lived alone.*

   HIS GIRLFRIEND LEAVE / NOW ASA LIVE ALONE

(50) *I haven't been to San Francisco since I was a little boy.*

   ME PAST TOUCH s-f ME CHILD / NOW PAST-CONT
   NOT-YET TOUCH s-f

In (46)–(48), we have causal situations, in (49) and (50) temporal ones, but in all cases no conjoining morpheme of any kind is present in ASL. In this respect, these examples are similar to all those already discussed.

In conclusion, I want to focus on the similarities of form represented in all the various ASL responses to complexities in English grammar. In every case we have two or three coordinate verb-argument clusters (I am purposely avoiding the word 'sentence') used to express something English uses a complex, subordinate structure to express. ASL uses the arrangement of these clusters in time and space to make their semantic relationships clear; English uses special-purpose morphemes and syntactic subordination. An explanation for this may lie in the differences in the two modalities within which these languages operate. It has been claimed that short-term iconic memory is much more limited than short-term echoic memory. This might provide a strong stimulus for languages in the visual modality to present information in smaller discrete chunks than is necessary for an oral language. This in turn encourages coordinate rather than subordinate organization of discourse. If the grammatical processing (assumed to take place in short-term memory) associated with each verb-argument chunk can be completed without reference to preceding or following chunks for **grammatical** information (i.e., coordination), no excessive strain will be placed on short-term memory. Disambiguation and the establishment of semantic relationships, which an oral language can afford to accomplish at a grammatical level, is performed at some more conceptual level by a visual language, since the lack of short-term iconic memory forbids complex grammatical processing.

The status of the few potential counterexamples mentioned earlier is unclear with respect to this explanation of the lack of subordination. It seems reasonable to suppose that a completely right-branching subordinate structure, together with a very common and basic verb at the top, does not present any processing problem. The semantic role of the embedded clause is completely determined in advance, and as long as there is no grammatical interaction with the higher verb, which there does not appear to be, there is no functional distinction between a subordinate and a coordinate structure, and in fact we cannot distinguish between the two. I think this suggests that, rather than consider this whole set of phenomena as a question regarding the availability of some grammatical construction in ASL, we should see them as clues to the ways in which the medium constrains the degree of grammatical/syntactic complexity that is permitted, because of constraints on processing.

In closing, let me reiterate that what I have attempted to demonstrate in this paper is the absence of a **syntactic** form in ASL, not of a linguistic function. It is easy to confuse the two notions, and to mistake a discussion of the evidence for and against the correlation of some syntactic form in ASL with syntactic forms used to accomplish similar functions in other languages, for a discussion of the **existence** in ASL of **any** mechanism—syntactically distinguished or not—which accomplishes that function. Thus, I am **not** claiming that ASL lacks the wherewithal to express certain linguistic function, which English expresses with marked syntactic forms, e.g., the restrictive relative clause, but simply that ASL uses no marked syntactic forms for that purpose. Moral: In doing field research on the structure of an exotic language, preconceptions are extremely dangerous. You will probably find what you are looking for, whether it is there or not.

ON THREE ASPECTS OF TIME EXPRESSION
IN AMERICAN SIGN LANGUAGE

Cathy Cogen

0. Introduction

Any language must provide surface representations for concepts of time like tense and aspect. Basic concepts of time include the time of the speech act, the time before the speech act, and the time after the speech act. In addition to a means for establishing temporal reference relative to the time of the speech act, the language must provide a means for making temporal reference relative to a pre-established reference time. That is, there must be a way to establish a reference time and then refer to time before and after. For example, the past perfect tense in English allows a speaker to refer to a time preceding a time previously established as before the speech act.

In American Sign Language (ASL), basic concepts of time are expressed relative to the signer's body along a time plane. Specific aspects of time, such as calendric units, are expressed within this system. However, more complex time locutions involving time reference relative to a time other than the time of the speech act require other devices, such as temporal ordering.

Time expressions and temporal reference in American Sign Language have been discussed previously. Fischer and Gough (1972) present an analysis of the uses of the perfective markers FINISH and NOT-YET; Frishberg and Gough (1973) and Friedman (1975b) describe the manifestation of temporal reference along the time plane, and the expression of time units within this system.

This paper will be concerned with the manifestation of time concepts in ASL, dealing specifically with the following topics: (a) the use of the time space for making temporal reference to one point or to a progression of points in time, focusing, in particular, on the use of PAST-CONTINUOUS as a temporal index; (b) the manner in which past and future indices combine with signs for calendric units; and (c) the representation of more complex time locutions, focusing on the expression of the concept of 'until'.

1.   The Manifestation and Use of the Time Space

In ASL, time relative to the time of the speech act is expressed within a vertical plane which extends forward and backward alongside the signer's body. The time space can be seen as divided into three primary areas. An imaginary line running down the side of the signer's cheek can serve as a base, relative to which we can describe the time spaces. The space from this line to the area immediately in front of the signer's body designates present time. For example, the signs NOW, HERE, and (TO) DAY are articulated in this area. The space extending forward from the body marks future time. A short movement forward from the base line on the cheek is associated with near future. For example, TOMORROW is signed with a fist, thumb extended ($\mathring{A}$-hand configuration), making contact at the base line on the cheek and brushing forward. A larger, more extended movement forward denotes more distant future. The sign WILL/FUTURE uses a flat, open palm (B-hand configuration), starting adjacent to the base line, and moving forward into future space. Very distant future is expressed by a stressed and reduplicated index.[1]

The space behind the base line and extending to the area behind the body refers to past time. Again, the area closest to the base line marks near past; the area behind the ear, farther from the base line, refers to more distant past. The sign YESTERDAY illustrates near past: with an $\mathring{A}$-hand configuration (fist with thumb extended) contact is made first at the base line on the cheek, and then just behind that line, toward the cheekbone, a point indicating near past. More distant past can be illustrated by the sign BEFORE/PAST, in which a flat open palm, facing backward, motions over the shoulder toward the space behind the ear. More recent past can be indicated by a smaller movement, ending in repeated contact with the shoulder, while a stressed or reduplicated index denotes very distant past.

In ordinary ASL discourse, the time of the speech act is unmarked time. The signer can establish temporal reference by the use of time adverbials (e.g., 'yesterday', 'every week'), perfective markers[2], or by indexic references to a point or set of points on the time plane. A sentence or discourse containing no temporal reference is interpreted as unmarked or present time, unless context indicates otherwise. The term 'indexic reference' as used here, includes the signs FUTURE and PAST already described, and PAST-CONTINUOUS, which is described below. Indexing reestablishes the time represented at the body as coreferential to the reference time.[3] Once temporal reference has been made, all discourse refers to that period of time, until new time reference is established.

Temporal reference along the time plane is quite consistent. Progression of time is expressed by progression of movement along these points of reference. For example, the notion 'as time goes on', as in (1), is expressed by a motion which begins with a flat open palm (B) facing the signer's ear, and moves slowly toward the future.

    (1) FUTÚRE (elongated) CHARLOTTE IMPROVE SIGN
       As time goes on, Charlotte's signing improves.

The meaning of 'as time goes on' includes the concept of past time: time that has been and is now in progress. The sign does seem to depict this notion. It differs from the sign for FUTURE, in that it starts farther back, close to the ear, indicating past time, and moves slowly forward, depicting time in progress.

PAST-CONTINUOUS is one sign which denotes a progression of time by indicating a set of points on the time plane. The following discussion describes how PAST-CONTINUOUS functions to establish temporal reference.

In the formation of the PAST-CONTINUOUS, both hands are held, index fingers pointing downward, near the dominant[4] shoulder which is in line with the ear and is within the area referring to past time. The wrists revolve slightly, so that the index fingers point toward the rear of the signer, as both hands move forward in an arc to the space immediately in front of the body—the space referring to present time. Thus, the sign is said to have the sense of 'it has been true up to now',[5] The visual image the sign creates within the time plane is consistent with that sense. It visually includes all points on the time plane between the past and the present.

PAST-CONTINUOUS creates a 'picture' of elapsed time. Its use does not seem to depend on the type of action that took place during the reference time; it can occur in constructions with durative or point-of-action verbs, statives, as well as 'psych' verbs. The sign PAST-CONTINUOUS has been translated into English as 'up to now', 'have been', 'ever since' and 'between then and now'. It does seem to serve a purpose similar to that served by these English phrases: it allows the signer to refer to a specific time span between the past and the present. As the 'picture' created by this sign suggests, its use does not imply anything about the future state of affairs, as we see from (2), and it does not seem to require a particularly long period of time, as we see from (3).

(2) a. ⌈ R ME PAST-CONTINUOUS WORK+ u-c   /ME q-u-i-t TODAY
　　　 ⌊ L   INDEX (left)

　　　 I have been working at U.C. I am quitting today.

　　 b. ⌈ R ME PAST-CONTINUOUS WORK++ u-c   / ME TEACH
　　　 ⌊ L   INDEX (left)

　　　 ⌈ R SIGN CLASS/ ME WILL CONTINUE NEXT SUMMER
　　　 ⌊ L

　　　 I have been working at U.C. I have been teaching a sign class. I will continue through(?) next summer.

(3) a. CHARLOTTE COLD++ PAST-CONTINUOUS/ MELT/ YESTERDAY
　　　 Charlotte has had a cold. It went away yesterday.

　　 b. LEORA JEFF TOGETHER++ SEVEN-YEAR/ WOW
　　　 Leora and Jeff have been together for seven years. Wow!

In (2a), the action described will end 'today', while in (2b), the action will continue. The PAST-CONTINUOUS can co-occur with a relatively short time period, while sentences indicating long periods of time do not always require the PAST-CON-TINUOUS.

PAST-CONTINUOUS indexes a set of points along the time plane, referring to that period of time which the signer wants to talk about. It functions in much the same way as the PAST and FUTURE indices, the difference being that PAST-CONTINUOUS indexes a progression of time between the past and the present.

It is not always necessary to use indexic reference to establish the reference time. For example, in the appropriate context, past durative and iterative action can be expressed by reduplication of the verb, without PAST-CONTINUOUS.

(4) ⌈ R ADAM QUESTION+++   TWO-HOUR
   | (alternating hands)
   ⌊ L   QUESTION+++

Adam has been asking questions for two hours.

(5) ANSWER++ QUESTION++ FIVE FIVE-HOUR

I have been answering questions for five hours.

(6) ⌈ R ME THINK-OVER GO l-a l-a FRIDAY SATURDAY SUNDAY
   |
   ⌊ L   THINK-OVER

I have been thinking of going to L.A. Friday, Saturday, and Sunday.

As in (4) and (6), a normally one-handed sign can be made with two hands, indicating that the activity has been going on intensively over a period of time. The reduplication in (4) may be accompanied by horizontal movement in an arc to one side, or from side to side.

That (4) and (6) describe action going on continuously from a point in time in the past up to the present would be made clear by the context of the discourse in which the utterances occur. The context could distinguish whether (4), for example, meant *Adam asked questions for two hours (last night)* or *Adam asked questions for two hours (up to now)*.

ASL constructions elicited from isolated English 'have been' sentences tend to occur with the PAST-CONTINUOUS, since out of context, this marker is needed to refer specifically to the time span up to the present.

(7) SHE PAST-CONTINUOUS SECRET / NOW SHE TELL-ME

She has been secretive up to now. Now she tells me (things).

(8) ME PAST-CONTINUOUS LIVE HERE SIX YEAR

I have lived here for six years.

(9) ME PAST-CONTINUOUS WORK+ INDEX (right) u-c NINE WEEK

I have been working at U.C. for nine weeks.

However, within a context where the time reference was clearly understood as 'up to now', the PAST-CONTINUOUS would most likely not be used. That is, as with other time indices, like PAST or FUTURE, once temporal reference has been made, all discourse refers to that time period, until new time reference is made. The PAST-CONTINUOUS in (7)- (9) is used to re-establish the time represented at the body as coreferential to the time 'up to now', in the same way that the PAST index establishes past reference in (10).

(10) ME PAST GO+++ LIBRARY DAILY NIGHT / NOW IT CLOSED NIGHT

I used to go to the library every night. Now it is closed at night.

Here, the PAST index allows the signer to talk about the period of time prior to the speech act. Then, NOW is a time adverbial which re-establishes the reference to present time. If (10) had occurred in a discourse in which past temporal reference had been established previously, it is likely that the PAST index would not have been signed.

Examples (11) and (12) can refer to the time span up to the present without the use of the PAST-CONTINUOUS.

(11) ME LIVE HERE SIX YEAR

I have lived here for six years.

(12) ME WORK++++ / TEACHER SIGN INDEX (left) u-c / WORK+++ / ME TODAY FINISH

I was working at U.C. until today.

It is not necessary to use the PAST-CONTINUOUS once the time span the signer is referring to is understood by the signer and the addressee. In fact, it may be that the PAST-CONTINUOUS occurred in examples (7)- (9) only because of the circumstances of the elicitation. These were all elicited from single English 'have been' sentences, out of context. In texts of normal discourse and story telling, many constructions occur which refer to the time from the past up to the present. Where temporal reference has been established as 'up to now' previously in the discourse, the PAST-CONTINUOUS is not used. Similarly in the elicitation of past tense constructions from single past tense English sentences, each sign construction occurred with a PAST index, while it is clear that in ordinary discourse, once the reference is established, it is not normally repeated with each utterance.

Examples (13) and (14) illustrate how the PAST-CONTINUOUS is used to establish new temporal reference.

(13) ME PAST+ TOUCH s-f ME CHILD PAST-CONTINUOUS TOUCH NOT-
      YET s-f

      I went to San Francisco as a child. Since that time I haven't been there.

(14) (past tense established by text)   ME GO SCHOOL MEET+ MANY
      FRIEND+ MEET+++ PAST-CONTINUOUS MANY YEAR MEET++
      FRIEND // BUT NOT CLOSE FRIEND

      *(When) I went to school, I made a lot of friends. Since then, a period of
      many years, I made a lot of friends, but not close friends.*

Temporal reference in (13) is first established by the use of a reduplicated past index,
denoting distant past when the signer went to San Francisco. The PAST-CONTIN-
UOUS then re-establishes the reference as the time span between the past and the
present. Similarly in (14), the PAST-CONTINUOUS re-establishes the time reference
from the past up to the present.

In this section, I have presented and discussed various aspects of the time-space
and temporal reference. In particular I focused on the PAST- CONTINUOUS which
functions in much the same way as the past and future time indices. Indexic references can be used to establish and/or re-establish temporal reference in ASL
discourse.

2. Calendric Units

We have seen some ways in which the space around the body is used for the
expression of basic concepts of time. The signs for calendric units are integrated
into this system. Frishberg and Gough (1973) and Friedman (1975b) have explored
this topic to some extent. The following discussion presents a reiteration, extension,
and refinement of some of their observations.

Friedman points out that the time of the speech act is unmarked time. That is,
the use of a lexical item (e.g., MONTH, DAY, NIGHT, YEAR) without any accompanying time reference indicates that period of time containing the speech act. For
example, DAY, without another time adverbial or index, means 'today'. However,
the signer has the option of signing NOW plus, for example, YEAR to mean 'this
year'. This is done for the purpose of emphasis or contrast.

Movements denoting past and future time can be combined with calendric
units to refer to the unit of time immediately preceding or following the unit
containing the speech act. The index may occur preceding or following the time
item, that is, TIME UNIT + INDEX (to past or future) or INDEX + TIME UNIT.
It is possible that the shape of the time item plays a role in determining whether
the index precedes or follows the time item. Those time items whose shape combines easily with the movement of the index may become lexicalized, and the form
that the index takes is associated with the shape of the time item with which it is

used. WEEK, for example, combines quite easily and consistently with time indices. The sign LAST-WEEK is made by signing a lexicalized form of WEEK+PAST. The dominant hand used in the formation of WEEK has the index finger extended (G-hand configuration), orientation away from the signer. However, in the formation of LAST-WEEK, the orientation of the articulator anticipates the past index and thus takes an orientation toward the signer. The articulator, in a G-hand configuration then brushes across a flat, open palm and in one continuous sweep, is thrown over the dominant shoulder, indexing past. However, many signers do not change the orientation of the dominant hand. WEEK is signed in the standard form, orientation of the articulator outward; the past index is made, maintaining the G-hand configuration and the outward orientation of the palm.

'Next week' is signed with the standard form for WEEK. The articulator, with the G-hand, orientation away from the signer, sweeps across a flat, open palm, and continues to move into future space, maintaining the G-hand shape.

Numeral incorporation occurs quite freely with the sign WEEK. TWO-WEEKS, THREE-WEEKS, and so on, can be signed by changing the shape of the articulator from the standard hand shape—index finger extended—to the hand shapes for TWO, THREE, and so on. Numerals above nine do not incorporate. In addition, numerals can combine with PAST and FUTURE indices. For example, 'two weeks from now' is signed with the same movement as NEXT-WEEK, but the articulator holds a TWO hand configuration. In TWO-WEEKS-AGO, the movement is the same as that of LAST-WEEK, but, again, the articulator holds the TWO hand shape.

The construction of MONTH+TIME INDEX does not allow assimilation as easily as WEEK. It seems that, at least with LAST-MONTH, either order, MONTH+INDEX, or INDEX+MONTH, is possible. Frishberg and Gough attribute the lack of assimilation with MONTH to the shape of the sign. They suggest that it may not be possible to.combine the downward motion of MONTH with an index to past in a smooth, easy movement.

The sign for NEXT-MONTH is formed with some variant of the sign for NEXT plus the sign for MONTH, in that order. NEXT can occur in citation form, both hands held with flat, open palms (B-hand configuration) facing the signer, one moving over the other. It can also occur as a simple movement of the articulator in a B-hand configuration, away from the signer toward future space.

MONTH can also incorporate numerals. It is normally formed by sliding the back of the index finger of the dominant hand down the side of the index finger of the nondominant hand. The orientation of the dominant hand is normally palm toward the signer. Normal orientation is maintained for numerals 'two' through 'five'. However, outward orientation of the palm tends to occur for numerals 'six' through 'nine'. The normal PAST index (flat palm motioning over the shoulder) is used in signing, for example, 'three months ago'. The numeral can be incorporated as described, or it can occur separately, THREE (ONE-)MONTH PAST. Moreover, the index to past can occur before or after MONTH, apparently without altering the meaning.

IN-TWO-MONTHS can occur with the numeral incorporated plus an index to the future. The future index can take the standard form of the sign WILL/FUTURE (flat, open palm motioning forward) or a form of the sign LATER, in which the articulator holding the *L*-hand (index finger and thumb extended) reaches out into future space.

In the basic sign for 'year', the dominant fist circles the nondominant fist, ending in contact, the dominant fist over the nondominant fist. LAST-YEAR and NEXT-YEAR are signed with a reduced form of YEAR. The sign consists simply of a single contact of the fists, combined with time indices to the past or future space. The dominant hand with index finger extended (*G*- or ONE-hand configuration) moves forward in NEXT-YEAR, or is thrown over the dominant shoulder in LAST-YEAR. Numerals can combine with the past and future indices only through 'four' or 'five'. Numerals above 'five' are signed separately and the normal past and future indices are used, for example, SIX YEAR PAST.

Habitual or periodic time reference is expressed by repetition of the time unit. Repetition is frequently used in ASL to denote repeated action or plurality. Brushing repetition is used in the signs for 'daily', 'every week', 'every month', 'every year'.

The sign DAILY is not based on the sign for 'day', which is formed in the area of present time on the time plane. Instead, DAILY is derived from the sign TOMORROW. Frishberg and Gough suggest that the complexity of the movement involved in DAY may not lend itself to an easy repeated movement. Moreover, every segment of DAY is a sign within the system: DAWN, MORNING, NOON, etc. The sign TOMORROW may be more accurately glossed as 'the next day', anchored to the reference time established in the sentence or discourse. For example, in a narrative, where past temporal reference has been established, the sign TOMORROW would be used for 'He returned home and **the next day** he . . .' Repeated brushing movement of this sign results in the meaning 'the next day and the next day . . .', or 'day after day after day . . .', that is, 'daily'.[6] The sign has come to mean 'every', when used with other repeated time items. For example, the sign for 'every week' commonly occurs as DAILY WEEK+++. The repeated movement of the articulator across the flat palm of the nondominant hand is accompanied by downward movement of the entire sign with each new formation, as if moving across each week on a calendar. Incorporation of numerals into this pattern can denote 'every two weeks', 'every three weeks', and so on.

'Every month' often occurs with DAILY plus a repeated form of MONTH, in a horizontal, arclike movement. Numerals can also be incorporated with DAILY-MONTH to denote 'every two (three, four . . .) months'.

'Every year' also occurs with DAILY. The reduced form of YEAR is used; 'every year' is a repeated form of the sign for 'next year'. Numerals can combine with past and future indices only through 'four' or 'five'. Numerals above 'five' tend to be signed separately and the normal past and future indices are used.

In each of these cases, the sign is repeated and re-formed to create the habitual reading. However, signs denoting parts of days, for example, NIGHT, MORNING,

AFTERNOON, are not re-formed to express regular intervals. Rather, contact is maintained as the entire sign moves smoothly to one side. 'Every night', for example, is formed with DAILY NIGHT (moving to one side).

Signs for the days of the week are formed with a rotating motion of the initial letter (from the manual alphabet) of the English word for each day. For example, the sign for MONDAY is a rotating *M*. THURSDAY is formed either with *T-H*, or simply *H*, in order to avoid confusion with the *T* for TUESDAY. The orientation of the hand can be either palm toward the signer or palm away from the signer. In signing, for example, EVERY-MONDAY, however, the circular motion is lost. 'Every Monday' is expressed by DAILY plus an *M*-hand configuration moving smoothly downward. SUNDAY is formed with both hands, flat palms facing away from the signer. EVERY-SUNDAY is made with DAILY plus both hands moving smoothly downward.

As mentioned earlier, the numerals 'ten' and above do not incorporate. Instead, the numeral occurs in isolation before the formation of the time item. In fact, all numerals can occur in this form, for example,

(15) ME STAY NEW YORK SIX (ONE)-MONTH

I'll be staying in New York for six months.

(16) HENRY START LEARN++ SIGN FOUR (ONE)-WEEK PAST

Henry started learning sign four weeks ago.

Numerals above 'three' or 'four' tend to occur in isolation more frequently than lower numerals. Often a numeral occurs in isolation before it is signed in the incorporated form as in,

(17) ME PAST WORK u-c PAST FOUR FOUR-MONTH

I was working at U.C. four months ago.

(18) ME PAST WORK THERE PAST (THREE) THREE-MONTH

I was working there three months ago.

This type of isolation tends to occur with numerals above 'three', probably because it aids visibility of the numeral. The numeral also occurs in isolation when it is stressed, for example,

(19) ME WALK+++ THREE THREE-HOUR

I have been walking for three hours!

The general tendency is to sign numerals 'one' to 'four' in the incorporated form, while numerals from 'five' to 'ten' tend to occur in isolation preceding the incorporated form.

We have seen how the signs for calendric units are integrated into the time plane. The signs combine with past and future indices, and numeral incorporation occurs within the system.

3. More Complex Time Locutions

The preceding discussion has presented and described some ways in which temporal reference can be established in ASL, relative to the time of the speech act. In addition to a means for expressing this type of temporal relationship, any language must provide a means for making temporal reference relative to a pre-established reference time.[7] Various devices exist among languages for this purpose. One option employed by many oral languages in the use of special lexical items. English, for example, can use words like 'before', 'after', 'then', and 'until' to express such temporal relationships.[8]

(20) a. *I left before he called.*
      b. *He called after I left.*
      c. *I left. Then he called.*

(20) illustrates three different surface forms describing the same sequence of events (though each has a slightly different focus). It is clear that English does not necessarily rely on temporal order to relate one time to another.

ASL, on the other hand, tends to rely on temporal ordering to convey notions expressed by the English 'before', 'after', 'then', and 'until'. Because of its visual modality, the signer can create an image which closely reflects the real-world situation. Reporting events chronologically, the signer creates a visual representation of the actual situation. From the visual representation, we infer time relationships and causality in much the same way as we would had we witnessed the real-world situation ourselves.

Though there are lexical items in ASL for 'before' and 'after', these signs are seldom used in ASL discourse.[9] Their usage would seem to reflect language closer to Signed English on the sign language continuum.[10] In ASL, these notions are most commonly expressed by means of chronological sequencing of temporal references, or in other words, by reporting events in real-world temporal order. For example, our informant was given the following story:

Leora and Asa were sitting and gossiping about Vicki. Vicki came up and Leora and Asa stopped gossiping. The three of them chatted for a while. Then Vicki left. Leora and Asa started gossiping again.

In answer to the question, 'When were Leora and Asa gossiping?' he replied:

(21) ⌈R ASA LEORA GOSSIP ABOUT VICKI/ VICKI   STOP GOSSIP
     ⌊L   COME

Asa and Leora were gossiping about Vicki. Vicki came. (They)
stopped gossiping.

The idea that the gossiping was going on before Vicki came is expressed by reporting the string of events in the order that they actually occurred. Asked when Asa
and Leora started gossiping again, the informant responded:

(22) ⌈ R VICKI GOSSIP
     ⌊ L   GO

Vicki left. (They) gossiped.

With the use of real-world temporal order, the signer tells us that the gossiping
began after Vicki left the scene. Whether Vicki's coming in (21) **caused** the gossiping to stop, or whether her leaving in (22) **allowed** the gossiping to continue, is a
question of the inference made from the temporal relationship between the events
described. Temporal ordering implies causality.

ASL differs from English in that it tends to rely on the use of temporal ordering to convey causal relationships. English, on the other hand, can express causal
relationships with a variety of surface forms. For example, (23 a–c) could describe
the same real-world situation.

(23) a. *I made him cry.*
     b. *I hit him and he cried.*
     c. *He cried because I hit him.*

Although (23b) contains no *CAUSE* morpheme, and no causal verb, it still conveys
the same causal relationship as do (23a) and (23c). The most common way to express this relationship in ASL seems to be as in (24):

(24) ME HIT HIM / HE CRY

     I hit him. He cried.

Again, (24) contains no *CAUSE* morpheme, and no causal verb, but temporal order
is maintained, from which we infer causality.

The following discussion is concerned with the manner in which the notion of
'until' is expressed in ASL. The principles of temporal ordering and causality presented above are important in determining the surface forms of 'until' constructions.

We can visualize the semantic notion expressed in English as 'until' very basically as a sequence of events or states occurring through time.

Until Phrase

Interval I ∧ Interval II

The period of time indicated by the 'until phrase' marks the end of the first interval. The 'until phrase' can simply indicate a point in time (e.g., 1975, yesterday), or it can describe a condition or event that in some sense causes a change, marking the start of the second interval. This distinction does not seem to be important as far as English surface structure is concerned. However, we will see that the distinction determines the form of the ASL structure, since temporal ordering of events implies causality.

The description of the new state of affairs that prevails in Interval II is not made explicit in English. 'Until' marks the point in time at which the first state of affairs ceases to prevail, and implies some sort of change in the situation, which is why a sentence like (25) is odd.

(25) ?Lewie was miserable until he moved to Arkansas, and now he's
     still miserable.

The second conjunct in (25) is unexpected because of the assumptions we make about the use of 'until'.

Essentially, ASL utilizes three surface forms for the expression of 'until'. One involves the use of the lexical item UNTIL, which is formed with two hands, both with index finger extended: the dominant articulator forms an arc ending with the tip of the index finger contacting the tip of the nondominant finger. The other two forms express the semantic content of 'until' in full, by means of ordered phrasing. Each of these different surface forms seems to provide a different focus. We will return to this distinction later.

Let us first discuss the forms that do not make use of the lexical item UNTIL. Consider the following examples:

(26) ME CAN'T MARRY YOU / FIRST MOTHER DIE / ME MARRY YOU
     I can't marry you until my mother dies.

(27) GIRL PRINCE SLEEP / KING COME / KISS / WAKE-UP
     The princess slept until the king kissed her.

(28) ⎡ R   ME NOW WITH ASA body turns right/ ME SEARCH HOUSE
     ⎣ L   INDEX (left)------------------------------ HOUSE

     ⎡ R   body turns slightly left FIND body turns left to
     ⎣ L   original position

     ⎡ R   MOVE (from place where Asa's house was originally established
     ⎣ L   in space to place where new house was set up)

     I'll be living with Asa until I find a new house.

Each of these examples provides a very vivid description of a series of events. What is expressed here is the full semantic content of the notion of 'until'. Notice how much more is depicted by the ASL construction in (28), for example, than in the English translation. Friedman (1975b) points out that with two available articulators, a signer is capable of articulating two phrases at the same time.

> The nondominant hand may also serve to maintain locative, temporal or pronominal reference while the dominant hand articulates the comment relevant to that reference. [p. 953]

(28) then, expresses the following:

(28') (a) I am now (staying) with Asa. (b) (In the meantime) I am searching for a house. (c) (When or after) I find it (d) I'll move out (of Asa's) into the new house.

'In the meantime' is expressed by holding the left hand index while simultaneously signing SEARCH to the right. The index is dropped to sign HOUSE, which is formed with two hands. The content expressed in (b) and (d) is not at all explicit in the English sentence. (d) expresses the content of Interval II, information which we must assume to be true from the English sentence in (28).

In (26)-(28), there is causal relationship between the 'until phrase' and the event of the second interval. In each case, the 'until phrase' states a condition, which, when satisfied, causes or allows the consequence specified in the last phrase. Striving for a visual representation of the real-world situation, the signer uses chronological sequencing of events, from which we can infer the causal relationship.

As I suggested earlier, the function of the 'until phrase' determines the form of the structure. In the following examples, causality is not involved.

(29) ASA NOT-KNOW WIFE PREGNANT/ FIND-OUT PAST TWO-MONTH

Asa didn't know his wife was pregnant until two months ago (i.e., he found out two months ago).

(30) LYNN SINGLE++/ SHE FINALLY MARRY/ TWO YEAR PAST/ 1973

Lynn was single until two years ago, 1973 (i.e., she finally married two years ago, 1973),

(31) CHARLOTTE WIDE-EYED/ SLEEP TIME 9

Charlotte was awake until 9:00 (i.e., she fell asleep at 9:00).

(29)-(31) simply relate two events in the order that they actually occurred. The 'until phrase' added to the end of the sentence just tells us **when** the new state occurred. It is the ordering of the 'until phrase' **between** the two intervals that creates the causal relationship.

(32) ASA SLEEP/ TIME 9/ GET-UP/ GO SCHOOL

Asa was asleep. (When) it was 9:00, he got up and went to school.

(33) ME CAN'T TELEPHONE YOU/ TIME 6/ ME TELEPHONE YOU

I can't call you. (When it is) 6:00, I'll call you.

Here, in (32) and (33), there is a causal relationship between the 'until phrase' and the second interval. (32) was elicited within a context where Asa was planning to get up at 9 o'clock, so that, when it was 9 o'clock, there was, in fact, cause for him to get up. In (33) apparently the signer knows that he will be able to call the addressee at 6 o'clock, and not before that time (in a sense, its becoming 6 o'clock causes, or at least allows, the signer to call). Returning again to (30), it is probably the case that 'two years ago' would not provide a cause for Lynn to get married. (Although it might be possible to create such a context, it is not a very usual or likely circumstance.) The same reasoning holds true for (31). In fact, a native signer has said that a construction like (34) is odd.

(34) *CHARLOTTE WIDE-EYED/ TIME 9/ SLEEP

Charlotte was awake until 9.

Most likely, (34) is unacceptable because the ordering suggests a causal relationship, and it would be quite unlikely that its being 9 o'clock could actually cause someone to fall asleep. (Again, we could probably create an unusual situation, where 9 o'clock could cause Charlotte to sleep, and perhaps in that case (34) would be acceptable.)

There is, then, a clear distinction between constructions like the following:

(35) ASA SLEEP/ GET-UP TIME 9

Asa slept until 9:00 (He got up at 9:00).

(36) ASA SLEEP/ TIME 9/ GET-UP

Asa slept until 9:00 (when it was 9:00, he got up).

A causal relationship is expressed in (36), but not (35). The notion of causality is inferred from the chronological representation of the events. (36) seems to focus on the causal relationship, while the focus in (35) is on the change in state or activity from the first interval to the second, with no causal relationship. In (35) the 'until phrase' serves to indicate when the first interval ended and the second began. The 'until phrase' in (36), however, represents a condition causing the change in state from Interval I to Interval II.

But notice that the relationship expressed in (36) is not considerably different from that expressed in (21)

(21) ⌈ R ASA LEORA GOSSIP ABOUT VICKI/ VICKI   STOP GOSSIP
     ⌊ L   COME

Asa and Leora were gossiping about Vicki. Vicki came. (They) stopped gossiping.

In both cases, a sequence of events is listed. Such a sequence of events could be used to express the notions of 'before', 'after', or 'until'. But, what exactly is the notion of 'until'? It denotes a relationship between time intervals, entailing notions of 'before' and 'after' and presupposing a change in the status quo from the 'before' period to the 'after' period (and includes perhaps some sense of causality).

As mentioned earlier, ASL has a lexical item UNTIL. I would suggest that it focuses on Interval I, rather than on the change from Interval I to Interval II, or on the causal relationship existing between the 'until period' and the second interval. The sign itself creates an image of progression of time up to one particular point. From the examples I have examined, it seems that, as its image suggests, the sign focuses on the time span up to the particular point in time where the first interval ceases to prevail. Consider, for comparison, (37) and (38).

(37) LYNN SINGLE++/ SHE FINALLY MARRY/ TWO YEARS PAST/ 1973

Lynn was single until two years ago, 1973.

(38) LYNN SINGLE++/ NOT MARRY SINGLE+/ UNTIL (slow movement) 1973/ MARRY

Lynn was single. She didn't marry until 1973. She got married.

While (37) seems to focus on Lynn's marriage in 1973, (38) seems to dwell on the fact that she was single, and did not marry in all the time up to 1973. In fact, the slow movement of UNTIL indicates a long period of time passing.

A similar difference in perspective is illustrated by (39) and (40).

(39) CHARLOTTE WIDE-EYED/ SLEEP TIME 9

Charlotte was awake until 9:00.

(40) CHARLOTTE TOSS-AND-TURN+++ UNTIL 3/ SLEEP

Charlotte tossed and turned (for a long time) until 3:00.

(39) describes two states of affairs concentrating on the fact that Charlotte fell asleep at 9 o'clock. In (40) the signer draws one's attention to Interval I, first by the use of the very graphic sign, TOSS-AND-TURN, from which one can actually

visualize a person tossing and turning uncomfortably in bed. The repetitiveness of
the sign indicates that the action continued for a long time. UNTIL then tells us
that the action continued during the time period all the way up to 3 o'clock. The
signer has presented a very vivid picture of that particular period of time. The
difference in focus between a construction with UNTIL and one expressing a causal
relationship is illustrated below. The informant was given the following story:

> Mark has to go in and talk to Lynn every week about his paper. When he
> finishes the paper, he won't have to go in every week anymore.

When asked how much longer Mark will have to continue his visits to Lynn, the
informant replied:

(41) MARK MUST GO SEE LYNN DAILY WEEK++++ UNTIL HE PAPER
WRITE FINISH

> Mark must go see Lynn every week until he finishes writing his paper.

Asked when Mark can stop going to see Lynn, the informant responded:

(42) FINISH PAPER / NOT MUST SEE LYNN

> When the paper is finished, he won't have to see Lynn.

While the first question leads to concentration or focus on the first interval, the
second question calls for focus on the causal relationship. Interval I in example
(42) is understood from the context of the utterance, and thus need not be stated.
The difference in focus is also illustrated by (43) and (44).

(43) $\begin{bmatrix} \text{R} & \text{MY FRIEND FROM l-a COME++ MY PLACE / COME++} \\ \text{L} & \hphantom{\text{MY FRIEND FROM l-a COME++ MY PLACE / }}\text{COME++} \end{bmatrix}$

$\begin{bmatrix} \text{R'} & \text{UNTIL 12 / DISSOLVE}^{11} \\ \text{L} & \end{bmatrix}$

> My friends from L.A. kept coming to my place until 12:00

(44) MY FRIEND FROM l-a MANY APPEAR++ / STOP TIME 12

> My friends from L.A. kept showing up. They stopped showing up at 12:00.

UNTIL in (43) seems to draw attention to the span of time leading up to 12 o'clock,
saying that the signer's friends just kept coming over all the way up to 12 o'clock.
(44) states a definite time at which the activity stopped, almost abruptly, and
focuses on that point.
Each of the three different surface forms used in ASL to express the concept
of 'until' reflects a difference in focus. Using temporal ordering and placing the
'until phrase' **between** the description of the first interval and that of the second
express a causal relationship between the 'until period' and the second interval.

Describing each interval in true chronological order and placing the 'until phrase' **after** the description of the second interval express the fact that one state of affairs changed to another at a particular time, without suggesting a causal relationship. The use of the sign UNTIL allows for particular focus on the first interval.

In practice, however, the sign UNTIL is used much less frequently than the other two options. This fact can be explained in terms of the motivating principle behind sign language. Signers tend to opt for the most accurate and complete visual analogue of the real-world situation. There must be a 'good picture' behind every sign language construction. The sign UNTIL does create a 'good picture' for the function it serves, namely to focus on the first interval of an 'until' sequence. But the general tendency is to describe the entire situation: the full semantic content rather than focusing only on Interval I.

The processes involved in the expression of 'until' are apparent in other aspects of the language. For example, temporal references in ASL normally occur in real-world temporal order. Causal relationships are most commonly expressed by means of temporal ordering. The sign UNTIL is similar to the sign PAST-CONTINUOUS, in that both are used to refer to a time period ending at a particular point in time.

This paper has presented some observations and discussion regarding the manifestation and use of the time space for establishing temporal reference relative to the time of the speech act, calendric units that are incorporated into this system, and more complex time locutions that integrate concepts of temporal order and causality.

It is hoped that the ideas presented here will stimulate further thought and discussion concerning these topics.

NOTES

1. 'Stressed' indicates that the movement is somewhat larger, and often slower than a normal future index. A stressed past index tends to reach back farther than the normal index to past, and sometimes occurs with palm facing the cheek (Frishberg and Gough, 1973). For detailed discussion of stress patterns in ASL, see Friedman, 1974a, 1976b.

2. For further discussion regarding perfective markers, see Fischer and Gough, 1972, and Friedman, 1975b.

3. Friedman (1975b) points out that the body of the signer is unmarked, representing present time, until temporal reference is made. Then, present time cannot be maintained, "since the time represented by the body can, by rights, be only one time (at a time)" (p. 943).

4. 'Dominant' refers to the right side in right-handed signers, the left in left-handed signers. The dominant hand serves as the main articulator.

5. Cf. Frishberg and Gough, 1973.

6. Cf. Frishberg and Gough, 1973.

7. This statement refers to the process by which a language expresses temporal relationships between events described in a discourse. For this reason, the phrases 'temporal relationship between events' and 'relationships between temporal references' are used interchangeably. The statement, then, does not refer to another process by which a signer uses adverbial phrases or indexical reference to establish temporal reference relative to a pre-established reference time as in

   (past reference previously established)   WORK FINISH / GO HOME //
   TOMORROW . . .
   He finished working, and went home. The next day . . .

   Having established a focal temporal reference as prior to the time of the speech act, the time of the speech act becomes irrelevant to the discourse. Thus, temporal references can be made relative to the established reference time, without establishing totally new time reference.

   This process is important and deserves further study and discussion. However, we are not concerned with it at the present time.

8. As mentioned earlier, English has another option for expressing this type of temporal relationship, namely, the past perfect tense.

9. This sign for the lexical item 'before' is not to be confused with the sign BE-FORE-PAST, used for indexic reference in the time space. The sign referred to here is formed in front of the chest, flat, open palms toward the signer; the back of the dominant hand begins in contact with the palm of the nondominant hand, and moves away from the nondominant hand, toward the signer. In the sign for 'after', the dominant palm begins in contact with the back of nondominant hand, and moves away from the signer.

10. Cf., Friedman, 1975b.

11. In this context, DISSOLVE means that the party gradually broke up.

REGULATORS AND TURN-TAKING IN
AMERICAN SIGN LANGUAGE DISCOURSE[1]

Charlotte Baker

0. Introduction

This paper provides an initial characterization of some multichannel[2] behaviors used to regulate dyadic conversation in American Sign Language (ASL). These behaviors are first classified according to the 'regulator' categories of Wiener and Devoe (1974) and then related to the turn-taking system formulated by Duncan (1973). Special attention is given to the unique role of eye gaze in the conversations of deaf persons. Finally, observed differences between the kinds and uses of regulators employed by deaf and hearing interactants are considered as contributing significantly to conflicts encountered in deaf-hearing social interaction.

1. The Turn-Taking System

Duncan's initial 'grammar of dyadic conversation' (1973) posits two mutually exclusive states for each participant: SPEAKER—a participant who claims the speaking turn at any given moment (Duncan, 1972), and AUDITOR—a participant who does not claim the speaking turn at any given moment (Kendon, 1967).

In this paper, the terms SPEAKER and ADDRESSEE will be used, the latter for obvious reasons (rather than AUDITOR) and the former because its usage to describe deaf interaction is in keeping with sign language itself. In ASL, one signs YESTERDAY ME-TELL-YOU ('Yesterday I told you') or INDEX SAY WHAT ('What did she say')—where signs referring to communication are made in the area of the mouth—rather than 'I signed to you' or 'What did she sign'.

Duncan describes the **mechanism of turn-taking** in terms of **signals** by which speaker and addressee indicate their respective states with regard to the speaking turn. Empirical investigations (Scheflen, 1963; Exline et al., 1965; Kendon, 1967; Duncan, 1972; Wiener et al., 1972; Argyle et al., 1973) have demonstrated that such signals are employed systematically with predictable results.

According to Duncan, a 'smooth exchange' of the speaking turn sequentially requires that (1) the speaker displays a turn signal—defined as the display of at least one of the following six cues: intonation (any pitch level and terminal juncture combination other than 22 | at the end of a phonemic clause), paralinguistic drawl, body motion (discontinuation/relaxation), sociocentric sequences (e.g., 'but um', 'or something', 'you know'), a drop in paralinguistic pitch/intensity, and syntax (completion of a grammatical clause); (2) the previous addressee switches to the speaker state, claiming the speaker turn; and (3) the previous speaker switches to the addressee state, relinquishing the turn.

Duncan observes that this smooth exchange (as well as the issuance of other signals and the event of simultaneous turns) occurred at **specific points**.[3] These points correspond to Duncan's unit of analysis which is bounded by the end of a phonemic clause and additionally marked by any of the turn signal behaviors listed above and/or other cues such as an unfilled pause or a turning of the speaker's head toward the addressee. Further description of these behaviors is found in Duncan, 1972 and 1973.

Duncan distinguishes **three speaker signals**[4] (as well as the 'unmarked'[5] state of 'no display of turn signals'): (1) the turn (or turn-yielding) signal; (2) the turn-claiming suppression signal (used to suppress attempts by the addressee to claim the speaking turn); and (3) the within-turn signal (apparently used to mark communication units "on a hierarchical level immediately lower than that of the speaking turn" 1973, p. 36). Addressee signals (including the "unmarked" state of 'no response') consist of (1) back-channel signals[6] (e.g., 'mm-humm', head nods, sentence completions, brief requests for clarification, and brief restatements, all of which do not constitute a turn or claim for a turn), and (2) turn-claiming signals (not described).

Duncan observes from his data that every addressee turn-claim in the absence of a speaker turn signal resulted in **simultaneous turns**. Simultaneous turns also occurred when the speaker displayed a turn-yielding signal, the addressee responded by initiating his/her own turn, and then the original speaker continued to claim the speaking turn.

A useful distinction proposed by Duncan differentiates **simultaneous talking** from simultaneous turns. Simultaneous talking occurs when the addressee's back-channel responses (which, as stated above, do not constitute a turn-claim) overlap with speaker verbalizations.

This distinction is particularly useful in describing signed conversation since the visual mode of the language seems to allow interactants to sign and observe another's signs without a loss of understanding, whereas in oral languages, it is more difficult to hear another's speech while talking.

Jaffe and Feldstein (1970) have shown that simultaneous speech in an oral dyad tends to be quite short, the mean duration being less than .5 second. This does not seem to be the case for ASL. The average length of simultaneous speech found in the data reviewed here is 1.5 seconds whereas the longest stretch lasts for 4.3 seconds.

2. Regulators

Wiener and Devoe (1974) have begun a systematic description of those behaviors in the visual, vocal, postural, and gestural channels that signal and/or monitor the initiation, maintenance, and termination of spoken messages in dyads. Also described as "acts which maintain and regulate the back-and-forth nature of speaking and listening between two or more interactants" (Ekman & Friesen, 1969, p. 82), these behaviors are called 'regulators'. Regulators convey information necessary for the regulation of a turn-taking system.

Wiener and Devoe distinguish **four sets of regulators**—initiation, continuation, shift, and termination regulators—each of which is further subdivided into addressor (speaker) regulators and addressee regulators.

Briefly, these sets describe (1) how a speaker initiates an exchange and how an addressee evokes a response from the speaker (initiation regulators); (2) how a speaker signals that encoding will continue after a short pause and how an addressee indicates listening and that the speaker may continue (continuation regulators); (3) how a speaker signals the end of a turn and how an addressee indicates a desire to begin a turn (shift regulators); and (4) how both speaker and addressee signal the termination of an exchange (termination regulators). Within these divisions is information about interactants' usage of eye gaze, vocal inflections, filled and unfilled pauses, head nods, postural shifts, hand and arm gestures, and facial activity (e.g., raised eyebrows, smile).

The correspondence of Duncan's signals with Wiener and Devoe's regulators is illustrated below.

	Duncan: signals	**Wiener & Devoe: regulators**
Speaker	turn signal	shift regulator
	turn-claiming suppression signal	continuation regulator
	within-turn signal	continuation regulator
	(no turn signal)	continuation regulator
Addressee	back-channel signal	continuation regulator
	turn-claiming signal	shift regulator
	(no response)	shift regulator

3. Regulators in American Sign Language

In the following section, regulators found in a small corpus of ASL will be presented and discussed.[7] The corpus was elicited from two dyads of deaf signers: Mary and Lisa (Set A)[8], Tom and Joe (Set B). Mary was instructed to ask Lisa how to play basketball, Tom was instructed to ask Joe about anything that interest him. Both conversations were videotaped, and the initial portions of each were analyzed for regulator behaviors.

In the portions used, the following number of signs was made by each participant: Mary—72, Lisa—58, Tom—58, Joe—82. The greater number of signs by Mary (questioner) as opposed to Lisa (respondent) in Set A may be explained by the difficulty Lisa experienced in understanding Mary's questions—a difficulty that required continual clarifications by Mary before Lisa could respond.

According to the Wiener and Devoe classification system, the following regulators were found (and will be discussed in detail after the taxonomy is presented):

A. Initiation Regulators

1. **Speaker**—initiates turn by
   a. Raising and extending hand(s) out of rest position[9]
   b. Followed by an optional indexing, touching, or waving a hand in front of addressee to get his/her attention[10]
   c. Optional head/postural lean forward, toward addressee
   d. Usually −GAZE when beginning a statement (after first making sure of addressee's attention)[11]
   e. Usually +GAZE when asking a question

2. **Addressee**—signals that speaker may initiate a turn by
   a. +GAZE
   b. Maintaining own inactivity—i.e., not signing

B. Continuation Regulators

1. **Speaker**—signals that encoding will continue after a proposition/information package or after a short pause by
   a. −GAZE
   b. Optional increase in signing speed
   c. Not returning to a rest position
      (1) Optional filling of pause with movements that indicate thinking (e.g., looking up, furrowing brow, slight shaking of index finger or palm, postural shift)
      (2) Optional holding last sign made (during pause)

2. **Addressee**—signals that decoding continues by
   a. Maintaining +GAZE
   b. Intermittent low-key changes in the physical state (e.g., head-nodding, smiling, postural shifts, facial activity expressing surprise, agreement, uncertainty, lack of understanding, etc.)
   c. Optional indexing the speaker after each proposition
   d. Optional short repetitions of some of speaker's signs

C. Shift Regulators

1. **Speaker**—signals turn-yielding by
   a. Return to +GAZE (if not already +GAZE)
   b. Optional decrease in signing speed near termination of turn

   c. Optional call for addressee response by
     (1) $Palm_a$ (palm up with heel raised higher than fingertips) and lowering hand(s)
     (2) Indexing addressee at end of speaker turn[12]
     (3) Holding last sign (as for questions)
     (4) Raising last sign (as for questions)
     (5) Concomitant question intonation carried facially or bodily
   d. Return to rest position

2. **Addressee**—signals turn-claiming during speaker turn by
   a. Optional increase in size and quantity of head-nodding, often accompanied by a concurrent increase in the size and quantity of indexing the speaker
   b. Optional switch to $palm_a$
   c. Movement out of rest position to get speaker's attention—may include indexing, touching, or waving hand in front of speaker
   d. Switching to ⁻GAZE when speaker is +GAZE—may include postural shift, looking up (as if thinking while preparing to sign), facial signaling of forthcoming question, disagreement, etc.
   e. Initiating turn (interrupting) and repeating first few signs until speaker is +GAZE and has yielded the floor or until speaker suppresses adressee's turn-claim

(The data here does not include any termination regulators.)

A-1.a

One important regulator peculiar to Sign (sign language) is the use of different **rest** positions, three of which are illustrated in the two data sets. The position referred to in this paper as **full-rest** corresponds to a maximally relaxed state in which the addressee is attentive to the speaker and is not physically preparing to perform or performing a sign. For one informant, Lisa, this position seems to include having both arms full length down at her sides, close to the body, with the hands relaxed in a slightly cupped shape. For Mary, this position means having her hands clasped, usually right over left (she is right-handed), at the central abdomen level, forearm resting against the body. Any hand/arm movement upward and/or outward from this position, then, can be viewed as a step toward increased muscular tension indicating a movement toward commencing "speech."

When the hand(s) is/are in **half-rest**, or at the waist with the palm(s) facing toward the addressee's own body ($palm_T$), the addressee is still demonstrating attentiveness to the speaker, but is either preparing to interrupt or anticipating that the speaker's turn will end soon and that the addressee will then respond. Interruption, itself, as well as the initiation of a turn, is often signaled by a changing of palm orientation (addressee shift regulator) so that the palm is facing upward and slightly toward the current speaker ($palm_a$), as illustrated in (1).

(1) Mary: (indexes Lisa) I KNOW NOTHING ABOUT BASKETBALL
      M   ....
      L   ....
      Lisa :   (in full-rest position)

      Mary: ? CAN YOU EXPLAIN BASKETBALL TO ME (rt. hold ME as lf.
      M   ....
      L   ....
      Lisa :   (raises lf. to mid-

      Mary: lowers to waist) (raises both hands) FIRST++ RULE
      M   ....
      L   ....
      Lisa :   chest, palm$_a$)   (lowers lf. to waist, palm$_T$)

In this example, Lisa, the addressee, maintains full-rest position until asked a
question. At that point, she begins to respond by raising her left hand, palm facing
upward and slightly toward her partner. However, before Lisa can answer, Mary
begins a new statement (clarifying her previous question). So Lisa turns her left
hand to full pronated position to signal attentiveness, but maintains it at half-rest
because she will soon be required to respond again.

As a speaker's cue, the hand held out palm up does not signal interruption or
turn-initiation since the turn is already in progress. Instead, it signals a termination
of encoding (speaker shift regulator) and is a way of calling for a response from
the addressee (usually accompanied by facially or bodily carried question intonation.[13]).

(2) Mary: (head in rt. tilt forward) . . . NOT UNDERSTAND WELL?
      M   ....
      L   ....
      Lisa :

      Mary: (lowers hands, palms$_a$)
      M   ....
      L   ....
      Lisa: (begins response)

In (2), Mary's question intonation is carried by a forward tilting of the head
and a concomitant hunching of the shoulders on the sign WELL. As she first calls
for Lisa to respond by switching the orientation of her palms to 'a' and then signals
the end of her turn by lowering her hands (speaker shift regulator), Lisa initiates
her response.

A variation of this call for a response, seen in (3), occurs when the speaker
indexes[14] the addressee after the termination of a proposition (also accompanied

by question intonation). Indexing refers to a signer's pointing with the index finger to a referent or the space designated for representing that referent. When an inter-actant indexes another interactant in a dyad, the index means YOU.

(3) Tom: YOU KNOW s-f b-y HEART (small forward lean)? YOU   GOOD!
    T   ....
    J   ....
    Joe :   (nods YES)

Quarter-rest position here refers to an addressee's resting one hand (usually the dominant hand) against the body above the waist. This position is primarily found during discourse involving a rapid exchange of turns since it maintains the dominant hand very close to neutral space[15] and, thus, requires the least amount of effort toward transfer into the speaker role. When one hand is in quarter-rest, the other is usually at half-rest.

The data reviewed for this study is too limited to make any generalizations about male-female differences in the use of these rest positions. However, in the female-female sequence (Set A), there was systematic use of full- and half-rest positions under the conditions already described, whereas both males seemed to prefer return to half-rest or quarter-rest when not signing and never had more than one hand in full-rest at a time. On the other hand, both male (Tom) and female (Mary) questioners maintained one or both hands at waist level (and above) more frequently than did their partners. One potential implication of these observations is that maintaining the hands closer to or within the signing space may be seen as a more aggressive stance.

A–1.b

Signed conversation differs uniquely from oral conversation in that a speaker cannot initiate a turn until the desired addressee looks at the potential speaker— i.e., an interactant cannot "say" something (and be "heard") if the other interactant is not looking.

This single constraint makes eye gaze one of the most powerful regulators in Sign since it determines when an interactant can speak. As a result, Sign conversants have developed a variety of ways of attempting to get the other's attention (+GAZE). Some of these are touching or indexing the desired addressee (meaning 'YOU, I want to talk to you'), waving a hand in front of the addressee, and other sharp movements designed to catch his/her attention.

In addition, there is an established convention in the deaf community by which third parties situated in closer proximity to the desired addressee will facilitate the speaker's attempt to get the addressee's attention by themselves attracting that attention and then indexing the person who wishes to speak to him/her. (Here the indexing means 'HE/SHE wants to talk with YOU'.)

Another little studied but often observed characteristic of deaf people which facilitates attention-getting (as well as attention-losing) concerns their unusual degree of sensitivity to visual stimuli. Deaf signers seem to be much more responsive to small movements in the periphery of vision (which are potentially linguistic) than are hearing persons.

However, one result of this sensitivity, noticed in the context of discourse, is an increased distractibility by visual stimuli from the environment in which communication takes place. This distractibility may partially account for other characteristics of signed discourse such as the unusually high degree of repetition by speakers of their own statements or of parts of those statements. Perhaps one function of this repetition is to insure the addressee's processing of the entire communication where parts of it might have been missed due to distractions from the environment. It does seem to be the case that the amount of repetition is increased in contexts where the addressee's attention is more easily distracted[16]—such as conversations held while eating.[17]

Due to the necessity of an addressee's maintaining consistent +GAZE on a speaker once the conversation has been initiated, this addressee +GAZE can reasonably be described as a given in effective signed discourse.[18] In addition, the location of addressee eye gaze is fairly predictable *a priori* as varying within a region extending from the speaker's eyes to his/her mouth.

It is socially rude in ASL discourse for an addressee not to maintain eye gaze on the speaker's face. However, pragmatically speaking, it is also necessary that this gaze be localized in the region described above because so much linguistic and regulatory information is carried by variations in the facial musculature and eyes of the signer.

For example, there are lexical items in ASL made solely by variations in a signer's facial musculature, as well as manual signs that are distinguished from each other solely by the facial expression that accompanies them (Baker, 1976a). Negation and interrogatives may be marked uniquely on the face, such as by a lowering or raising of the eyebrows (Stokoe, 1960; Bellugi & Fischer, 1972). In addition, eye movements can have a variety of linguistic functions, such as pronominal reference and emphasis (Baker, 1976b).

A-1.c

As illustrated in (2) and (3), questions can be signaled by inclining the head or upper portion of the body toward the addressee. Similarly, such a forward movement can be used as a back-channel response (B-2.b) by the addressee indicating interest, surprise, etc., depending upon what other responses are concomitant to it. When initiating an exchange, a speaker may also lean his/her head or body toward the addressee to signal 'Now I'm going to direct this communication to you', and the movement conjointly serves to capture the addressee's attention.

A-1.d, e

Initial perusal of the data concerning the occurrence of speaker +GAZE and −GAZE suggests a great deal of similarity between its use in Sign and its use in English. Kendon (1967) has reported that speaker gaze-shifts are systematically coordinated with the timing and boundaries of utterances and result in predictable addressee responses. A speaker's return to +GAZE has at least three functions: (1) to check on addressee decoding, (2) to signal the boundary of an information package, and (3) to signal a termination of encoding.

These same three functions are apparent in signed discourse, as illustrated in (4) where Joe is responding to Tom's question, 'What have you been doing in the last few days?' Joe replies, 'Two nights ago, I watched a movie called *Dirty Harry* and another, *Magnum Force*, starring Clint Eastwood'. Tom thinks Joe has said it was a 'dirty movie' (rather than a movie entitled *Dirty Harry*) and responds, 'Oh, it was a dirty movie! Was it good?' Joe then corrects him, 'Not dirty. It wasn't a dirty movie' and begins to describe the movie, 'it was a story about a detective in San Francisco'.[19]

(4) Tom: YOU d-o YOU d-o LAST-FEW-DAYS d-o YOU LAST-FEW-DAYS
    T   ....
    J ....
    Joe :   TWO

    Tom: d-o+ (holds this last sign)
    T ....
    J   ....
    Joe :   NIGHT PAST ME WATCH MOVIE TITLE DIRTY h-a-r-r-y

    Tom:
    T ....
    J ....
    Joe: AND WELL m-a-g-n-u-m f-o-r-c-e ACT b-y c-l-i-n-t EAST

    Tom: ? DIRTY MOVIE GOOD+
    T ....
    J ....
    Joe: w-o-o-d   DIRTY NOT DIRTY MOVIE

    Tom: DETECTIVE + + + + (indexes Joe) s-f
    T ....
    J   ....
    Joe : ABOUT DETECTIVE+ STORY DETECTIVE ACT IN s-f

Notice, first of all, how Joe seems to mark the boundaries of each constitutent/ information package by a return to +GAZE: (a) TWO NIGHT PAST (b) ME WATCH

MOVIE (c) TITLE DIRTY h-a-r-r-y (d) AND WELL m-a-g-n-u-m f-o-r-c-e (e) ACT b-y c-l-i-n-t EAST w-o-o-d (f) DIRTY NOT (g) DIRTY MOVIE (h) ABOUT DETEC-TIVE STORY DETECTIVE (i) ACT IN s-f.

Researchers in Sign have been particularly troubled by the problem of discern-ing 'sentence' boundaries in ASL.[20] The data presented here suggests that shifts in eye gaze may be a productive source of information for locating these boundaries and facilitating the discussion of ASL syntax. One potential problem, however, may arise when trying to decide when a speaker is returning to +GAZE to check on decoding as opposed to when the +GAZE marks the boundary of an information package. It is certainly possible (and probable) that the two occur together—a hypothesis supported by Kendon's data demonstrating that addressee back-channel responses (signaling decoding) occur much more often when the speaker is +GAZE (where speaker +GAZE usually occurs at phrase boundary pauses—p. 40).

In any case, speaker eye gaze in Sign varies fairly systematically with the func-tion of the utterance (questions, statements, and exclamations are reviewed here), its length (the number of information packages), and according to the desire of the speaker to continue or discontinue his/her turn. The termination of a turn is always marked by a return to +GAZE so that the addressee can initiate a turn.

In both of the data sets discussed in this paper, speakers usually maintained constant +GAZE during questions and exclamations, whereas other statements were initiated with −GAZE after the speaker was sure of addressee +GAZE. These results are presented below in Table 1. Parentheses denote those utterances which at initiation overlapped (in time) with the other interactant's signing. At any point where overlap occurs in Sign, both signers will be +GAZE, except (a) when an addressee anticipates a speaker question and begins to respond (−GAZE) prior to its completion, and (b) when an addressee tries unsuccessfully to claim a turn (inter-rupt), and the speaker maintains his/her turn by not looking at the addressee.

The one case of a −GAZE exclamation, illustrated in (5), occurred when Mary tried unsuccessfully to interrupt Lisa and then quickly signed RIGHT! (in the absence of any turn-yielding signals) at the end of Lisa's statement, 'If you walk with the ball, the referee calls "walking" '. Here the −GAZE exclamation may be seen as a way of capturing the floor (turn).

(5) Lisa: IF   WALK
        L
        M   ....
    Mary: (full-rest) (begins to raise rt.) (returns to full-rest)

    Lisa: CALL 'WALKING'
        L   ....
        M   ....
    Mary: RIGHT! . . .

The three cases of −GAZE questions (all by Tom) are not as easily explained. The first, illustrated at the beginning of (4), occurred at the initiation of a conversa-

Table 1

Speaker Eye Gaze at the Initiation of Questions, Exclamations, Statements

		+GAZE	⁻GAZE
Questions	Mary	7(1)	–
	Lisa	1	–
	Tom	3	3
	Joe	–	–
		11(1)	3
Exclamations	Mary	–	1
	Lisa	–	–
	Tom	3	–
	Joe	2	–
		5	1
Statements	Mary	(1)	7
	Lisa	2(6)	3
	Tom	(1)	4
	Joe	1(2)	14
		3(10)	28

tional exchange. Prior to the question, Tom was looking down, thinking about what to ask Joe, and the ⁻GAZE here may be a carry over from that period. The second and third ⁻GAZE questions were asked in the middle of the speaker turn— one after a statement and the other, after an exclamation. Since these ⁻GAZE-initiated questions occurred in the middle of the speaker's turn, the ⁻GAZE may have been used to hold the floor (continuation regulator). Both questions terminated with +GAZE.

Two of the (nonoverlapping) statements initiated with +GAZE were simple repetitions of what the speaker had just said. Kendon's data from oral discourse reveals that speakers tend to be ⁻GAZE as they begin a long utterance (lasting 5 seconds or more) and that they return to +GAZE by the end of the utterance (p. 33). He suggests that one explanation for the ⁻GAZE initiation is the speaker's need for a certain amount of advance planning

> even if it is a matter of selecting, from among a number of alternatives, which of a number of well-rehearsed phrases shall be used. (p. 31)

This advance planning, then, may necessitate the speaker's withdrawing his/her attention from the addressee as the speaker concentrates on what next to say.

Goldman-Eisler's (1958, 1961) work on hesitations supports this hypothesis with the findings that (a) hesitations tend to precede novel combinations of words, and (b) hesitations are more common during speech which involves abstract and interpretative thought, rather than mere description. Thus, the two cases of +GAZE statement initiation in the Sign data may be partially explained by the fact that they were repetitions and as such, required no planning.

The third +GAZE-initiated statement, seen in (6), occurred at the termination of Tom and Joe's conversational exchange. Joe was unable to express himself clearly (he was trying to explain why he liked the Berkeley area), and the +GAZE may have been a way of calling for help from Tom—who did respond with the equivalent of 'Yes, I understand what you mean.'[21]

(6) Tom: WHY YOU LIKE HERE LIKE BERKELEY
     T ....
     J ....
   Joe: WELL   a TO z a TO z

  Tom: ALL IN
     T ....
     J ....
   Joe : ALL IN   WELL HAVE ITALY FOOD TO CHINA FOOD WELL

  Tom:
     T ....
     J ....
   Joe : THINK FOOD WELL OTHER PLACE NOT HAVE ALL IN NOT

  Tom: 'THAT'+
     T .... (Both then simultaneously lower their hands to half-
     J .... rest, palms$_T$)
   Joe: HAVE WELL

A–2.a

As discussed earlier (A-1.b), a speaker may not initiate an exchange without first capturing the addressee's attention. Addressee +GAZE, then, is a way of signaling to the speaker that he/she may initiate the exchange.

A–2.b

Since any hand/arm movement upward and/or outward from rest position is a move toward commencing speech (excepting head-scratching, etc., which is often initially confused for speech), an addressee's maintaining a rest position (+GAZE) signals that the speaker may begin.

B-1.a

Since an addressee cannot effectively claim a turn without speaker +GAZE, the speaker signals that encoding will continue after the completion of an information package by switching to −GAZE right after the unit's boundary is marked by +GAZE. Similarly, the speaker signals that encoding will continue after a short pause by maintaining −GAZE during the pause.

B-1.b

As observed by Padden (personal communication), one way for a speaker to signal that encoding will continue after an information unit and that the addressee should not interrupt is to increase the speed with which the signs are made. When the signing speed is increased, the signs, themselves, may or may not be decreased in size, but are never increased.

B-1.c:1,2

Since returning to a rest position signals the end of a turn, the speaker, during a pause, will maintain one or both hands in the signing area either by 'filling' the pause with small movements that indicate planning what next to say or by holding the final position of the last sign (analogous to 'open inflection' in oral languages). As will be reported in (C-1.c:1), holding the last sign +GAZE is a speaker shift regulator, whereas holding −GAZE is a continuation regulator.

B-2.a,b

After speaker initiation, the addressee continues to signal attentiveness and decoding by maintaining +GAZE and by making intermittent back-channel responses such as head-nodding and facial variations indicating the addressee's reaction to each speaker proposition. Such back-channel responses seem to occur more frequently in signed discourse than in oral conversation. However, careful analysis of their frequency was not made in this study.

B-2.c

Addressees sometimes seem to mark and indicate their understanding of each speaker proposition by indexing the speaker after each signed proposition is completed. Concomitant with appropriate facial activity, indexing can also mean, for example, 'Hmm, that's interesting' or 'So that really happened!'.

B-2.d

Another back-channel response that occurs quite frequently in Sign and that accounts for approximately 42% of the sign overlap found in both data sets is the addressee's short repetitions of some of the speaker's signs. Such repetition is illustrated in examples (4) and (6), as well as in (7).[22]

(7) Tom: YOU MOVE HERE ? (ONE) FOUR YEAR PAST (holds last sign)
     T   ....
     J   ....
     Joe :   FOUR YEAR PAST FOUR YEAR PAST

In both sets of data, approximately 30% of the discourse involved either full or partial overlap of one interactant's signs with the other's signs. Both kinds of overlap are illustrated in (8).

(8)   (partial)   (full)
     Mary: RIGHT?   REALLY NOT FAIR REALLY
     M   ....
     L   ....
     Lisa : (raises rt.) NOT FAIR   NOT FAIR

             (partial)
     Mary: FUNNY (lowers palm$_a$)
     M   ....
     L   ....
     Lisa: DRIBBLE (lowers palm$_a$)

Included as an instance of partial overlap is the case of one interactant's hand(s) moving toward the position where a sign will be made as the other interactant is making a sign. This inclusion is justified by its relevance to speaker eye gaze: excluding cases in which the speaker suppresses an addressee turn-claim by not looking at the addressee, a speaker will almost always be +GAZE as an addressee moves toward the initiation of a sign.

C-1.a,b

As discussed earlier (A-1.d,e), a speaker signals turn-yielding by returning to and maintaining +GAZE; This may be accompanied by a decrease in signing speed as the speaker nears termination of the final proposition. Thus, a decrease in signing speed (+GAZE) is a speaker shift regulator, whereas an increase in signing speed (−GAZE) is a speaker continuation regulator.

C-1.c:1,2

Also discussed earlier (A-1.a) was the speaker's optional use of palm$_a$ or of indexing to call for a response from the addressee at the termination of a turn. The index is usually held until the addressee initiates a turn (or waives the turn), and the palm$_a$ is lowered gradually during the first stages of this initiation. An interesting instance of both interactants signaling turn completion and waiting for the other to respond was seen in (8). Here both Mary and Lisa simultaneously lowered their palms$_a$ while maintaining +GAZE.

C-1.c:3,4,5

One common way of signaling that a question has been asked and that the addressee should respond is to hold the last sign (+GAZE) with concomitant facial-ly/posturally expressed question "intonation." Friedman (1974a,b, 1976b) observes that this final sign in a string is held for at least 30–40 VTR (videotape recorder) fields (1 field = 1/60 sec.)—which is approximately one-half second longer than a sign is usually held in a nonquestion utterance.[23] Both Bellugi and Fischer (1972) and Friedman (1974b, 1976b) also observe that the final sign in a string may be raised slightly as one cue that a question is being asked. This finding is supported in the data reviewed here, but only in those cases where the final sign is also held longer.

The 'smooth exchange' of roles is facilitated by these 'calling' devices such that the addressee becomes speaker (begins signing) before the old speaker returns his/her hand(s) to rest position.

C-1.d

Return to rest position marks the final stage of the turn exchange for the old speaker (new addressee).

C-2.a

Similar to its function in oral conversation, an increase in the size and quantity of head-nodding can signal addressee turn-claiming. It is a way of communicating 'Yes, yes, yes, I understand fully what you are saying, and I have something to add'.

This head-nodding is often accompanied by a similar increase in the size and quantity of indexing the speaker where the downward movement of the head concurs in time with the downward movement of the index. Both then punctuate each other with increasing speed until the final nod and index reach a considerable size and mark the end of decoding and the subsequent initiation of encoding. Most speakers will yield their turn when confronted with this highly effective and intense turn-claiming signal.

C-2.b,c

Illustrated in (1) was the addressee's use of palm$_a$ to signal a desire to initiate a turn. However, the turn, itself, is not effectively claimed until the addressee begins signing with the addressee's attention. As mentioned previously, one way of trying to capture the addressee's eye is to touch, index or wave a hand in front of him/her.

C-2.d

Once the speaker's attention has been elicited, the addressee may then switch to ‾GAZE to hold the floor. An unusual illustration of the use of ‾GAZE in attempting to claim the right to speak is seen in (9).

(9) Lisa: IMAGINE   PEOPLE BOY   (lowers rt. to waist) DRIBBLE
     L   ....
     M   ....
     Mary: (begins to raise rt.) (MUST) WHAT ? DRIBBLE   MEAN

As Lisa begins her statement, Mary starts to initiate a question. Lisa notices
Mary's movement (Lisa becomes +GAZE) at which point Mary tries to gain the
floor by discontinuing her gaze on Lisa. Lisa tries to overcome the interruption by
continuing signing ⁻GAZE. However, Mary still proceeds with her interruption—
which Lisa realizes when she return to +GAZE at BOY. Lisa then yields her turn
by lowering her hands out of the signing space. At this point, Mary knows she has
the floor and shifts to ⁻GAZE until the conclusion of her question when Lisa
begins to respond.

C-2.e

Another way of capturing the floor is to initiate signing and then repeat the
first few signs in sequence or in an altered order until the other interactant is +GAZE.
This alternative is often employed as an attention-getting device for the initiation of
a conversational exchange, especially when there are other distractions in the environment (such as during eating). It is also an aggressive way of interrupting a present
speaker's discourse—which may result in the speaker's extending an upturned palm
(palm$_1$) toward the speaker (meaning 'Stop!') to suppress the addressee's turn-claim.

An extremely rude way of claiming the turn is to hold the speaker's hand/arm
to keep him/her from signing. This action, though, is rarely seen and usually results
in anger on the part of the speaker—similar to that which would be aroused in oral
conversation if the addressee put a hand over the speaker's mouth!

4. Implications for Deaf-Hearing Interaction

This paper reports some initial findings on how turn-taking is regulated in
American Sign Language. It should be clear from these results that turn-taking in
the context of Sign is as systematically structured and as highly developed as it is in
other cultures. Since turn-taking is a system that determines the appropriate form
of one major kind of social interaction, that is, discourse, differences between the
system used in Sign as opposed to that for English can yield insights into the problems arising from deaf-hearing social interaction.

One of the most basic problems confronted in deaf-hearing interaction concerns
the different use of eye gaze between the two cultures. Hall (1963) notes that (hearing) Americans engage in mutual eye gaze much less than Arabs and Greeks, for
example. In addition, Argyle and Dean (1965) and Argyle and Ingham (1972) have

demonstrated that the amount of both gaze and mutual gaze will decline with the proximity of the (hearing) interactants (as an avoidance of intimacy).

Kendon (1967) reports that mutual gazes between previously unacquainted (hearing) interactants tend to last for little more than one second (p. 28). However, Exline (1963) and Exline and Winters (1965) have demonstrated that context and sex of interactants as well as their roles (speaker/addressee) are major influencing factors in the amount of time spent in looking at the other interactant as well as in the amount of mutual glances.

On the other hand, effective communication in Sign requires a consistent maintenance of addressee eye gaze on the speaker, and periods of mutual gaze extending longer than 5 seconds are not uncommon (especially among females engaged in non- or less competitive discourse). Deaf persons frequently comment that hearing people seem to be inattentive to and uninterested in what is being said. Even more disturbing is the fact that hearing people are often perceived as being hostile because they avoid the intimacy of mutual eye gaze (which, as discussed in A-1.b and elsewhere, is essential to the language).

In addition to the differential use of eye gaze, another major disparity in the total communicative activity between deaf and hearing people is the higher frequency and degree of facial activity in deaf people's conversation. Schiff (1973a,b), who has conducted research on the differences between the hearing and deaf person's perception of facially expressed emotion, inadvertently highlights a problem arising from this difference when he writes,

> In this language (Sign), emotional intensity is indicated by the abruptness, velocity, and prolongation of the gestural motion with which the sign is performed as well as by rather extreme (to the hearing person) facial grimaces. (1973b, p. 73)

Not only do the facial displays appear as "extreme" to hearing people, but they also seem to be disturbing, as revealed by Schiff's use of the word 'grimace'. Many (or most) hearing people appear to experience discomfort by deaf people's greater "mobility" with facial movements; consequently their own resultant use of the face in Sign is highly controlled.

On the other hand, since the face seems to play an important role as a carrier of "intonation" in Sign, many hearing people who sign are often secretly criticized by deaf people as being boring "monotones." The often remarked smallness and tightness of their signs also contributes to this characterization.

Another difference in deaf and hearing signers' use of the face has been observed by Stokoe and Battison (1975) as a difference in linguistic code. They report that a certain facial expression when shown on videotape

> [was] interpreted as 'emphatically negative' by hearing signers, and 'emphatically positive' by deaf signers. This is clearly a code conflict. Actual misunderstandings based on this particular expression have been observed. (p. 19)[24]

Hearing counselors with deaf clients often report difficulty in knowing when their client has finished signing his/her thought and when it is appropriate to respond. However, the timing of such exchanges is very important in the development of a good relationship between counselor and client—as it is for any relationship. For example, some people feel slighted when their last syllable is chopped by another's turn initiation. Responding too quickly may give the impression that you are not as interested in what has just been said as you are in your own reply. On the other hand, a late response is sometimes associated with lack of understanding, possible disagreement, or even disinterest—all of which may make the other person uncomfortable. Proper timing of turn exchanges requires an ability to "read" and respond to each other's shift regulators.

Many hearing people find it extremely difficult to follow effectively conversations between two or especially, three or more deaf interactants. The hearing person does not usually know where to look in time to pick up each turn initiation. By the time the location of the present speaker is discovered by the hearing person, part of the communication has been missed, or the turn itself may already have shifted to another interactant. That can be a very frustrating experience, and it is similar to the frustration most deaf people experience when they try to follow hearing people's conversations by lip reading (which already involves substantial guesswork).[25]

Even when hearing people are signing and speaking simultaneously, there is a strong tendency to rely still on oral language behavior to signal turn-taking. In addition, many of what are sudden, unselfconscious movements to the hearing person, such as scratching or raising a hand to the mouth to cover a yawn, are distracting to the deaf participant because the movements are potentially linguistic and thus, might be perceived as turn initiations.

These and other problem areas for deaf-hearing social interaction (c.f., Padden and Markowicz, 1975; Stokoe and Battison, 1975) are issues that should be confronted in the classroom where nonsigners (hearing and deaf) are being taught to communicate in Sign. However, rarely are such issues even mentioned, and most beginners either learn "the hard way" or never learn how to cross the sociolinguistic boundaries separating hearing culture from deaf culture.

NOTES

1. I am grateful to Robbin Battison for his many helpful comments on an earlier version of this paper, to Paul Ekman and Lars von der Lieth for their many helpful criticisms, to William Stokoe for serving as my advisor during the difficult latter stages of this draft and for allowing me to use the facilities of the Linguistics Research Lab at Gallaudet College to continue my research, and

especially to Carol Padden for the many hours she spent critically reviewing my observations with her own insightful, native intuitions.

2. Wiener and Mehrabian (1968) define 'channel' as "any set of behaviors in a communication that has been systematically denoted by an observer, that is considered by that observer to have coding possiblities, and that can be studied (at least in principle) independently of any other co-occurring behaviors (p. 51)." Baker (1976a) distinguishes at least five separate channels of ASL discourse: the eyes, the face, the head, the hands and arms, and the total body posture of the signer.

3. These specific points are called 'transition-relevance places' by Sachs, Schegloff, and Jefferson (1974) who also maintain that all turn-transfer is coordinated around these points/places.

4. A recent paper by Duncan, "On the structure of speaker auditor interaction during speaking turns" (*Lang. Soc.* 2, 161–180), proposes some changes in terminology as well as makes several additions to kinds of signals transmitted in the turn-taking system. This paper, unfortunately, arrived too late to modify the review of Duncan's work presented here.

5. Duncan's use of the term 'unmarked' is questionable since 'no cue' can, itself, be a cue. For example, Wiener and Devoe observe that some speakers, during a pause, will intermittently look at the addressee and seem to require some form of addressee decoding regulator before continuation of encoding (cited in Robbins, 1974). In addition, an addressee's nonemission of a continuation regulator can function as an addressee shift regulator (Wiener and Devoe, p. 55).

6. Duncan notes that these signals are analogous to Kendon's 'accompaniment behavior' and Dittman and Llewellyn's (1968) 'listener response.'

7. For purposes of this discussion, the following additions to the transcription system presented in the introduction to this volume will be used:

$palm_T$	orientation of palm facing toward signer (fingers down)
$palm_L$	orientation of palm facing away from signer (fingers up)
$palm_a$	orientation of palm facing up and slightly away from signer (adapted from Stokoe, 1965)
rt.	right hand
lf.	left hand
+GAZE	for interactant specified, positive eye gaze on other interactant, continuing until otherwise specified
–GAZE	for interactant specified, negative (no) eye gaze on other interactant, continuing until otherwise specified
....	period of +GAZE corresponding to time line (transcription of GAZE follows a suggestion by Battison)

(CAPS)   a sign which transcriber(s) are not certain was actually present on the tape

(lower
  case)   information regarding nonsign movements

8. I am grateful to Lynn Friedman for the use of her tape and preliminary transcript of Set A.

9. A discussion of three types of rest positions distinguished in the two data sets begins on page 219.

10. See Stokoe, 1965, for the earliest discussion of how signed conversations are initiated.

11. More recent work (Baker, 1976b) has shown that this shifting to −GAZE at the initiation of statements is particularly true of competitive turn exchanges. However, there may be very little of this kind of shifting in less competitive sequences.

12. See Covington, 1973, for a discussion of this use of indexing (pointing with the index finger).

13. Intonation in Sign still awaits systematic study. However, some cues that appear to function like question intonation are: raising the eyebrows (Friedman, 1974b), retracting the eyelids (commonly referred to as 'widening' the eyes), inclining the head forward toward the addressee (with an optional sideways tilt), and raising (hunching) the shoulders.

14. See Friedman, 1975b, for a discussion of the use of indexing in pronominalization, Lacy, 1974, for its role as a nondeictic anaphor, and Mandel for a more general discussion of its significantce.

15. Neutral space is that area of the signing space (described by Friedman, 1975b) in which a very large number of signs are made. The signing area approximates a rectangle extending from the waist to about 6″ above the head, the width of which is determined by the signer's lax arm spread. Neutral space has no well-defined boundaries, but generally refers to the area in front of, but not in contact with, the signer's chest.

16. The amount of repetition also seems to vary between individuals as well as with the speaker's attitude toward the communication—e.g., if the addressee is less interested, he/she may not maintain consistent +GAZE, and the speaker would need to repeat more.

17. I am grateful to Carol Padden for showing me her tape of a dinner conversation and pointing out the high degree of repetition in that discourse.

18. Exceptions to this rule (where not predictable as attempts to interrupt) occur rarely and seem to be predictable when they do occur. For example, when the

speaker performs a sign out of the visual signing space (e.g., DRIBBLE, made with the palm below the waist), the addressee may be required to look away from the eye gaze region in order to discern what sign is being made. Another observed exception occurs when the speaker is fingerspelling a word, and the addressee anticipates what it is before the spelling is completed. One informant commented that it is boring to continue looking and that the disruption of +GAZE is a way of indicating to the speaker that completion of the finger-spelled word is unnecessary.

19. At the 1975 meeting of the Chicago Linguistic Society, Garnes and Bond gave an interesting paper on 'slips of the ear'. Klima and Bellugi (1975) have talked about 'slips of the hand' in signed discourse. Perhaps similar research on 'slips of the eye' would prove productive.

20. Bellugi and Fischer (1972) have proposed that a proposition in ASL be considered equivalent to a simple underlying sentence. In their study, they counted as underlying propositions "all main verbs or predicates which had overt (or covert) subjects" (p. 16). There is a problem with this kind of definition because it is not readily, if at all, able to take into account the use of space in ASL. For example, Robbin Battison and King Jordan are presently conducting an experiment in which one deaf signer is given a picture to describe, and a second deaf signer must choose the correct picture from a total of 36 similar photos. These descriptions involve locating and describing objects, such as furniture or the distinguishing features on a particular kind of car or the arrangement of three seated girls as they are actually present in the photograph.

Informal observations of the videotaped results suggest a lack or extreme paucity of verbs (as we know them) in each description. To continue using Bellugi and Fischer's definition, we would either have to say the signers were not using 'sentences', or we would have to begin talking about 'covert' verbs (e.g., 'deleted' copulas), or we would have to redefine what a 'verb' is in ASL. None of these alternatives is immediately satisfactory or possible.

21. Free translation:

Tom—Why do you like Berkeley?
Joe—Well, it has everything. Berkeley has Italian food, Chinese food, all kinds of food. Well, other places don't have that kind of variety.
Tom—Yes, I know what you mean.

22. Free translation:

Tom—When did you move here? One, oh, four years ago.
Joe—   Four years ago.

23. This one-half second continuation may be more meaningful to the reader if it is known that signing rate seems to vary (contextually and individually) between 2.3–2.5 signs per second (Bellugi & Fischer, 1972) and 3.12 signs per second (Baker, 1976a).

24. This difference may be relevant to the work of Paul Ekman (1972) and his associates on universals of facial expressions.

25. One frequent result of this mutual frustration, explained to me by Terrence O'Rourke (June 1976: personal communication), is that a deaf (or hearing) person will often try to control the discussion by maintaining the floor as long as possible. When the deaf (or hearing) person is speaking, he/she does not need to be scrambling to follow the conversation.

REFERENCES

Argyle, M., & Dean, J. (1965), "Eye-contact, distance and affiliation," *Sociometry*, **23**, 289–304.

Argyle, M. & Ingham, R. (1972), "Gaze, mutual gaze, and proximity," *Semiotica*, **6**, 32-49.

Argyle, M., Ingham, R., Alkema, F., & McCallin, M. (1973), "The different functions of gaze," *Semiotica*, **7**, 19–31.

Baker, C. (1976a), "What's not on the other hand in American Sign Language," *Papers from the Twelfth Regional Meeting of the Chicago Linguistics Society*, University of Chicago.

Baker, C. (1976b), "Eye-openers in ASL," *California Linguistics Association Conference Proceedings*, San Diego State University.

Battison, R. (1971), *Some Observations on Sign Languages, Semantics, and Aphasia*, Ms., University of California, San Diego.

Battison, R., Markowicz, H., & Woodward, J. (1973), "A good rule of thumb: variable phonology in American Sign Language," to appear in Shuy & Fasold, eds., *New Ways of Analyzing Variation in English* (Vol. 2), Georgetown University Press.

Bellugi, U. & Fischer, S. (1972), "A comparison of sign language and spoken language: rate and grammatical mechanisms," *Cognition: International Journal of Cognitive Psychology*, **1**, 173–200.

Bellugi, U. & Klima, E. (1974), "Aspects of sign language and its structure," to appear in Kavanagh, J., & Cutting, S., eds., *The Role of Speech in Language*, MIT Press, Cambridge, Mass.

Chomsky, N. (1965), *Aspects of the Theory of Syntax*, MIT Press, Cambridge, Mass.

Chomsky, N. (1971), "Deep structure, surface structure, and semantic interpretation," in Steinberg, D., & Jakobovits, L., eds., *Semantics: An Interdisciplinary Reader in Philosophy, Linguistics, and Psychology*, Cambridge University Press, London.

Cooper, W. E., & Ross, J. R. (1975), "World order," *Papers from the Parasession on Functionalism*, University of Chicago.

Covington, V. (1973), "Juncture in American Sign Language," *Sign Language Studies*, **2**, 29–58.

Dittman, A., & Llewellyn, L. (1968), "Relationship between vocalizations and head nods as listener responses," *Journal of Personal & Social Psychology*, **9**, 79–84.

Dowty, D. (1972), *Studies in the Logic of Verb Aspect and Time Reference in English*, Doctoral dissertation, University of Texas, Austin.

Duncan, S. (1972), "Some signals and rules for taking speaking turns in conversations," *Journal of Personal & Social Psychology*, **23**, 283–292.

Duncan, S. (1973), "Toward a grammar for dyadic conversation," *Semiotica*, **9**, 29–46.

Ekman, P. (1972), "Universals and cultural differences in facial expressions of emotion," in Cole, J., ed., *Nebraska Symposium on Motivation*, University of Nebraska Press, Lincoln.

Ekman, P., & Friesen, W. (1969), "The repertoire of nonverbal behavior: categories, origins, usage, and coding," *Semiotica*, **1**, 49–98.

Exline, R. (1963), "Explorations in the process of person perception: visual interaction in relation to competition, sex, and need affiliation," *Journal of Personal and Social Psychology*, **31**, 1–20.

Exline, R., Gray, D., & Schuette, D. (1965), "Visual behavior in a dyad as affected by interview content and sex of respondent," *Journal of Personal and Social Psychology*, **1**, 201–209.

Exline, R. & Winters, L. (1965), "Affective relations and mutual glances in dyads," in Tomkins, S., & Izzard, C., eds., *Affect, Cognition and Personality*, Springer, Verlag, New York.

Fant, L. J., Jr. (1972), *Ameslan: An Introduction to American Sign Language*, Joyce Motion Picture Co., Northridge, California.

Fillmore, C. J. (1968), "The case for case," in Bach, E., & Harms, R.T., eds., *Universals in Linguistic Theory*, Holt, New York.

Fischer, S. (1973a), "Two processes of reduplication in the American Sign Language," *Foundations of Language*, **9**, 469–480.

Fischer, S. (1973b), "Sign language and linguistic universals," to appear in the *Proceedings of the Franco-German Conference on French Transformational Grammar*, Athaenium, Berlin.

Fischer, S. (1975), "Influences on word order change in American Sign Language," in Li, C. N., ed., *Word Order and Word Order Change*, University of Texas Press, Austin.

Fischer, S., & Gough, B. (1972), *Some Unfinished Thoughts on Finish*, Ms., Salk Institute for Biological Studies, La Jolla, California.

Fischer, S., & Gough, B. (to appear), "Verbs in American Sign Language," in Bellugi, U. & Klima, E., eds., *The Signs of Language*, Harvard University Press, Cambridge, Mass.

Friedman, L. A. (1974a), *On the Physical Manifestation of Stress in the American Sign Language*, Ms., University of California, Berkeley.

Friedman, L. A. (1974b), *A Comparative Analysis of Oral and Visual Language Phonology*, Ms., University of California, Berkeley.

Friedman, L. A. (1975a), "Phonological processes in the American Sign Language," *Proceedings of the First Annual Meeting of the Berkeley Linguistics Society*, 147–159.

Friedman, L. A. (1975b), "Space, time, and person reference in American Sign Language," *Language*, **51**, 940–961.

Friedman, L. A. (1976a), "The manifestation of subject, object, and topic in American Sign Language," in Li, C. N., ed., *Subject and Topic*, Academic Press, New York.

Friedman, L. A. (1976b), *Phonology of a Soundless Language: Phonological Structure of American Sign Language*, Doctoral dissertation, University of California, Berkeley.

Friedman, L. A., & Battison, R. (1973), *Phonological Structures in American Sign Language*, NEH Grant Report AY-8218-73-136.

Frishberg, N. (1975a), *The Case of the Missing Length*, Ms., National Technical Institute for the Deaf, Rochester, New York.

Frishberg, N. (1975b), "Arbitrariness and iconicity: historical change in American Sign Language," *Language, 51*, 696–719.

Frishberg, N., & Gough, B. (1973), *Morphology in American Sign Language*, Ms., Salk Institute for Biological Studies, La Jolla, California.

Garnes, S., & Bond, Z. (1975), "Slips of the ear: errors in perception of casual speech," *Papers from the Eighth Regional Meeting of the Chicago Linguistics Society.*

Goldman-Eisler, F. (1954), "On the variability of the speed of talking and on its relation to the length of utterances in conversation," *British Journal of Psychology, 45*, 94–107.

Goldman-Eisler, F. (1961), "The distribution of pause durations in speech," *Language and Speech, 4*, 232–237.

Hall, E. (1963), "A system for the notation of proxemic behavior," *American Anthropologist, 65*, 1003–1026.

Hockett, C. F. (1966), "The problem of universals in language," in Greenberg, J., ed., *Universals of Language* (2nd edition), MIT Press, Cambridge, Mass.

Jaffe, J., & Feldstein, S. (1970), *Rhythms of Dialogue*, Academic Press, New York.

Jones, N. (1975), *On Expressing Plurality in American Sign Language*, Ms., University of California, Berkeley.

Kendon, A. (1967), "Some functions of gaze direction in social interaction," *Acta Psychologica, 26*, 22–63.

Klima, E., & Bellugi, U. (1975), "Perception and production in a visually based language," to appear in the *Annals of the New York Academy of Science.*

Lacy, R. (1974), *Putting Some of the Syntax Back into Semantics*, Ms., University of California, San Diego.

Lakoff, G. (1971), "On generative semantics," in Steinberg, D., & Jakobovits, L., eds., *Semantics: An Interdisciplinary Reader in Philosophy, Linguistics, and Psychology*, Cambridge University Press, London.

Lakoff, G. (1972), "Hedges: a study in meaning criteria and the logic of fuzzy concepts," *Papers from the Eighth Regional Meeting of the Chicago Linguistics Society,* University of Chicago.

Liddell, S. K. (1975), *Restrictive Relative Clauses in American Sign Language*, Ms., Salk Institute for Biological Studies, La Jolla, California.

Long, J. S. (1918, reprinted 1949), *The Sign Language: A Manual of Signs*, Athens Press, Iowa City, Iowa.

Madsen, W. J. (1972), *Conversational Sign Language II: An Intermediate-Advanced Manual*, Gallaudet College Press, Washington, D.C.

McCawley, J. (1971), "Where do noun phrases come from?" in Steinberg, D., & Jakobovits, L., eds., *Semantics: An Interdisciplinary Reader in Philosophy, Linguistics, and Psychology*, Cambridge University Press, London.

Padden, C., & Markowicz, H. (1975), "Crossing cultural group boundaries into the deaf community," Paper presented at the Conference on Culture and Communication, Temple University, Philadelphia (March).

Riekehof, L. (1963), *Talk to the Deaf*, Gospel Publishing House, Springfield, Mo.

Robbins, S. (1974), *Regulator Behavior in Restricted and Elaborated Code Using Groups*, M.A. thesis, Clark University.

Ross, J.R. (1976), "The sound of meaning," Paper presented at the Second Annual Meeting of the Berkeley Linguistics Society.

Sacks, H., Schegloff, E., & Jefferson, G. (1974), "A simplest systematics for the organization of turn-taking for conversation," *Language, 50*, 696–735.

Saussure, F. de (1959), *Course in General Linguistics*, Philosophical Library, New York.

Scheflen, A. (1963), "Communication and regulation in psychotherapy," *Psychiatry, 26*, 126–136.

Schiff, W. (1973a), "Social perception in deaf and hearing adolescents," *Exceptional Children, 39*, 289–297.

Schiff, W. (1973b), "Social-event perception and stimulus pooling in deaf and hearing observers," *American Journal of Psychology, 86*, 61–78.

Schlesinger, I. M., Presser, B., Cohen, E., & Peled, T. (1970), *Transfer of Meaning in Sign Language*, Working paper no. 12, Hebrew University of Jerusalem.

Siple, P. (1973), *Constraints for a Sign Language from Visual Perception Data*, Ms., Salk Institute for Biological Studies, La Jolla, California.

Stokoe, W. C. (1960), "Sign language structure: an outline of the visual communication system of the American deaf," *Studies in Linguistics, Occasional Papers 8*, University of Buffalo.

Stokoe, W. C. (1972), "Classification and description of sign languages," in Sebeok, T. A., ed., *Current Trends in Linguistics, 12*, Mouton, The Hague.

Stokoe, W., & Battison, R. (1975), "Sign language, mental health, and satisfying interaction," Paper presented at the Michael Reese Medical Center Workshop, Toward Understanding the Mental Health Needs of Deaf Adults, Chicago, Ill.

Stokoe, W. C., Casterline, D., & Croneberg, C. (1965), *A Dictionary of American Sign Language on Linguistic Principles*, Gallaudet College Press, Washington, D.C.

Talmy, L. (1975), *Figure and Ground in Complex Sentences*, Ms., Language Universals Project, Stanford University.

Trager, G. & Smith, H. (1957), *An Outline of English Structure*, American Council of Learned Societies, Washington, D.C.

Wiener, M. & Devoe, S. (1974), "Regulators, channels, and communication disruption," Research proposal, Clark University.

Wiener, M., Devoe, S., Rubinow, S., & Geller, J. (1972), "Nonverbal behavior and nonverbal communication," *Psychol. Review, 79,* 185–214.

Wiener, M., & Mehrabian, A. (1968), *Language Within Language: Immediacy, a Channel in Verbal Communication*, Appleton-Century-Crofts, New York.

INDEX

Relativization, 183ff, 187
Repetition, 31–32, 34, 212, 222, 228
Rest positions, *see also* Regulators, 219ff, 226
Role-switching, *see* Body movement

S

Scalar elements, *see* Analogic phenomena,
    Discreteness, nondiscreteness
Semantic domains, 118ff
Sentence boundaries, 182, 223ff
Sign Language continuum, 3, 139, 206
Signed English, 3, 183, 206
Simultaneous articulation, 4–5, 209
Simultaneous talking, 216, 224, 228
Stress, 30–31, 34
Syntactic subordination, 181ff
Syntactic theories, 111ff, 130ff

T

Temporal reference, *see also* Indexing,
    51–52, 77, 197ff
    adverbials, 51, 201
    calendric units, 51, 202ff
    complex time locutions, 206ff
    establishment of, 198, 201
    real-world temporal order, 206ff
    times of day, 52–53
    time plane, 8, 41, 51, 77, 197, 198
Topic, 164–165
Transcripts, interpretation, 10–11
Turn-taking signals, *see also* Regulators,
    215ff
    back-channel, 216, 222, 227–228
    turn-claiming, 216, 229
    turn-claiming suppression, 216
    turn-yielding, 216, 228
    within-turn signal, 216
Two-handed signs, *see also* Morpheme
    structure conditions, 13–14, 23, 30, 37,
    42

U

Unmarked (neutral) components, 37, 40
    neutral hand shapes, 14, 22, 33

V

Verbs
    bodily anchored, 145ff
    classes, 143ff

compound verbs, 189–190
durative, 200
experiencer-anchored, 140ff, 191
iterative, 200
multidirectional, 5, 76, 138, 143ff, 145,
    168
multiorientational, 5, 147ff
nonmultidirectional, 139ff
one-place predicates, 140ff, 191
reduplication of, 200
semantic classification, 143ff, 145
Visual acuity, 40

W

WH-words, 183
Word order, 5, 137ff, 183

A
B 7
C 8
D 9
E 0
F 1
G 2
H 3
I 4
J 5